Esoteric Islam in Modern French Thought

New Directions in Religion and Literature

This series aims to showcase new work at the forefront of religion and literature through short studies written by leading and rising scholars in the field. Books will pursue a variety of theoretical approaches as they engage with writing from different religious and literary traditions. Collectively, the series will offer a timely critical intervention to the interdisciplinary crossover between religion and literature, speaking to wider contemporary interests and mapping out new directions for the field in the early twenty-first century.

Series editors: Emma Mason and Mark Knight

ALSO AVAILABLE IN THE SERIES:

The New Atheist Novel, Arthur Bradley and Andrew Tate
Blake. Wordsworth. Religion, Jonathan Roberts
Do the Gods Wear Capes?, Ben Saunders
England's Secular Scripture, Jo Carruthers
Victorian Parables, Susan E. Colón
The Late Walter Benjamin, John Schad
Dante and the Sense of Transgression, William Franke
The Glyph and the Gramophone, Luke Ferretter
John Cage and Buddhist Ecopoetics, Peter Jaeger
Rewriting the Old Testament in Anglo-Saxon Verse, Samantha Zacher
Forgiveness in Victorian Literature, Richard Hughes Gibson
The Gospel According to the Novelist, Magdalena Mączyńska
Jewish Feeling, Richa Dwor
Beyond the Willing Suspension of Disbelief, Michael Tomko
The Gospel According to David Foster Wallace, Adam S. Miller
Pentecostal Modernism, Stephen Shapiro and Philip Barnard
The Bible in the American Short Story, Lesleigh Cushing Stahlberg and Peter S. Hawkins

Esoteric Islam in Modern French Thought

Massignon, Corbin, Jambet

Ziad Elmarsafy

BLOOMSBURY ACADEMIC
LONDON • NEW YORK • OXFORD • NEW DELHI • SYDNEY

BLOOMSBURY ACADEMIC
Bloomsbury Publishing Plc
50 Bedford Square, London, WC1B 3DP, UK
1385 Broadway, New York, NY 10018, USA
29 Earlsfort Terrace, Dublin 2, Ireland

BLOOMSBURY, BLOOMSBURY ACADEMIC and the Diana logo are trademarks of Bloomsbury Publishing Plc

First published in Great Britain 2021
This paperback edition published 2022

Cover design by Eleanor Rose
Cover image © Tim Bird / Getty Images

A catalogue record for this book is available from the British Library.

A catalog record for this book is available from the Library of Congress.

ISBN: HB: 978-1-7809-3824-0
PB: 978-1-3502-0018-0
ePDF: 978-1-7809-3694-9
eBook: 978-1-7809-3654-3

Series: New Directions in Religion and Literature

Typeset by RefineCatch Limited, Bungay, Suffolk

Contents

Acknowledgements

This book started out as something very different. It metamorphosed into its current form over several years, institutions, jobs, cities, discussions, emails, meals, drinks, concerts, operas, and occasional quarrels with colleagues and friends in France, the Netherlands, the UK, and the USA. This section bears witness to my immense gratitude to those named in the following lines, as well as those who, for a variety of reasons, are not.

The project would never have come this far, nor indeed would it have begun, without the initial persuasive approach of the editors of the Bloomsbury's New Directions in Religion and Literature series; namely, Emma Mason and Mark Knight. Their patience and support, along with those of David Avital, Lucy Brown, Ben Doyle, and the rest of the editorial and production teams at Bloomsbury, kept the project alive even when I wanted to give up. The fact that they accepted a book so unlike the one that I proposed years ago is a testament to their broad vision and sense of possibility. Joanna de Groot's insight and intelligence were instrumental in transforming the project from an amorphous mass of ideas and themes into something more structured and readable. Arthur Bradley was an inspiring friend and careful reader from start to finish. Christian Jambet gave generously and sincerely of his time and counsel, both by correspondence and in person, even on the day when France won the World Cup. The impact of Derek Attridge's lessons about creativity, reading, and responsibility, and Adam Phillips's injunctions about grandiosity and against self-betrayal, will be legible everywhere in this work. I am deeply indebted to them all.

My new colleagues, friends, and neighbours at King's College London and in London itself have been a wonderful source of companionship, information, and humour. In particular, I would like to thank Russell Goulbourne, Michael Luck, Paul Readman, Johanna Malt, Patrick ffrench, Raphael Woolf, Max Saunders, Rebecca Dean and Rayne Small for their sage and practical advice and a general lifting of spirits, as well as some timely interventions that kept things going when they would otherwise have stopped. The technological assistance of the King's IT team over the past four years is hereby gratefully acknowledged.

Engaging feedback from audiences at King's College London, the University of Chicago, the University of Leiden, the University of Manchester, and the University of York helped to mark the stark contrast between those parts of the project that worked and those that did not. Librarians at York, the Maughan Library at King's, Senate House, the British Library, and the Bibliothèque nationale de France, all helped to ensure that the parts that worked continued to do so. I am profoundly grateful to my hosts and interlocutors at these locations, especially Anne Vila, Daniel Desormeaux, Matthew Campbell, James Williams, and Santanu Das, all of whom kept me talking; Kenneth Clarke, who sorted out my misunderstandings of the *fedeli d'amore*; David Ricks, who embodies the term, 'Master of Illumination;' Elaine Morley, whose initiation into hermeneutics was critical in setting the direction of the project; Thomas Pavel, whose use of the word 'wisdom' is always instructive; Kazuyo Murata and Carool Kersten, who both taught me a great deal about the reach and limits of intellectual beauty; and Martin Stokes, whose presence remains a constant reminder of the powers of music, language, and spirituality. Phiroze Vasunia's and Andrew Laird's kind comments about an early reading of al-Suhrawardī were essential to keeping him and his readers in the present volume. Matthew Bell set me straight about hidden aspects of Goethe, while Michael Silk shed light on the Orphics. I have learned much about Catholicism from Sanja Perovic, Robert Priest and, indirectly, from David Todd. The long-delayed debate with Wen-Chin Ouyang about the relative merits of Barthes and Derrida as Sufis will have to await another occasion. Kenneth Reinhardt was a very helpful guide to key aspects of Lacan. Conversations with Alain Messaoudi and Françoise Jacquin were pivotal in forming my views of Massignon. Brian Cummings and Simon Ditchfield made me think about the links between religion and critique in novel and exciting ways. Renée Champion kept me in the loop on current intellectual trends in France, even as she asked important 'What about…?' questions, not all of which will be answered in the following pages. Daniel Rivet's and Michel Fani's admonitions about writing (*Beddak tiktub!*) ensured that it actually happened, albeit at a slower pace than they or I wished. Both also taught me much about some key post-May '68 fictions and publications. Annie Kent was the sternest and wittiest taskmaster of them all.

Two trips to the Institut Mémoires de l'édition contemporaine (IMEC), the first to explore part of the Derrida archive and the second to commemorate his legacy, proved fruitful and revealing on multiple counts. All my thanks, therefore, to the staff of the IMEC, and to the co-organisers of the 'Penser avec Derrida où qu'il soit' conference in 2014, Safaa Fathy and Carlos Lobo, for bringing about a turning point in my thinking through exchanges with Gil Anidjar, Alain David, Eberhard Grüber, Benjamin Mayer Foulkes, Yuji Nishiyama, and Sherif Younis. Pierre Joris was particularly generous with his time and advice in Caen, Paris, and elsewhere. Although I have been unable to use all of the ideas that emerged from these encounters in the present volume, I hope that they will feed into future publications.

For hospitality that would have made Massignon proud and increased my appetite for just about everything, I would like to thank Hugh Haughton, Kit Fan, Pat Palmer, Oussama Himani, Julian Ingle, Francesca Orsini, Peter Kornicki, Gerald Maclean, Donna Landry, Michael Fend, Amanda Lilly, Felicity Riddy, Jachi and Philippe Siu-Jedar, Wakako Siu, Daniel and Françoise Rivet, Neil Vickers, Sarah

Richmond, Arthur Bradley, Abir Hamdar, Adam Phillips, Judith Clarke, Martin Stokes, Lucy Baxandall, Alastair Hamilton, Jan Loop, Bernhard Klein, Irene Musumeci, Safaa Fathy, Jane Darcy, Jūratė Levina, Mary Malone, and Elizabeth Tyler. Michael Fend, Amanda Lilly, and Elizabeth Tyler also steadied my hand as I struggled with endless decisions about cover images. Emma Major consistently came through with jokes and witty correspondence when the need for such things was at its greatest. Claire Westall's quiet pragmatism was a beacon of sanity in tumultuous times.

The institutional and personal welcome that I received from Drs. Mohamed Keshavjee and Walid Ghali, together with the Ismaili Centre, London, the Institute for Isma'ili Studies, and the Aga Khan University, have been a wonderful reminder of the worldly manifestations of many of the ideas in play in this book. A larger-scale welcome from colleagues and collaborators at the Université Paris Diderot (now Université de Paris) – Frédéric Ogée, Antoine Cazé, Clarisse Berthezène, Fatou Esteoule, Federico Tarragoni, Mi-Kyung Yi, and Catherine Marcangeli – expanded the universe of possibilities and kept that excitement going in the life of the mind.

Four dear friends and teachers – Josué Harari, Assia Djebar, Jon Stallworthy, and Jean Denaro – left during the writing of this book. I hope that my eternal appreciation reaches them, wherever they may be.

The final word of thanks goes, as ever, to my family, whose unflinching support, humour, and steady increase over the years means more than words can say.

Abbreviations, Transliterations and Translations

EI2	*Encyclopaedia of Islam, Second Edition*
EM	Louis Massignon, *Écrits mémorables*
GA	Martin Heidegger, *Gesamtausgabe*
HW	G.W.F Hegel, *Werke*

Full bibliographic information is provided in the bibliography.

For all transliterations from Arabic and Persian, I have used the *IJMES* system without the final *ha.* I have used popular forms of certain terms (Qur'an, Muhammad) wherever it seemed likely that readers would have encountered them, rather than the *IJMES* transliteration.

As a general rule, I have placed English translations in the body of the text with the originals in a footnote, and provided references to key passages in published English translations where necessary. Some departures from this rule were necessary in the second chapter in order to call attention to Corbin's use of language in his approach to and translations from Heidegger. All English translations of the Qur'an are taken from the Khalidi translation.

References to multilingual works (such as Corbin's editions and translations for the *Bibliothèque iranienne* series) refer to material assuming that the books are read from left to right – in order: Corbin's translation, commentary, and original text – with section/paragraph numbers added for additional clarity. References to multivolume works separate volume and page by a colon, thus 1:20 means volume 1, page 20.

Introducing the Guest

If the past few centuries have taught us anything, it is that the division between the seemingly rational and the apparently irrational is endlessly negotiable. Not only has religion returned as a peculiarly powerful determinant of social and political life over the past half century, but the place and explanatory force assigned to it keep changing. We speak of 'faith', 'belief', 'culture' and much else in modes that both address and conjure away the inexplicable, however troubling it may be, but our lives grow increasingly unpredictable anyway, and that unpredictability is often phrased in terms of a certain idea of religion.

This book will address some responses to that unpredictability by a group of French specialists of Islam. It is not another book about Islam 'and' the West, whatever the conjunction may mean. This is a book about Islam in, of, and around the West; about their coexistence, and about ideas and figures emanating from both turning up in unexpected places. It is also a book about decisions; in particular, the decision to dedicate a human life to something unusual; to make a point of hosting strange ideas in one's mind as one might host a guest at a meal, and to dedicate one's life to that curious form of hospitality. Henry Corbin (1903–1978), one of the people who made such a decision, and to whom one of the chapters in this book is dedicated, concluded his monumental four-volume study of Islam in Iran, *En Islam iranien*, as follows:

> And this is perhaps the thing that best summarizes the teaching that the philosopher owes to the hospitality of Islam in Iran. But

> there is no spiritual hospitality without reciprocity, without the received guest being internally a guest who welcomes as well. For, without this reciprocity, there is no hope of *understanding*.[1]

For Corbin, his followers and interlocutors, reciprocity, hospitality, and understanding go together. It is difficult to imagine what a capacious intellect like Corbin's might have held at the precise moment when these lines were composed, but he might have been thinking of his former teacher, Louis Massignon (1883–1962), who was often preoccupied with the ethics of hospitality as a mode of comprehension, speech and thought. Indeed, Corbin's conclusion contains a strong echo of Massignon's key statement, 'To understand the other, one does not need to annex him but become his guest.'[2]

What happens, then, when other people and ideas are received, or when they receive us as guests? One short, if obvious, answer, is 'complications.' Every act of hospitality contains, as Derrida reminds us, more than a hint of hostility.[3] It is no coincidence that one of the places in which Derrida makes this point is in a seminar that brought together the works of Levinas and Massignon on the question of hospitality. The presence of a guest changes us, not always for the better, and vice versa, no matter how kind or generous we or they might seem (see *Tartuffe*). And yet people visit each other every day, and the principles of coexistence and sharing endure, even as humanity keeps marking new lows of exclusion and violence. Without

1 'Et tel est peut-être ce qui condense au mieux l'enseignement dont le philosophe est redevable à l'hospitalité reçue en Islam iranien. Mais il n'est pas d'hospitalité spirituelle sans réciprocité, sans que l'hôte accueilli ne soit intérieurement un hôte qui accueille. Car, sans cette réciprocité, il n'est point d'espoir de *comprendre*.' Henry Corbin, *En Islam iranien. Aspects spirituels et philosophiques*, 4 vols. (Paris: Gallimard, 1991), 4:460.

2 'Pour comprendre l'autre, il ne faut pas se l'annexer, mais devenir son hôte.' Louis Massignon, *Écrits mémorables*, ed. Christian Jambet, 2 vols (Paris: R. Laffont, 2009), 2:248.

3 Jacques Derrida and Anne Dufourmantelle, *De l'hospitalité* (Paris: Calmann-Lévy, 1997); Jacques Derrida, 'Hostipitality,' in *Acts of Religion*, ed. Gil Anidjar (New York and London: Routledge, 2002).

hospitality and the changes that it creates, neither sense-making nor understanding would be possible.[4]

The guest in question over the course of this book is Islam, or rather a certain esoteric and otherworldly idea of Islam. I use the term 'esoteric' as a translation for the Arabic term, *al-Bāṭin* – the interior, the hidden, the spiritual – as opposed to the visible, exterior (*al-Ẓāhir*) aspect of a given thing or phenomenon. The opposition between *Ẓāhir/Bāṭin* and exoteric/esoteric can be applied to anything, and indeed operates as a universal structural principle in numerous currents of Islamic thought. In his important study of Western Sufism, Mark Sedgwick adds an important qualifier to the opposition between the exoteric and esoteric: the latter is seen by its adherents as the more valuable part of the opposition.[5] One related term that should be introduced is the *waliyy* (pl. *awliyā*ʾ), which is usually translated by 'friend' or 'lover [of God]' or, in Shīʿī contexts, by 'successor [to Muhammad]'. More generally, *waliyy* designates a Sufi Saint or a Shīʿī Imām. In both Sufi and Shīʿī traditions, the *awliyā*ʾ are those who preserve and transmit the esoteric.[6] This is related to the view that sees the passage of time as a series of revelations, with one cycle of revelation, transmitted by the prophets (the cycle of *nubuwwa*, or prophecy), succeeded by another, transmitted by the *awliyā*ʾ (the cycle of *walāya*). Corbin sees in the opposition between the exoteric and the esoteric the entire scriptural vindication of Shīʿism, adding that Sufism might be considered an exploration of all esoteric aspects of Islam.[7] Our focus will accordingly be on those aspects of Islam that

[4] Derek Attridge, *The Work of Literature*, First ed. (Oxford: Oxford University Press, 2015), 303–305.

[5] Mark J. Sedgwick, *Western Sufism: From the Abbasids to the New Age* (New York: Oxford University Press, 2017), 5.

[6] Corbin, *EII*, 1:219–284. On the idea of the *walāya* as the love (*dilection*) of God and the esoteric core of the prophetic tradition (*Bāṭin al-nubuwwa*), see *EII*, 1:248–251.

[7] Henry Corbin, *L'Imagination créatrice dans le soufisme d'Ibn ʿArabî* (Paris: Entrelacs, 2006), 98–99.

are driven by the *Bāṭin* and transmitted, for the most part, by *awliyāʾ*; namely Shīʿism, Sufism and Illuminationism, and those thinkers who devoted their lives and careers to them, thereby permanently shaping a certain idea of Islam in France: the aforementioned Louis Massignon, his student, Henry Corbin, and Corbin's student, Christian Jambet (1949–). This version of Islam now holds a central place in modern French intellectual life. One additional claim is that, far from remaining otherworldly, each of these thinkers has firmly inscribed esoteric Islam within the actual concerns of the world, successively demonstrating the social and political import of the esoteric. Indeed, the esoteric might be seen as the mechanism that enables the insertion of Islam into everyday life in non-Islamic spaces (such as 'the West').

Nor are examples of that insertion lacking. The pattern of increasing familiarity between Muslims and non-Muslims for reasons related to imperialism, migration and war over the past two centuries is well known. Less familiar, however, are examples of the inscription of esoteric ideas in the annals of literary criticism and theory. We might, by way of example, mention the appearance of Corbin's work in Lacan's. Lacan's seminar on ethics (Seminar VII) explicitly refers his audience to Corbin's monograph on the Sufi philosopher and thinker Ibn al-ʿArabī by way of emphasizing the links between courtly love and the Sufi tradition, and the idea that certain forms of poetic creation had a decisive influence on ethics.[8] Nor is this all. The curious end of Lacan's March 1960 lecture, 'Discours au catholiques', invokes Ibn al-ʿArabī's encounter with Ibn Rushd (Averroes):

> Thus let not the philosopher stand up, as happened to Ibn ʾArabî, to greet me overflowing with signs of his consideration and friendship, to end up embracing me and saying, 'Yes.'

[8] Jacques Lacan, *Le Séminaire de Jacques Lacan. Livre VII. L'Éthique de la psychanalyse* (Paris: Seuil, 1986), 178.

> Of course, like Ibn ʾArabî, I would end up saying 'Yes' to him. And his joy would be heightened when he observed that I had understood him.
>
> But, realizing what incited his joy, I would have to add, 'No.'[9]

It is, as usual, difficult to fully understand what Lacan is getting at here. Why would he put himself in the position of the mystic, and not just any mystic, but the most important theorist of Islamic mysticism? Why would he conclude his lecture by saying something like, 'I now find myself in a position comparable to that of Ibn al-ʿArabī before Averroes'? Lacan explicitly foregrounds the place of psychoanalysis, as before this passage he says: 'This is not my place, which is by the bedside of the patient who speaks to me.'[10] But even taking this into account, it is hard to be conclusive. One possibility is that he is trying to inscribe psychoanalysis in a region beyond the limits of reason, just as Ibn al-ʿArabī himself went beyond those limits to fathom the full powers of the creative imagination in Corbin's account.[11] What interests me more than the meaning of this passage, however, is the fact that Lacan thought nothing of concluding a public lecture in Brussels in 1960 in this allusive, enigmatic fashion. This demonstrates the currency of the esoteric in European academic circles in the mid-twentieth century.

Another example comes from a very careful reader of Corbin; namely, Harold Bloom. It will probably stand as one of the greatest curiosities of literary criticism's very rich history in the twentieth and

9 Jacques Lacan, *The Triumph of Religion: Preceded by Discourse to Catholics*, trans. Bruce Fink (Cambridge: Polity, 2013), 52. The original reads:

> Aussi, que le philosophe ne se lève pas, comme il arriva à Ibn ʾArabî, pour venir à ma rencontre, en me prodiguant les marques de sa considération et de son amitié, et pour finalement m'embrasser et me dire « Oui ».
>
> Bien entendu, comme Ibn ʾArabî, je lui répondrai en lui disant « Oui ». Et sa joie s'accentuera de constater que je l'aurai compris.
>
> Mais prenant conscience de ce qui aura provoqué sa joie, il me faudra ajouter – « Non ». Jacques Lacan, *Le Triomphe de la religion* (Paris: Seuil, 2005), 65; Corbin, *Imagination créatrice*, 62–63.

10 Lacan, *Triumph*, 52; *Triomphe*, 64–65.

11 I am grateful to Kenneth Reinhardt for this suggestion.

twenty-first centuries that Harold Bloom was a great fan of Henry Corbin. Bloom refers to Corbin as a genius in his preface to the 1998 edition of *Alone with the Alone*, the English translation of Corbin's *L'Imagination créatrice dans le soufisme d'Ibn ʾArabî*. Invoking Hegel's description of Shakespeare's characters as 'free artists of themselves', Bloom extends the comparison: 'The Sufis, interpreting the Koran, like the Kabbalists and Gnostics interpreting the Bible, also were "free artists of themselves".'[12] The components of this remarkable statement are worth pondering, if only because of the addition of Sufism to a series of otherwise heterogeneous keywords: Sufism, Gnosticism, art, interpretation, the self. How does Sufism operate as a tool that helps Bloom reflect on being a 'free artist' of the self?

Part of the answer comes in a book that Bloom published around the same time, *Omens of Millenium: The Gnosis of Angels, Dreams, and Resurrection*. Here Bloom takes on two questions that seemed, at the time, to be major preoccupations in American cultural life: angels and the end of the twentieth century. Faced with an American approach to these questions that he finds spiritually lacking, Bloom makes the case for Gnosticism as a *fin-de-siècle* true religion. In Corbin's angelology and discussions of esoteric themes, Bloom finds,

> [T]he best corrective we all of us could have to the softness of our current, popular, commercialized angelology. The image of the angel can be of use to us only insofar as we are capable of seeking Gnosis, by a hard path of spiritual rebirth. Our popular cult of angels patronizes those formidable beings [. . .] What we make into an empty image could still retain its enormous power, but only if approached again with all the powers of the mind and spirit.[13]

12 *Alone with the Alone: Creative Imagination in the Sūfism of Ibn ʾArabî*, New ed. (Princeton, NJ: Princeton University Press, 1998), xvi; Georg Wilhelm Friedrich Hegel, *Werke*, ed. Eva Moldenhauer, Karl Markus Michel, and Helmut Reinicke, 20 vols. (Frankfurt am Main: Suhrkamp, 1986), 15:562.

13 *Omens of Millennium: The Gnosis of Angels, Dreams, and Resurrection* (New York: Riverhead, 1997), 202.

This second approach, featuring 'all the powers of the mind and spirit', constitutes the core of the free art of the self that Bloom demands. Thus, whether seen as a corrective to a contemporary malaise, or a way of situating imagination within and between the idioms of psychoanalysis and philosophy, Corbin's account of the esoteric offers a vocabulary and method to thinkers trapped in a difficult discursive situation where words would otherwise fail.

The failure of words, or beliefs, or ideas, is constantly in the background of this book, and of the three thinkers who animate it. From Massignon's nervous breakdown in Iraq, after which he made the decisive shift to mysticism, devotion, and the study of al-Ḥallāj, to the violent horrors of the mid-twentieth century that called everything into question and drove Corbin to seek certainty in Shīʿism and Gnosticism, to Christian Jambet's break with certain revolutionary positions in favour of the study of Ismaʿīlism and early modern metaphysics, the esoteric consistently functions as a solution of sorts. The foregoing possibilities of failure might therefore be linked to the keyword associated with each thinker in the following chapters: Massignon and desire, Corbin and certainty, Jambet and resurrection.

Louis Massignon's towering status as a student of Islam and Sufism has a strong aesthetic background mediated both by his father, the sculptor Pierre Roche, and the novelist Joris-Karl Huysmans, best known as the author of the novel, *À rebours*, and for his leading role in the Catholic revival of the turn of the twentieth century. As a devout, queer Catholic, Massignon's engagement with desire and Islam was both unsurprisingly difficult and unusually productive. From the influence of Huysmans, whom Massignon calls his 'first teacher',[14] to his love for Luis de Cuadra, who catalysed Massignon's relationship to Islam and the Arabic linguistic and mystical universe, to his later

[14] *EM*, 1:129.

alliance with Mary Kahil, with whom he founded the *Badaliya* association, Massignon spent most of his life caught up in impossible networks of desire and seemingly endless substitutions of one object for another. And it is this substitution that became the core of Massignon's ethics and politics: from the constant substitution of host for guest, from praying for other sinners to actually desiring that one be tormented in their place, the language of self-sacrifice infuses his ideas and writing. The possibilities opened up by desire were in evidence from Massignon's student days, when Massignon wrote a *mémoire* on the vocabulary of love in Honoré d'Urfé's *L'Astrée*, a novel in which gender fluidity plays a prominent part.[15] He returned to this topic in his work on the technical origins of the language of Sufism, a project that further emphasizes the importance of desire found in his monumental hagiography, *La Passion de Husayn Ibn Mansûr Hallâj*, which is dedicated to Huysmans. Although much is often made of Massignon's description of al-Ḥallāj as the 'Qur'anic Christ' based on the latter's well-known utterance, 'I am the Truth [*Anā al-Ḥaqq*]' (cf. Jn 14.6), I will argue that the key to Massignon's reading of Sufism and the esoteric inheres in his interpretation of a poem by al-Ḥallāj that declares the primacy of desire above all else. This notion of 'essential desire', as Massignon called it, creates a framework that enables us to see his subsequent work – on gender, love, language, and politics – as an exploration of the value of desire as an effective way of bridging cultural gaps and creating solidarity. For Massignon, Sufism and the esoteric thus open up a (primarily) literary method of thinking about desire that unites humanity in a common love of the divine.

Whereas Massignon's interest in Sufism was informed by his Catholic identity and his interest in literature, his student Henry Corbin was a staunch Protestant who saw in the esoteric a path

[15] Mary Louise Gude, *Louis Massignon: The Crucible of Compassion* (Notre Dame, IN: University of Notre Dame Press, 1996), 11.

towards certainty defined in phenomenological and hermeneutic terms. Corbin discovered Sufism and Heidegger simultaneously – he was Heidegger's first French translator, and was advised by Massignon to read al-Suhrawardī at the same time. He was also a committed student of modern Protestant theology and Hegel, often serving as the only credible interlocutor at Alexandre Kojève's well-attended 1930s seminar on the reading of the *Phenomenology* that proved formative for the likes of Bataille, Lacan, Queneau, and others. Corbin's reading of al-Suhrawardī's stories became the basis for an entire spiritual anthropology that assigned paramount importance to the process of *kashf*, or revelation, and saw in Shīʿī Islam the spiritual ground that enables the genesis of Sufism. Through a revolutionary reading of the history of Islamic thought focused on both al-Suhrawardī and Ibn al-ʿArabī, Corbin brought to light multiple key genealogies that ran from the dawn of Islamic philosophy to the contemporary period, thereby reversing Ernest Renan's claims about the waning of Islamic philosophy after Averroes.[16] For Corbin, the esoteric thus operates as the source of certainty in thought and the touchstone of the truth.

Of all the names cited in this study, Jambet's is arguably the most peculiar. He is the only one who is still alive. Unlike Massignon and Corbin (who would later become his thesis supervisor and mentor), Jambet has prominent leftist leanings, came quite late to the study of Islam, and spent much of his youth as an activist in left-wing groups as a Maoist and committed member of the *Gauche prolétarienne*. Having discovered the appalling realities of totalitarian regimes in the former USSR and China, however, he abandoned this version of political activity (without jettisoning the aim of making the world a better place) and underwent a self-imposed 'deprogramming' with his intellectual companion, Guy Lardreau. Together, they wrote a number of works that aimed at re-inventing philosophy and politics untainted

[16] Ernest Renan, *Averroès et l'Averroïsme. Essai historique* (Paris: Calmann-Lévy, 1869), 2.

by the dogmas that had, in their view, infected them (*Apologie de Platon*, *L'Ange*, *Le Monde*). Under Corbin's tutelage, Jambet quickly mastered the history and content of Islamic philosophy, without which, he argued, one could not possibly make sense of Western thought. Jambet continued Corbin's work on thinkers based in Iran and Central Asia, most notably Mullā Ṣadrā of Shirāz, who occupies a central role in his philosophy. Rethinking revolution in light of Islamic history was a key part of this process: in 1990 he published a landmark study of the Ismaʿīlī Resurrection proclaimed at Alamūt, seeing in this event the culmination of revolutionary thinking in Sufi and Shīʿī political theologies. He has also continued his work as a translator and mediator between multiple cultures and genres, spanning the range from Sufi and Shīʿī works to key readings of Western philosophy and an annotated translation of *The Ballad of Reading Gaol*. Throughout this immense (and growing) *œuvre*, Jambet consistently returns to the phenomenology of the hidden and the revealed as an interpretive framework. Like Corbin, he relies on Islam's esoteric traditions as the royal road to the truth, understood as that which must be revealed. He differs from Corbin in his reading of the political: for Jambet, there is a continuum between esoteric thought and political efficacy. It is thus possible for him to speak coherently of Mao as a gnostic (understood in the Islamic sense of *ʿIrfān* – arguably a version of Sufism) in his 1983 study of Corbin's thought, *La Logique des orientaux*. The esoteric enables this strange qualification.

At this stage, one version of a summing up would be to say that the esoteric reminds us that language is hospitality (Massignon), that being is interpretation (Corbin) and that fidelity is resurrection and immortality (Jambet).

*

Although this is not the first time that these writers have been presented to the anglophone reading public, it is, I believe, the first time that they have been presented together in a framework that focuses on *how* their ideas work, rather than on whether or not they do, in a perspective that tilts away from Islamic studies and towards philosophy and theory (writ large). That said, their work has attracted the attention of researchers and scholars worldwide, predominantly in the fields of religion, theology, and Islamic studies. The story that I aim to tell inscribes them in a more interdisciplinary space while calling attention to the necessity of thinking about them together. Where I differ from my predecessors is in the insistence on the coexistence of ideas taken from the vast corpus of esoteric Islam and the corpus of Western ideas: I contend that Massignon must be read alongside Lévi-Strauss, Mauss, and, naturally, Huysmans; Corbin with Heidegger, Goethe and Luther; Jambet with Badiou and Lacan; all in the spirit of what Lévi-Strauss once called *bricolage*.[17] The provenance of an idea matters but should not foreclose the fate of that idea. Ideas derived from esoteric Islam should not be treated esoterically, or indeed as being somehow without a place in the worldly sphere. Esoteric Islam is not a niche subject; some familiarity with the philosophical and aesthetic aspects of Sufism, Shīʿism and the esoteric more generally should be part of every critic's and every theorist's arsenal, not least because of the methods of reading and possibilities of interpretation that it entails.

Some of those methods are evident in the work of my predecessors. Quite apart from the voluminous writing dedicated to each of our three thinkers in French, and the writing that they devoted to each other – Corbin wrote on Massignon, and Jambet wrote on and edited both – there is a significant body of work that engages with their legacy in English and outside the field of Islamic studies. Perhaps the most important mediator between Massignon and his anglophone audience

[17] *Œuvres*, ed. Vincent Debaene, Bibliothèque de la Pléiade (Paris: Gallimard, 2008), 576–577.

is Herbert Mason, whose *Memoir of a Friend* stands as the best short, single-volume introduction to the subject. In a key essay included in what I consider his most important book, Edward Said presented Massignon alongside Renan as thinkers 'so integral to the French culture of their epochs – Renan from 1850 to 1900, Massignon from 1900 to 1960 – as to give their work on Islam and even Islam itself a far greater status and authority for a non-Orientalist cultural public than could have happened in England and perhaps elsewhere in the West.'[18] Over the course of numerous monographs and articles, Mary Louise Gude has analysed in detail the relationship between conversion, mysticism, compassion, and literature across Massignon's *œuvre*. Patrick Laude's work underlines the notion of interiority and an inner (read: esoteric) Islam in the work of Massignon and Corbin alongside René Guénon and Frithjof Schuon, seeing in each thinker a source of multiple pathways leading to 'hidden layers of meaning and consciousness.'[19] Laude's claim about the textual character of Massignon's and Corbin's engagement with Islam is important, but I am not entirely sure that the opposition between the textual and the non-textual always stands up to Massignon's reading of desire and Corbin's of being.[20] Over the course of a series of monographs, Tom Cheetham has presented Henry Corbin's thought and works to the anglophone public in frameworks that combine archetypal (Jungian) psychology and ecological philosophy in a highly creative, independent style, pleading for an idea of the world and humanity that privileges the imagination.[21] Elsewhere,

[18] Edward W. Said, *The World, the Text and the Critic* (Cambridge, MA: Harvard University Press, 1983), 274.

[19] Patrick Laude, *Pathways to an Inner Islam: Massignon, Corbin, Guénon and Schuon* (Albany, NY: State University of New York Press, 2010), 31.

[20] *Pathways*, 57.

[21] Cheetham has written several books inspired by his very original readings of Corbin, but see, for starters, *The World Turned Inside Out: Henry Corbin and Islamic mysticism* (Woodstock, CT: Spring Journal Books, 2003); *Green Man, Earth Angel: The Prophetic Tradition and the Battle for the Soul of the World* (Albany, NY: State University of New York Press, 2005).

in registers that literary specialists would call theoretical, Peter Hallward reads Deleuze's ideas on creation – especially being as creation – against those of Corbin to explore the fate of the self through the processes of dematerialization and illumination.[22] Jambet's early works, especially those co-authored with Lardreau, attracted quite a bit of commentary, much of it critical, in relation to the emergence of the movement known as *la nouvelle philosophie*.[23] Far too little seems to have focused on the far larger corpus of his work as a specialist of Islam. There are exceptions, however, such as Anthony Paul Smith, who has used Corbin and Jambet to reformulate our understanding of nature and revolution.[24]

As will quickly become clear, I have been influenced by these readings, along with many others. My objective differs as much by its focus as by its modesty from what others have done in this area. My aim is to show how and why the three thinkers at the heart of this study work, as one might speak of a textual system or system of ideas 'working'. I believe that there is much to be gained from presenting them together, and from tracing ideas, themes and vocabularies across their thought and writing. Inevitably, much has been excluded. It will ultimately be up to my readers to decide whether my approach and included material work, but I hope nonetheless that they will find some instruction and pleasure in the pages that follow.

[22] Peter Hallward, *Out of this World: Deleuze and the Philosophy of Creation* (London; New York: Verso, 2006), 82–85.

[23] Full references for this polemic will be provided in chapter 3 below, but see also Gayatri Chakravorti Spivak and Michael Ryan, 'Anarchism Revisited: A New Philosophy,' *Diacritics* 8, no. 2 (1978).

[24] Anthony Paul Smith, 'NATURE DESERVES TO BE SIDE BY SIDE WITH THE ANGELS: nature and messianism by way of non-islam,' *Angelaki* 19, no. 1 (2014), https://doi.org/10.1080/0969725X.2014.920640; Anthony Paul Smith, 'The Speculative Angel,' in *Speculative Medievalisms: Discography*, ed. The Petropunk Collective (Brooklyn, NY: Punctum Books, 2013).

1

Louis Massignon: In the Beginning Was Desire[1]

'It is as Creator that God is truth.'[2]

Desire, in the pre-eternity of pre-eternities is the Absolute;
In Him, by Him, of Him it appears; in Him it appeared.
Desire is not contingent, since it is the attribute
Of attributes for the one whom it killed and whom it restores to life.[3]

'They say that the Badaliya *is an illusion; for one cannot put oneself in the place of another, and that it is a lovers' dream* [une rêverie d'amoureux].' *Massignon to Mary Kahil, 16/1/1955*[4]

1 In addition to sources cited in the introduction, this chapter relies heavily on biographical works by Rocalve, Destremeau and Moncelon, as well as the editorial annotations in the excellent edition of Massignon's writing, the *Écrits mémorables* by Christian Jambet, Souad Ayada, François Angelier, and François L'Yvonnet. Their influence should be assumed even when they are not cited directly.

2 'C'est en tant que Créateur que Dieu est vérité.' Massignon, *EM*, 1:445.

3 Louis Massignon, *The Passion of al-Hallāj: Mystic and Martyr of Islam*, trans. Herbert Mason, Bollingen Series 4 vols (Princeton, NJ: Princeton University Press, 1982), 1:366. Massignon's French translation of this poem reads as follows:

Le Désir, dans la prééternité des prééternités est l'Absolu
En Lui, à Lui, de Lui Il apparaît, en Lui il a paru
Le Désir n'est pas contingent, puisqu'il est l'attribut
D'entre les attributs pour celui qu'Il a tué et qu'Il ressuscite *EM*, 1:463.

The Arabic original shows Massignon's liberties as a translator:

العشق في أزل الآزال من قدمٍ
فيه به منه يبدو فيه إبداءُ
العشق لا حدث إذ كان هو صفة
من الصفات لمن قتلاه أحياءُ

Cf. Ruspoli's commentary and translation of this poem. Stéphane Ruspoli, *Le Message de Hallâj l'expatrié. Recueil du 'Dîwân', 'Hymnes et prières', 'Sentences prophétiques et philosophiques'* (Paris: Cerf, 2005), 100, 242–244.

4 'On nous dit que la Badaliya est un leurre, car on ne peut pas se mettre à la place d'un autre, et que c'est une rêverie d'amoureux. Il faut répondre que cela est, que ce n'est pas une rêverie, mais une souffrance que l'on reçoit sans l'avoir choisie et dont on conçoit la

Louis Massignon was arguably the most important modern French student of Islam. The name most frequently associated with Massignon is Ḥusayn ibn Manṣūr al-Ḥallāj, the tenth-century Sufi and poet who was crucified, ostensibly on charges of heresy, and forms the centre of Massignon's intellectual universe. Massignon calls al-Ḥallāj the 'Qur'anic Christ' ('le Christ coranique')[5] adding in an early letter that he believed that, given the way in which he died (betrayed, imprisoned, tortured, crucified, burned), al-Ḥallāj had died a Catholic Christian, like Massignon himself.[6] Al-Ḥallāj is also known as the 'perfect lover' of God in divers poetic traditions of the Muslim world.[7] Nevertheless, Massignon never lost sight of the fact that al-Ḥallāj was, in Herbert Mason's words, 'first and last a Muslim, and a witness of the Qur'an's spiritual treasury of inspiration.'[8] As we will see, the jarring coexistence of these two seemingly irreconcilable identities is symptomatic of Massignon's method and thought.

The importance of al-Ḥallāj for Massignon is such that it is often difficult to separate where the former ends and the latter begins. Massignon was a mystic, but he was no hermit: in addition to his vast

grâce, la visitation cachée du fond de l'angoisse de compassion qui nous saisit; et que c'est l'entrée dans le Royaume de Dieu et que cette souffrance nous saisit; certes, elle paraît impuissante, mais puisqu'elle exige tout, Quelqu'un qui est en croix la partage avec nous, et la transformera au dernier jour.' Louis Massignon and Mary Kahil, *L'Hospitalité sacrée* (Paris: Nouvelle Cité, 1987), 293.

5 Louis Massignon, *La Passion de Husayn Ibn Mansûr Hallâj : martyr mystique de l'Islam, exécuté à Bagdad le 26 mars 922 : étude d'histoire religieuse*, 4 vols. (Paris: Gallimard, 1990), 1:76; Massignon, *Passion English*, 1:36.

6 'L'examen détaillé des textes de son procès, de longues discussions à ce sujet avec mes amis musulmans, m'ont amené à la conclusion (provisoire) que Hallâdj mourut implicitement (et peut-être même explicitement) chrétien catholique, unissant à la pratique du sacrifice de soi la croyance dans le sacrifice du Verbe fait chair, homme-Dieu (cela est explicite).' Letter to Paul Claudel, 8 August 1908. Paul Claudel and Louis Massignon, *Correspondance 1908–1953: braises ardentes, semences de feu*, Nouvelle édition renouvelée et augmentée ed., ed. Dominique Millet-Gérard, Les Cahiers de la *NRF* (Paris: Gallimard, 2012), 39.

7 *Passion English*, 1:li. The importance of this attribute for Massignon may be seen from the fact that it precedes the mention of *Anā al-Ḥaqq* in the foreword to the original thesis of *La Passion de Husayn ibn Mansûr Hallâj*.

8 Herbert Mason, *Memoir of a Friend: Louis Massignon* (Notre Dame, IN: University of Notre Dame Press, 1988), 25.

output and constant preoccupation with travel and pilgrimage, Massignon's lifelong and tireless commitment to the cause of justice in the Arab and Muslim worlds, primarily, though not exclusively, in France's former colonies, puts him far ahead of his contemporaries. His many years of teaching at the Collège de France placed him squarely at the heart of French intellectual life in the twentieth century.[9] This chapter will focus on Massignon's view of the other, which he interprets and uses in terms of a human intersubjective and intercultural reality involving language, desire and hospitality. We will proceed in four stages, covering Massignon's key events in Massignon's early life, followed by explorations of the role of desire, language, hospitality and human rights in his work.

Truth: Visitation and Expression

Like most *sui generis* thinkers, Massignon combined multiple influences with his own native genius. Many of these influences worked by defusing crises and conjuring away violence, both of which were a steady part of Massignon's life, both in terms of his engagement with the Arab and Muslim worlds and his own internal struggles. A devout Catholic, Massignon spent much of this youth pondering the

9 Quite apart from Massignon's relationships with Huysmans, Claudel, Maspero, Mauriac, and many other thinkers and writers, one indicator of the central place that he occupies in French intellectual life may be seen in the distribution lists of the various texts and editions that make up the *Trois prières d'Abraham*. Among the hundreds of names on the distribution lists of the various editions we find those of Breton, Genet, Dumézil, Leiris, Lévi-Strauss, Michaux, Merleau-Ponty, and Lacan. Louis Massignon, *Les Trois prières d'Abraham* (Paris: Cerf, 1997), 149–174. Although the responses of Massignon's interlocutors were variable – some were immediately drawn to the text, while others, such as Roger Martin du Gard found it impenetrable – Genet's reply to Massignon gives an idea of just how much the latter was appreciated by his contemporaries: '[C]haque mot a un éclat, un prolongement très lointain: le ton de votre voix est inoubliable.' *Trois prières*, 166. An even more dramatic evocation of Massignon's life as mystic and worldly intellectual may be seen in Herbert Mason's diary, parts of which were published in *Memoir*, 59–167.

incontournable questions of grace and free will.[10] His reflections in this area were inflected both by his homosexuality and by the emerging post-symbolist moment in *fin-de-siècle* France: Massignon's father, Pierre Roche, was a well-known and well-connected sculptor and, unlike his wife (Massignon's mother), a convinced rationalist. Massignon experienced his first crisis of faith in his late teens – a process that would continue for many years – as an antidote to which his father sent him to see the novelist Huysmans, who by that point had become a key figure in the *fin-de-siècle* Catholic revival and living in his retreat at Ligugé.[11] These were the years of Huysmans's final works – the series that began with *Là-bas* and culminated in *L'Oblat* and *Sainte Lydwine de Schiedam*. In other words, this was the moment where the novelist's aesthetic became inseparable from his religious experience, and, as the opening of *La Cathédrale* demonstrates, Huysmans was really turning the relationship between art and religion into a manifesto. Not for nothing is Massignon's study of al-Ḥallāj dedicated to Huysmans. In addition to the spiritual aesthetics of Huysmans's late period, the doctrines of vicarious suffering and reparative compassion that Huysmans propagated (particularly in his *Sainte Lydwine*) had a deep impact on both Massignon and his

[10] Unless otherwise indicated, all biographical information about Massignon is taken from Christian Destremeau and Jean Moncelon, *Louis Massignon*, Tempus (Paris: Perrin, 2011). For biographical information about Huysmans I have relied mainly on Robert Baldick, *The Life of J.-K. Huysmans* (Sawtry: Dedalus, 2006). On the relationship between Huysmans and Massignon with an emphasis on aesthetics and style, see also Mary Louise Gude, 'J.K. Huysmans, Louis Massignon, and The Language Of Mysticism,' *Religion & Literature*. 30, no. 2 (1998); Dominique Millet-Gérard, 'Massignon et Huysmans: "silhouette d'or sur fond noir"', *Bulletin de l'Association des Amis de Louis Massignon*, no. 20 (2007).

[11] The Catholic revival is covered very thoroughly by both Griffiths and Gugelot. Richard Griffiths, *The Reactionary Revolution: The Catholic Revival in French Literature, 1870–1914* (London: Constable, 1966); Frédéric Gugelot, *La Conversion des intellectuels au catholicisme en France, 1885–1935* (Paris: CNRS, 2010). I am deeply grateful to Robert Priest for his assistance and advice on this matter. One significant difference between Griffiths and Gugelot is that Griffiths argues that the revival was not 'in the main, a movement of intellectuals'. *Reactionary Revolution*, 21. Gugelot, on the other hand, focuses specifically on the intellectuals who were caught up in the revival.

contemporaries, sometimes leading to cases where a chain of conversions to Catholicism is triggered by one person's suffering.[12] The idea that one could suffer for another, or that through one's suffering save another, founds Massignon's particular view of history as a continuum punctuated by exempla of self-sacrifice, starting with al-Ḥallāj and extending through Joan of Arc, Marie-Antoinette, Charles de Foucauld, Gandhi, and culminating in the *Badaliya*, the sodality that he founded with Mary Kahil in 1934 with the express purpose of fasting and praying for others, specifically Muslim others. The very idea that one can save the world through compassion illustrates Massignon's firm belief in the powers of desire. As Herbert Mason puts it, the key to Massignon's mystical theology is 'to be found in the actualizing mystery of substitution: of surrender of one's self spontaneously by unexpected transferent grace for the sake of another. It is the transference in suffering of love between lover and Beloved.'[13]

Massignon's fascination with the languages of love and the terminology of desire marks a key node along this axis joining art and religion. The thinking that went into his dissertation on *L'Astrée* would eventually translate into his second thesis on the development of the language of early mysticism in al-Ḥallāj. Wherever we look, we find this relationship between religion and art structuring Massignon's thought, and, moreover, that this relationship is always thought through the linguistic and literary registers rather than the plastic or visual ones. This relationship works through conflicts that were both internal and external – between Massignon's crises of faith and increasing terror of his homosexuality, as well as the periodic conflicts that shook both Europe and the Middle East, among which we might list the establishment of French and Spanish protectorates in Morocco

[12] Gugelot, *Conversion*, 397–401; Griffiths, *Reactionary Revolution*, 149–222.

[13] 'Louis Massignon, Catholicism, and Islam: A Memoir Reflection,' *Spiritus: A Journal of Christian Spirituality* 8, no. 2 (2008): 206, https://doi.org/https://doi.org/10.1353/scs.0.0021.

in 1904, the Tangiers Crisis the following year, the Young Turks revolt in 1908 and the Italo-Turkish War in Libya, the Agadir crisis, the first and second Balkan Wars and eventually, the First World War. Always and everywhere, there seemed to be war within and war without. And in Massignon's case, the link between the two was language: specifically, the Arabic language.

Massignon mastered Arabic with lightning speed, eventually being appointed to teach university courses, delivered in classical Arabic, on the history of philosophical vocabulary at the New Egyptian University (now Cairo University) in the academic year 1912–13. Not only did Massignon fall in love with the language and the place in which it was spoken; he fell in love with its speakers. On his way to Egypt in 1906, Massignon met a young Spaniard, Luis de Cuadra, who had converted to Islam and spoke fluent Arabic. Cuadra taught Massignon that understanding and self-abandonment went together: 'Pour comprendre, il faut se donner'[14] – an early version of what will become Massignon's credo for relating to others; 'To understand the other, one does not need to annex him but become his guest.'[15] The oscillation between the use of military language and the language of hospitality here is deliberate, as is the ambiguity in the French word *hôte*, which means both host and guest. For Massignon the antidote to colonial violence, whether it exists in fact or as a possibility, is hospitality; and the thing that makes hospitality work is language. Quite apart from the importance of giving and belonging in both contexts – we belong to a language as we 'belong' to our hosts and guests – Massignon is building a model of intercultural contact that depends on completely decentring oneself in order to prepare for the arrival of the other; or indeed to abandon oneself to the other's disposition. Both speaking and hosting bear an important relationship

[14] *EM*, 1:xxxix–xl.
[15] *EM*, 2:248; Mason, *Memoir*, 89.

to the truth. Making a false promise – breaking one's word after one has given it (*parole donnée*) is the equivalent of failing to uphold a sacred duty by betraying one's guest. The two institutions of language and hospitality become the axes that frame Massignon's spiritual and political geography.

Massignon had an intense erotic relationship with Luis de Cuadra, along with several other liaisons in Egypt.[16] Massignon described this phase of his life as 'voluntary servitude' or, more exactly, 'volunteer slavery' (alluding to La Boétie's term: *esclavage volontaire*) to whatever the present moment might bring, a total self-abandonment to desire. Elsewhere Massignon would speak of being 'held captive' by his desires, and of movement or travel as a suitable antidote. In mid-1907 he wrote to his friend the novelist Jean-Richard Bloch that he was 'soaked in Arabic – and more penetrated by Islam than I want to admit.'[17] The important difference between 'giving oneself' and 'being a guest' might be resolved through an expanded understanding of the term 'hospitality.'[18] Being a guest of the other, now understood as complete self-abandonment to the other's desire, can only function in a context of what might be called total hospitality: a situation where hospitality is not limited to food and shelter, but can, and indeed should, include love and sex. This, it would seem, is the condition under which hospitality and language come closest to each other and

[16] Although the affair ended with Massignon's return to Europe and departure for Iraq in 1907, Massignon continued to pray for Luis de Cuadra until the end of his life. Laure Meesemaecker, *L'Autre visage de Louis Massignon* (Versailles: Via Romana, 2011).

[17] '[i]mbibé d'Arabe – et pénétré d'islam plus que je ne veux me l'avouer.' *EM*, 1:xl.

[18] Derrida's work on the subject is of paramount importance on this point. Like Massignon, Derrida emphasizes the extent to which the coming of the stranger is actually supposed to trouble the host, to the point of becoming a substitute for the host, without which trouble and substitution there would be no hospitality (or what Derrida calls 'absolute hospitality'). Hospitality necessarily contains hostility. Derrida and Dufourmantelle, *De l'hospitalité*, 29–44. Derrida cites, with approval, Levinas's statement that language *is* hospitality. *De l'hospitalité*, 119. Derrida also presents an extended and very detailed reading of passages from Massignon's *L'Hospitalité sacrée* dealing with the themes of sacrifice, exile (being a stranger), and substitution, but without treating the relationship to al-Ḥallāj. Derrida, 'Hostipitality,' 364–382.

work best together. In this version of hospitality, sexuality operates not (or not only) as the result of self-abandonment, but also, to borrow a phrase, as a cure for classification, as a way out of the too rigid certainties and compartmentalizations that divide self and other, host and guest, Muslim and non-Muslim and so on. Furthermore, this version of language-hospitality, now conceived as one complex operation which we might call hospitalanguage, invites a new understanding of belonging that necessarily involves the other: we are not ourselves, cannot possess ourselves or be ourselves, until we engage in this abandonment to the other.[19]

Nor did Massignon's adventures in the hospitalanguage complex end there. In 1907, he was sent on a mission by the French Ministry of Education to explore a number of sites around Baghdad. This trip ended badly. Massignon's caravan left Baghdad in Spring 1908 with a group of guards, guides and sundry assistants. Massignon embarked on an affair with a fellow traveller, Jabbūrī, which immediately triggered jealous responses from other members of the caravan. It also turned out that Massignon was being used as a pawn in the rivalry between the German and French governments. After about a month on the road in this very tense atmosphere, as well as further conflicts and thefts, Massignon stopped the expedition, and took a riverboat, the *Burhāniyya*, back to Baghdad.

---

[19] It is perhaps no accident that shortly after meeting Luis de Cuadra, Massignon found the project that would define his entire career: al-Ḥallāj. While reading ʿAṭṭār's *Memorial of the Saints* (*Tadhkirat al-awliyā*ʾ), Massignon came across a verse that decided his intellectual destiny: 'Two *sajdas* (prostrations) suffice in love (as at dawn, and in war).' The adjacency of love and war, in this text and in Massignon's life more generally, is not insignificant, as he himself explains: 'J'ai été très frappé d'un mot de Hallâj dont la beauté m'avait frappé par un paradoxe: « Dans la prière d'amour, il n'y a pas besoin de plus de deux prosternations, de deux rak'a, mais l'ablution qui la valide doit avoir été faite *dans le sang.* » C'est un paradoxe apparent: le sang répandu est impur, surtout chez les Musulmans; oui, mais le sang du martyr ... Le martyr chez les Musulmans on l'enterre tel quel; on ne le lave pas, on ne lave pas un martyr, le sang est pur parce que le sang c'est de l'esprit. Chez les Mystiques, chez les Sémites, ce témoignage du sang, c'est le témoignage de la vie, de la vie de l'esprit ...' *EM*, 2:265.

Once aboard the boat Massignon had what can only be described as a nervous breakdown. As soon as he boarded, he was the object of disapproving gazes and comments about his behaviour and sexuality, threatened, and called a terrorist and a spy. After several failed attempts at escape and suicide, he experienced what he called 'The Visitation of the Stranger' ('La Visitation de l'Étranger'). The title that Massignon chose for this event when he related it in writing contains a by now familiar grouping of elements. It is neither vision nor revelation, it is a *visitation* by a *stranger*, a visit by an other, who appears as a combination of divine and human attributes, masked, as Massignon puts it, by Massignon's own appearance ('masqué sous mes propres traits'). This visitation turns everything in Massignon's world upside down even as he creates it anew. The principle of that re-creation is language, as witness the terms in bold in the following extract:

> No **name** remained in my memory (not even my own) that could have been **shouted** at Him to free me from His scheme and let me escape His trap. Nothing left, that is, but the **recognition** [*aveu*] of His sacred aloneness: acknowledgement of my unworthiness, the transparent shroud between us, the intangibly feminine veil of **silence** which disarms Him and becomes iridescent with His coming: through **His creative word**. [...]
>
> By a 'finalist' reversal of effects on causes, of **intersigns** on archetypes, as most men experience only when dying. And this would be an excuse if I did not propose further, here, to search through the biographies of the mystics for an **ersatz technical vocabulary** in order to 'enter into the presence' of the One whom no **Name** *a priori* dare **evoke**, neither 'You' nor 'I' nor 'He' nor 'We,' and if I did not transcribe simply a **cry** that is of course imperfect but poignant **uttered** by Rumi (quatrain 143) in which the essential, insatiable, and transfiguring divine Desire flows forth from the depths of our **silent** and naked **adoration**, at night:
>
> The One whose beauty made the Angels jealous has come in the morning twilight, and He looked into my heart:

He was crying and I cried until the coming of the dawn, then He **asked** me: 'of the two of us, who is the lover?'[20]

The visitation of the Stranger – God as the ultimate guest, as it were – gives rise to a situation where language fails utterly. The host, Massignon, has nothing left to give, not even words, and it is only as he emerges, slowly from this reverie that he begins to speak again, begins to name again, and the names that he keeps repeating are his own (*Je suis Louis Massignon*) those of Jabbūrī and al-Ḥallāj, as well as the term associated with al-Ḥallāj, *al-Ḥaqq*. These elements – his name, that of al-Ḥallāj, Jabbūrī (who represents desire) – become the axes that re-structure his mental universe. The experience of hospitality that 'saved' Massignon was not simply that of being a guest of the Arabs, but rather that of being a host, of receiving the divine guest – the Stranger – in a way and in terms similar to those of the culture of the Arabian desert. Once again, the common denominators of all these experiences are hospitality and language.

---

[20] *Testimonies and Reflections: Selected Essays of Louis Massignon*, ed. and trans. Herbert Mason (Notre Dame, IN: University of Notre Dame Press, 1989), 41–42. The language of Massignon's original is particularly powerful, including his translation of Rumi:

> Aucun **Nom** alors ne subsista dans ma mémoire (pas même le mien) qui pût Lui être **crié**, pour me délivrer de Son stratagème, et m'évader de Son piège. Plus rien; sauf **l'aveu** de Son esseulement sacré: reconnaissance de mon indignité originelle, linceul diaphane de l'entre-nous deux, voile impalpablement féminin du **silence:** qui le désarme, et qui s'irise de Sa venue: sous **Sa parole créatrice**. [...]
>
> Par un retournement « finaliste » des effets vers les causes, des **intersignes** vers les archétypes, tel que la plupart des hommes ne le réalisent qu'en mourant. Et cela m'est une excuse si je ne propose plus, ici, de chercher dans les biographies des mystiques un **vocabulaire** technique d'ersatz pour « entrer en présence » de Celui qu'aucun **Nom** *a priori* n'ose **évoquer**, ni « Toi », ni « Moi », ni « Lui », ni « Nous », et si je transcris simplement un **cri**, imparfait, certes, mais poignant, de Rumi où le Désir divin, essentiel, insatiable, et transfigurant, jaillit du tréfonds de notre **adoration silencieuse** et nue: la nuit.
>
> Ce Quelqu'un, dont la beauté rend jaloux les Anges, est venu au petit jour, et Il a regardé dans mon cœur;
>
> « Il pleurait, et je pleurais; et puis Il m'a demandé: "de nous deux, dis, qui est l'amant ?" » *EM*, 1:6–7.

Once Massignon had experienced this moment of hospitality and rescue in Iraq – this living experience of the sacred[21] – he found himself, like al-Ḥallāj, possessed by an even stronger desire to bear witness to his beliefs, and to the new self that was born at that moment. Gabriel Bounoure compared the experience of being touched by the sacred in this way to being turned inside out like a glove.[22] This pattern of reversibility produces multiple and varied effects throughout Massignon's life and work. On one hand, there is Massignon's description of the believer's soul 'conceiving' God as the divine Guest.[23] On the other hand, there is the history of vicarious suffering and reparative compassion aiming to save the greatest of sinners. Huysmans's relationship with the Satanist Abbé Boullan, who served as the model for Dr Johannès in *Là-bas*, is a key link in Massignon's commitment to this doctrine.[24] It is not merely a question of praying for, or substituting oneself for, others. It is, rather, a matter of going as

[21] I allude to Massignon's phrase, 'experience vitale du sacré chez les autres,' which occurs in a commemorative speech that he pronounced in 1959 in honour of Charles de Foucauld. Massignon credits Foucauld with helping him reconcile, or rather abandon altogether, the opposition between science and faith: 'Foucauld m'a fait sortir du problème classique des rapports entre la science et la foi, de la théorie pure, par ce que j'ai observé, vécu dans la collision opposant la foi monothéiste monolithique des musulmans à la technique perforatrice de pénétration colonial de la culture occidentale, dans ce choc qui nous a fait retrouver [. . .] la foi chrétienne dans la blessure d'une compassion divine, de combattants devenus fraternels.' *EM*, 1:125; *Testimonies*, 22. Griffiths presents a sceptical take on Foucauld, arguing that Massignon 'attributed his own attitudes to those of his contemporaries who had any sympathy for Islam' and therefore could not see 'in Foucauld the many traits which were at variance with his own concepts.' *Reactionary Revolution*, 253. One possible reason for this difference in outlook is Massignon's desire to preserve differences in frameworks of social and spiritual unity.

[22] 'Condition étonnante, où le moi parait à lui-même fonctionner au rebours et au-delà de lui-même, comme si une « *ruse de Dieu* » le retournait comme un gant. Massignon reprendra indéfiniment dans sa réflexion cet entrelacement, ce nœud de significations, cette réversibilité.' Gabriel Bounoure, 'Louis Massignon, itinéraire et courbe de vie,' in *Louis Massignon*, ed. Jean-François Six, Cahiers de l'Herne (Paris: L'Herne, 1970), 46.

[23] Bounoure describes Massignon's 'Visitation de l'Étranger' thus: 'Vouloir témoigner, n'est-ce pas une orgueilleuse ambition, une duperie de l'amour-propre, comme si nous avions constamment à notre disposition les moyens d'accès qui conviendraient au Deus absconditus. Il faudrait au croyant, pour le soutenir dans ce rôle de témoin, un don spécial lui permettant de « concevoir Dieu, comme une femme, aveuglément ».' Bounoure, 'Louis Massignon, itinéraire et courbe de vie,' 48.

[24] Griffiths, *Reactionary Revolution*, 130–138; Massignon, *EM*, 1:140–143.

far as one can in this direction, of sacrificing oneself for the sake of the worst sinners; which leads to a particular interest in the figure of Satan. The latter brings us to the intersection of Massignon's desire and expertise: al-Ḥallāj considered Satan to be the most devout of the monotheists, one whose preaching is equal to that of Muhammad; an idea he sets out in his *Ṭāwasīn*.[25] There was thus formed an indissoluble link in Massignon's mind between desire, al-Ḥallāj, and the doctrine of mystical substitution extending to the impure and satanic. This version of *concordia oppositorum* was a way of managing the frightening unpredictability of desire and the divine, of forces that drove Massignon into the arms of strange people, lands, languages, and actions, all governed by an inscrutable, terrifying deity.[26]

Al-Ḥallāj's theopathic declaration, *Anā al-Ḥaqq*, which might be translated 'I am the Truth' or 'I am the Real' (or in Herbert Mason's eloquent translation, 'God is in me as the Truth'[27]), can also be read, as it was by his detractors, to mean 'I am God', since *al-Ḥaqq* is one of the 99 Most Beautiful Names of God, and is indeed a term often used to designate God in Sufi writing. For Massignon, its echoes of Jn 14.6 ('I am the way and the truth and the life') foreground al-Ḥallāj's Christ-like reality. In his analysis of mystical language, Massignon maps the semantic field of the term, derived from the Arabic triliteral root ḤQQ, before adding a variant translation of al-Ḥallāj's utterance:

> *ḤQQ. ḥqq*. (1) in law, an ambivalent term, 'debt' or 'claim'; (2) in Hellenistic philosophy, the truth (objective truth, as opposed to *ṣidq*, subjective sincerity); (3) in mysticism, very early, the implied subject of the inspired saying, of the preaching that personalizes

[25] *Passion English*, 3:308–315; *Passion*, 3:326–333; Peter J. Awn, *Satan's Tragedy and Redemption: Iblis in Sufi Psychology* (Leiden: Brill, 1983), 122–135.

[26] Awn, *Satan's Tragedy and Redemption: Iblis in Sufi Psychology*, 188–192.

[27] *Memoir*, 25.

> and realizes; the (open) Real, Creative Truth in act. Because of the Sufis, this dynamic term, fundamentally Ḥallajian and closely tied to the Qur'an (50:41: *ṣayḥa bi'l-Ḥaqq*; cf. 42:17) became the common name for God in the Turkish, Persian, and Indian lands. The statement attributed to Ḥallāj, '*Anā al-Ḥaqq*,' is well known: 'My "I" is the Creative Truth.'[28]

The relationship that al-Ḥallāj proposes, and Massignon believes, about the link between the self and the other (both human and divine) provides the core of Massignon's immense body of scholarship. Much of al-Ḥallāj's writing is about opening the self up to the other, about somehow making space within the self for the other, being a host to the other, and allowing oneself to be changed – or indeed completely erased – as a result of this encounter.[29] Furthermore, this is not only a description of the mystical experience in al-Ḥallāj's work, but it also becomes a template for Massignon's political and ethical views about the (human) other. Massignon's work on al-Ḥallāj shows him to be a key thinker about the act of literary creation, which is itself understood as an effect of the hosting of the other within the self. This complex process of hospitality and substitution, operating in both sacred and human registers, has echoes throughout Massignon's *œuvre*, inflecting his work on culture, language, politics and human rights.

[28] Louis Massignon, *Essay on the Origins of the Technical Language of Islamic Mysticism*, trans. Benjamin Clark (Notre Dame, IN: University of Notre Dame Press, 1997), 28. '*ḤQQ*. *Ḥaqq*. 1° en droit, terme ambivalent, « dette » ou « créance ». 2° en philosophie héllenistique, la vérité (objective : opp. à *ṣidq*, sincérité subjective) 3° en mystique, de bonne heure, le sujet éminent de la phrase inspirée, de la prédication personnalisante et réalisatrice, le Réel (ouvert), la Vérité Créatrice an acte. Ce terme dynamique, fondamentalement hallagien, en relation étroite avec le Qur'ân (50, 31 : sayha bi'l Haqq ; cf. 42, 17), est devenu, à cause des sûfis, le nom commun de Dieu en pays turc persan, et indien. – On connait le mot fameux, prêté à Hallâj : « Ana'l Haqq », « Mon » « Je », c'est la Vérité Créatrice.' *Essai sur les origines du lexique technique de la mystique musulmane* (Paris: Cerf, 1999), 38.

[29] Once again, Herbert Mason sums it up well : 'He [al-Ḥallāj] spoke of his "Beloved," his "Friend," "You," as filling him with His presence to the point where his only self was Himself and he could no longer even remember his own name.' *Memoir*, 26. 'Friend' and 'Beloved' are frequently-used Sufi terms for God.

One of the many possible translations of *al-Ḥaqq* in this context is *la Vérité Créatrice*, the Creative Truth.[30] In an early article, Massignon provides a reading of this idea that combines both thomist and Islamic sources:

> Veritas est adaequatio rei et intellectus – Deus = veritas veritatum – [Truth is the adequation of thing and mind – God = truth realized] – It is as Creator that God is truth [. . .]
>
> The Ḥallājian vocabulary expressly designates in *al-Ḥaqq* pure divine being, – the creative substance, – insofar as it is opposed to creation, *al-Khalq*. *Al-Ḥaqq* is not just one of the names of God here [. . .] it should be understood in the sense that Muʿtazilism imposed on the contemporary [i.e. ninth-century CE] philosophical lexicon pure God, – the Creator.[31]

God's truth is the divine capacity for creation, understood as something that completely transcends any conceivable attribute or accident. Furthermore, coming to terms with God as Creative Truth in the manner of al-Ḥallāj leads to a reproduction of the creative process: the ecstatic who grasps this reality proceeds not only to declare it in speeches, poems and theopathic utterances; he becomes incapable of *not* articulating it. The secret of Sufism is found in the process triggered once the ascetic has understood and assumed, in his innermost self, the creative Truth that is God – he can now experience

30 Massignon's commitment to the truth antedates his discovery of al-Ḥallāj. Bernard Guyon argues that this explains Massignon's style: 'Parce qu'il avait vécu longtemps dans l'atmosphère austère, rigoureuse, puritaine, janséniste, du scientisme positiviste, il a eu d'abord et n'a jamais abandonné une foi laïque en l'existence d'une vérité scientifique qu'il faut rigoureusement respecter. D'où la confiance qu'il a toujours fait naître chez ses interlocuteurs agnostiques qui refusaient pourtant de le suivre dans son itinéraire mystique. D'où l'extrême précision, la rigoureuse construction de ses phrases. Elles n'ont jamais rien de mou, de vague, de mouvant: rien qui tremble, qui papillote, qui sente l'impressionnisme.' Bernard Guyon, 'Jalons pour une étude du style de Louis Massignon,' in *Louis Massignon*, ed. Jean-François Six, Cahiers de l'Herne (Paris: L'Herne, 1970), 108.

31 'Veritas est adaequatio rei et intellectus – Deus = veritas veritatum – C'est en tant que Créateur que Dieu est vérité. [. . .]

Le vocabulaire hallâgien désigne expressément en *al-Haqq* la pure essence divine, – la substance créatrice, – en tant qu'opposée à la création, *al-Khalq* –. *Al-Haqq* n'est pas ici simplement un des noms de Dieu [. . .] il faut le prendre tel que le mo'talizilisme l'imposait au lexique philosophique contemporain [. . .] Dieu tout pur, – le Créateur.' *EM*, 1:446.

the divine visitation that enables the connection between the transcendent source of creation and his self, his *Anā*.[32]

Massignon refers to this internal grace by the term that al-Ḥallāj's detractors used against him: *ḥulūl,* or the descent of the divine spirit into the human form. The term is also used as the basis of arguments against the divinity of Christ. Massignon, however, uses *ḥulūl* in its widest possible sense to refer to the penetration of the divine spirit into the spirit of the mystic, thereby totally transforming the latter, but without any possible confusion between the human and the divine. Here we see another instance of differences preserved in unity. The grace of divine visitation imprints and informs the heart of the mystic, who is then transported to a permanent state of unity of being, which progressively transforms his attributes to the point where he acquires his definitive self:

> *Hulūl*, the keystone of Hallajian dogmatics, is the *divine imprint* [in Arabic, *Inṭibāʿ al-Ḥaqq*] in the saint's heart, which finds itself transported to a permanent state of a Unity of being, where – after the transformation of his *ṣifāt* [attributes] – he finds himself 'transubstantiated' into divine being, with neither confusion nor destruction, and thus acquires his definitive, supreme personality : *Anā*.[33]

Asceticism thus becomes a way of cultivating, preparing the self so that it might reach a stage where it is 'imprinted' by divine grace, and so that God might speak through it.

If we were to seek a moment where Massignon commits to an interpretation of *Anā al-Ḥaqq*, it might be the following:

32 '[C]e n'est qu'après s'être démontré qu'en droit, Dieu est insaisissable, – et comme « en dehors » de la créature, – que le mystique peut comprendre et goûter dans leur réalité la grâce interne des visitations divines, – quand Dieu pénètre « au-dedans » du cœur.' *EM*, 1:446.

33 'Le *hulûl*, clef de voûte de la dogmatique hallâgienne, – c'est *l'information divine* [in Arabic, *Inṭibāʿ al-Ḥaqq*: the imprint of *al-Ḥaqq*] dans le cœur du saint, qui se trouve alors transporté dans un état permanent d'Union essentielle où, – après la transformation de ses *sifât* – il se trouve « transubstantié » en essence divine, – sans confusion ni destruction, – et acquiert ainsi sa personnalité définitive, suprême, *Ana*.' *EM*, 1:447.

> [Al-Ḥallāj] seeks the way to surrender his heart to the *Nutq*, to the vital utterance of the inmost divine creative liberty. Sanctity is a '*clairaudience*' that expresses itself. He feels he will reach it only by the strictest discipline in his observance of prescribed religious duties and the most stringent purification of his heart. And when his speech becomes only a pure, divine, inspired utterance, he will and must speak, in order to oppose with it, not only the Shīʿites, who reserve to the Imāms the *hadith qudsī*, but also the Sūfīs, who fear that public use of theopathic utterances would set in motion legal repression. But Love cannot keep quiet: 'I am the Truth' means 'God is wholly within me.'[34]

Massignon describes the discipline to which al-Ḥallāj subjected himself during a year-long stay in Mecca. The point of this exercise was precisely to open himself up, body and soul, to the sound of the Other, to become 'clairaudient', as Massignon puts it: to hear and transmit the words of the wholly Other. Elsewhere Massignon spells out the details of this discipline: fasting and orality serve not only to cleanse the soul, but also to prepare the ascetic for the possibility of receiving and re-transmitting the pure message of divine origin. This process is not necessarily voluntary. Massignon quotes al-Ḥallāj as saying that *al-ʿibāra qayʾ*: expression is vomiting; a literal ex-pression of what is within the self.[35] If the self cannot contain what is within

[34] *Passion English*, 1:23. '[C]omment soumettre son cœur au *Nutq*, à l'énonciation vitale de l'essentielle liberté divine créatrice? La sainteté est une « clairaudience » qui s'énonce. Il sent qu'il n'y arrivera que par la plus stricte discipline d'observance dans les rites prescrits et la plus dure ascèse du cœur. Et, quand sa parole ne sera plus qu'une pure énonciation divine, inspirée, il parlera, dût cela le mettre en conflit, non seulement avec les shîʿites, qui réservent aux Imâms les hadîth *qudsî*, mais avec les sûfis, qui craignent que l'usage en public de locutions théopathiques ne déclenche la répression légale. Mais l'Amour ne peut se taire: « je suis la Vérité » signifie « Dieu est tout en moi. »' *Passion*, 1:63.

[35] *Passion*, 3:37–38n., cf.1:236. Laude goes further, arguing, in light of Massignon's reading of al-Ḥallāj and the visitation of the stranger, that, 'A true person is therefore much more than an individual, a true person is a guest – the guest of a "foreign" presence accepted as messenger of the One who alone "can say truly 'I', in us."' *Pathways*, 63. Cf. Massignon's remarks on the relationship between testimony and personhood below and *EM*, 1:55–56, where Massignon describes the word as an involuntary prayer; 'un psaume, une prière « arrachée » hors de nous-mêmes.' *EM*, 1:55.

it – the natural outcome of the discipline to which the ascetic subjects himself, which leads to the divine *logos* descending into the self – then that which is within it must perforce be expressed. In al-Ḥallāj's case, this was aided and abetted by his strong opposition to the behaviour of hermits who shut themselves off from the world, keeping to themselves the spiritual benefits of their practice. Al-Ḥallāj, for his part, cannot help communicating his message to the entire world, by virtue of his 'fraternal compassion'.[36] The indicator that this message of compassion, creativity, and hospitality have reached their audience can be perceived in a key aspect of Muslim life: the *basmala*, the phrase 'In the Name of God', which is traditionally recited at the start of any significant act, including reading the Qur'an and eating a meal. To recite this phrase is, for al-Ḥallāj, to express the creative 'fiat' (=*kun*, 'be!'),[37] by which God creates the universe, in order to realize it here and now. This realization occurs by according to this divine guest of our soul and our body the most sacred of rights; asylum, hospitality.[38]

[36] 'Il [Ḥallāj] a rompu, parce qu'excédé par le dessèchement de cœur et les hypocrites « corrections fraternelles » de ces ermites qui cultivent leur perfection en vase clos, gardant pour eux les paroles de vie qui pourraient sauver les autres en ne font que les intoxiquer, eux. Mais il y a acquis et en retient l'essentiel, une technique de vie spirituelle, ascétique et mystique, où son élan les a dépassés, une voie vers Dieu le Réel, *al-Haqq*, une psychagogie dont il est résolu à communiquer, par compassion fraternelle, la méthode aux laïcs de tous les milieux.' *Passion*, 1:236.

[37] As in the phrase that occurs repeatedly in the Qur'an, *kun fayakūn*: '[God commands that something] be, and it is.' Cf. Q36:82: 'His [God's] wont, if He desires anything, is but to say to it: "Be!" and it is.' This creative imperative and the ideas attached to it will recur frequently in the rest of this study, across the work of Massignon, Corbin and Jambet.

[38] 'Dire « au Nom de Dieu ... » (=réciter la *basmala*), c'est, pour Hallâj, exprimer le « fiat » (=*kun*) créateur en Dieu même (Stf. [i.e. Sulamī's commentary on the Qur'ān, *Ḥaqā'iq al-tafsīr*]): afin de le réaliser hic et nunc: en accordant à cet hôte divin, de notre âme et de notre corps, le plus sacralisant des droits d'asile, l'hospitalité, *iqrâ*, *ikrâm al-Dayf*, *dakhâla*, *ijâra*. – Dire à Dieu « je T'aime, je Te rends grâces », c'est se donner à Lui, c'est mourir avec Lui du même Désir qu'Il a de lui-même, en Se le disant, Lui, dans le même éternel instant présent, suprême, où cette parole inouïe d'anéantissement amoureux Le ressuscite: et nous ressuscite: « ceux que le Désir tue, Il les ressuscite » [i.e. the fragment cited in the epigraph to this chapter].' *Passion*, 1:393; *Passion English*, 1:344–345. For Massignon's gloss on al-Daylamī's extract and al-Ḥallāj's poem, see *Passion*, 1:413–415; *Passion English*, 1:365–367. For the originals see Massignon, *Essai*, 359 (Sulamī) and 448 (Daylamī).

When we recite the *basmala* we find ourselves in this union with the singularity of the wholly Other.[39]

Desire as Alpha and Omega

Massignon describes al-Ḥallāj not only as the Qur'anic Christ, but (arguably more significantly) as 'a man of desire'[40] whose mysticism is oriented by that very desire:

> If he directs all of his desires through outpourings of love to God, it is to prove that the divine Spirit alone can 'fulfil' these desires, can vivify them through the supernatural gift of the self, that efficacious sacrifice without which our demonstrations of adoration (*da'wā*) and renunciation, our complete abandonment of the divine will, are of no value in uniting us with God.[41]

If God is *al-Ḥaqq*, God is also *'ishq*, or desire understood as longing. Desire is the mechanism by which Islam *becomes* Islam: elsewhere Massignon argues for the centrality of testimony in Islam (see below).[42] Al-Ḥallāj's theopathic interjections and effusions are there to bear witness to the fact that the only possible realization of desire can be in God.

Massignon refers to the notion of 'essential desire' in al-Ḥallāj's doctrine, which is to say that the being of God *is* desire, that desire is

[39] 'L'on « se retrouve » conforme à sa finalité prédestinée, dans l'union essentielle de l'Esseulement.' *EM*, 1:453. Cf. Ibn al-'Arabī's and Corbin's ideas about being 'alone with the alone' in chapter 2, below.

[40] *Passion English*, 3:3.

[41] *Passion English*, 3:5–6. 'S'il oriente par des effusions d'amour tous ses désirs vers Dieu, c'est pour attester que l'Esprit divin seul peut 'réaliser' ces désirs, les vivifier par ce don surnaturel de soi, ce sacrifice efficace, sans lequel nos protestations d'adoration (*da'wā*) et de protestation, nos adorations pléniers au choix divin sont sans valeur pour nous unir à Dieu.' *Passion*, 3:10–11.

[42] The importance of testimony in Massignon's thought is not limited to Islam, as witness this sentence about the commemoration of Huysmans: 'La conviction qui réunit les amis de Huysmans pour défendre purement sa mémoire, ne dépend pas de l'objectivité de sa conversion, mais de la véracité expérimentale de son témoignage [...] Témoignage de l'écrivain d'abord, avant le témoignage du mystique.' *EM*, 1:140–141.

creation's beginning and end. The key document in support of this reading is the poem by al-Ḥallāj cited in the epigraph to this chapter. Much of al-Ḥallāj's output, and Massignon's analysis, is concerned with connecting this eternal desire to truth (*al-Ḥaqq*) and hospitality in a sacred triangle. The idea that those who are killed by desire are promised eternal life is central to Massignon's reading of al-Ḥallāj as messianic martyr and witness. Massignon describes Ḥallāj's message as a *psychagogie*. Just what Massignon intends this to mean is not necessarily easy to discern. In French, the term is often used to describe necromancy and the magic rituals used to invoke the spirits of the dead. Massignon, however, seems to be using it in a register closer to its etymological meaning: al-Ḥallāj was a leader and guide of the souls and minds of his audience, liberating and awakening their souls to the realities of the *al-Ḥaqq* and *ʿishq* by a process not unlike Socrates' maieutics. The resonance of the term with necromancy and magic underlines the uncontrollable aspects of the process: as is the case with any creative endeavour, there is no telling where the process will go or where it will lead. No amount of prediction or calculation can foretell the outcome in the hearts and minds of al-Ḥallāj's audience. Nor is the goal of this process entirely private: the aim of al-Ḥallāj's psychagogy is not only to purify certain individuals but to restore a fallen social order through spiritual revolution. This is one of the most important lessons that Massignon learns from al-Ḥallāj: social and political change do not come about through struggle and conflict alone, but through a synthesis of struggle and vow, action and desire.[43]

In Massignon's account, the lead prosecutor in al-Ḥallāj's trial is Ibn Dāwūd, author of *The Book of Venus* (*Kitāb al-Zahra*), which develops a theory of courtly love diametrically opposed to al-Ḥallāj's

[43] We will return to this theme below, but one particularly striking example is found in Massignon's treatment of the premonitions and predictions that foretold the fall of Constantinople in 1453. *EM*, 2:336–344. Massignon reads this series of events, from early *ḥadīths* to the actual conquest of 1453, as the result of what he calls *la surhistoire*: an 'additional' history of prayer and spiritual work. *EM*, 2:338–339.

view of desire.[44] In line with the precepts of the Ẓāhirite (exoteric, literalist) school of thought, which he led, Ibn Dāwūd considers love as an illness, something that progresses in recognizable stages, can be diagnosed and, therefore, is wholly inapplicable to God.[45] Indeed, the majority of Baghdad's theologians taught that 'God cannot love Himself.' Al-Ḥallāj's doctrine of primordial desire as *the* definition of God, and the basis of the proper human relationship to Him, therefore proved threatening: God cannot be identified with an illness, nor can He fall ill. Ibn Dāwūd sees desire as a doctor sees a disease: something perfectly predictable and knowable, in a certain time and place, according to external, visible signs. Al-Ḥallāj, on the other hand, re-inscribes this desire everywhere: both within (by saying the *basmala*, for instance) and without the self, both within God and between the Sufi and God, both within the believer's heart and in his public preaching in the squares of Baghdad.

Al-Ḥallāj emphasizes the infinity and unknowability of desire through its identification with God. Massignon repeatedly stresses the fact that Ḥallāj was the only one to have equated God's being (*essence*) with desire, and that desire is the thing that makes Islam what it is – displacement, ex-patriation:

> It is expatriation through desire; in Islam the love of God is only conceivable, very paradoxically, as Desire, as an interminable ascension towards an Inaccessible uncircumscribed [One] [. . .] Al-

[44] *Passion*, 1:386–390.

[45] It bears pointing out that the idea of love as an illness, and homosexuality as an 'infection' is also found in Massignon's 'La Prière sur Sodome' (*Trois prières*, 36-43). The biggest differences between Massignon and Ibn Dāwūd would seem to be in the former's insistence on interiority and his rejection of courtly or Uranian love. Cf. Gabriel Bounoure's commentary on this aspect of the link between desire and language: 'L'égoïsme esthétique, n'étant qu'une présence jalouse à soi, un refus d'hospitalité, un refus de l'autre et de l'objet, ne lui inspirait [=à Massignon] que dégoût. La fermeture lui paraissait condamnée par la parole poétique elle-même, qui est accueil, participation, élan de feu: la part féminine du poète lui avait montré la perversion de l'uranisme et le "*sérieux chrétien*" avait remplacé chez lui le jeu artiste.' Bounoure, 'Louis Massignon, itinéraire et courbe de vie,' 52.

> Ḥallāj is the only one who dared to write that in God, being is Desire (*ʿishq*).[46]

Al-Ḥallāj's death was thus a moment of supreme self-expatriation, the summit of divine desire:

> It is a matter of supreme expatriation, an ascetic mortification of the spirit, of the peak of divine desire, as when Abraham offers the son that he promised. 'The ecstatic's desire is satisfied when the One that he loves is in him, Alone.' [i.e. al-Ḥallāj's declaration, '*Ḥasb al-wājid ifrād al-Wāhid lahu*'].[47] Stripped of all the mental representations that the ecstatic had of Him (and in which Iblīs [Satan] was caught as in a trap of crystal) God becomes pure Desire.[48]

At the summit of the mystic's journey, at which point God has transcended every possible comparison and qualification, we are left with God as Desire (or more accurately Desire desiring Itself: *ʿIshq Dhātī*). In this respect, al-Ḥallāj completely overturns the received ideas and representations of God as an Ancient of days or distant

[46] 'C'est un expatriement par le désir ; l'amour de Dieu, en Islam, n'est concevable, très paradoxalement, que comme Désir, ascension jamais achevée vers un Inaccessible incirconscrit [. . .] Hallaj est le seul à avoir osé écrire qu'en Dieu même, l'essence est le Désir *('ishq)*.' *EM*, 1:409.

[47] For reasons that will be obvious in the context of monotheism, the themes of isolation and solitude (*esseulement*) are of particular importance to al-Ḥallāj and Massignon. On al-Ḥallāj's statement linking the ecstatic saint and the isolated (*esseulé*) God – one of his last according to his biographers – see *Passion*, 1:663–665; *Passion English*, 1:613–614; *Essai*, 448–449. In addition to providing multiple translations of al-Ḥallāj's penultimate declaration, Massignon goes even further in his gloss on *ifrād* (solitude): 'The solitude of God divesting Himself of all majesty, being only a poor, and naked, Desire.' *Passion English*, 1:614. ('Esseulement de Dieu se privant de toute majesté, n'étant qu'un pauvre, et nu, Désir.' *Passion*, 1:665.) Herbert Mason's translations of al-Ḥallāj's phrase include: 'All that matters to the ecstatic is the increasing solitude of his Only One, in Himself' *Passion English*, 1:613; 'All that matters [. . .] for the ecstatic [. . .] is the Solitude [. . .] of his One in Himself' *Passion English*, 1:614; and elsewhere, 'All that matters for the ecstatic is that his Only One bring him to His Oneness.' Herbert Mason, *Al-Hallaj* (New York and Abingdon: Routledge, 1995), 32.

[48] 'Il s'agit d'un expatriement suprême, d'une ascèse mortifiant l'esprit, de la cime du désir divin; comme dans Abraham offrant le fils de la promesse. « Le désir comble l'extatique, quand Celui qu'il aime est en soi, tout Esseulé. » Dépouillé des plus hautes représentations mentales que l'extatique s'était faites de Lui (et où Iblis s'est pris comme dans un piège de cristal), Dieu est alors un pur Désir.' *EM*, 1:412.

Demiurge, re-inscribing, within the structure of the Unknown and Unknowable (*al-Ghayb*), a free Intention, appealing to this always open infinity.[49]

Language and Hospitality

Massignon's code of conduct dictating hospitality to and with the other comes from an article first published in the journal *Arabica* in 1954. The article unfolds in a theoretical space spanned by Massignon's interests in Islam and Sufism on the one hand, and his discovery of structuralism via Troubetzkoy and Lévi-Strauss on the other, bolstering his own views of language and philology as the foundation of the human sciences. The title of the article, 'Réflexions sur la structure primitive de l'analyse grammaticale en arabe' alludes to Lévi-Strauss's *Structures élémentaires de la parenté* (1949). The reflections in question revolve around a view of the Arabic language as a privileged conduit to the truth (what he calls *le vrai*, 'the true', which is a rendition of al-Ḥallāj's *al-Ḥaqq*[50]) as revealed in the Abrahamic monotheisms. The truth in question here is not constative but performative: Massignon makes much in his writing of the central importance of the *shahāda*, the confession of faith and performative speech act by which a person becomes a Muslim, in Muslim life. It is this very act that becomes a marker of both individual dignity and collective democracy: 'The human person in Islam is *testimony* above all, which makes Islamic society level, democratic and jealously

[49] 'Dire que l'Essence divine est Désir, *Ishq Dhâtî* (Hallâj) [. . .] c'est réintégrer, au-dedans de la structure essentielle du Mystère Divin, *al-Ghayb*, qui n'est pas un état, mais un Acte, une Vie donnée, une Intention libre, un Appel à cette Infinitude actuellement ouverte, et pour toujours, même à nous, insectes d'un instant ; une Nudité démasquée, pudique et désarmée, triomphale, de l'Être supérieur, qui n'apparaît aux yeux humains qu'à travers l'ablution non sanglante des larmes.' *EM*, 1:478.

[50] Nevertheless, Massignon does follow the standard procedure of translating al-Ḥallāj's locution by 'I am the Truth' ('Je suis la Vérité!') elsewhere. *EM*, 1:444–452.

individualistic.'[51] This sort of witnessing will become a key counterpart to the infinite chain of responsibilities and substitutions that constitute Massignon's ethics and politics. In Massignon's scheme, the Arabic language provides this privileged conduit to *al-Ḥaqq* in its constant evocation of the absence and inaccessibility of God. In this respect it always resists the temptation to reduce the wholly other to the same:

> Arabic is the language of the tears of those who know that in His essence God is inaccessible and that everything is best this way. If he comes into our midst, it is as a Stranger who interrupts our normal life, like a moment of rest from work, and then passes on.[52]

The truth contained within the Arabic language is the inaccessibility of God, and the ephemeral nature of his grace and presence within us.

This divine impermanence is coupled with the defining themes of hospitality and compassion in Massignon's reflections on the structure of Arabic. The discovery of both the language and the truth to which it leads are the result of the experience of hospitality: 'As a foreign guest of the Arabs, I found in their language this contact, this communicable consciousness of that which is true.'[53] Proceeding

[51] La personne humaine est, en Islam, avant tout, un *témoignage* ; ce qui fait de l'Islam une société nivelée, démocratique, jalousement individualiste.' *EM*, 1:781. Elsewhere Massignon argues that Islam is testimony above all else: 'L'Islam est avant tout témoignage oral, profession de foi, shahâda « au Nom de Dieu ».' *EM*, 1:643; *Testimonies*, 45. Cf. Edward Said's eloquent gloss on this aspect of Massignon: 'To testify is to speak, and to speak is to move from yourself toward another, to displace yourself in order to accommodate another, your opposite and your guest, and also someone absent whose absence opposes your own presence. The irony of this is that you can never directly come together with another: your testimony can at best accommodate the other, and this of course is what language does and is, antithetically – presence and absence, unless in the case of the shahid (martyr) the self is obliterated for the sake of the other, who because of the martyr's love is more distant, more an Other than ever.' Said, *The World, the Text and the Critic*, 286.

[52] *Testimonies*, 14. 'L'arabe est la langue des larmes : de ceux qui savent que Dieu, dans son essence, est inaccessible, et que tout est bien ainsi. S'il vient en nous, c'est comme un Étranger, qui rompt notre vie normale à la manière d'un intervalle délassant du travail, et il passe.' *Trois prières*, 141.

[53] 'Hôte étranger des Arabes, j'ai trouvé un jour dans leur langue ce contact, cette conscience communicable du vrai.' *EM*, 2:247.

methodologically along lines that echo those of the structuralists, Massignon sets out the 'groups' that span the linguistic possibilities of the Arabic language – the 28 consonants, trilateral roots, the three vocalizations and what he calls *involution* (Arabic *taḍmīn*), that is, the fact that every Arabic root contains multiple verbal forms within itself in another example of the same containing the other. The structure of *involution*, along with the complementary operation of *takhrīj* (adding letters to bring out the meaning contained in a linguistic root),[54] forms the linguistic basis for the experience of the other:

> I have sometimes dreamt of writing, on the bases of these four groups, an introduction 'from within' to the study of Arabic, a sort of 'Fatima, or Arabic through the Veil of Exile' in the manner of S. Reinach's 'Cornelia, or Latin without Tears,' so that the readers might 'expatriate' their desire for understanding outside their norms; decentring it, as Copernicus did the Ptolemaic universe, passing like a geometer who transforms his system of Cartesian co-ordinates into polar co-ordinates centred on the axis of the other. To understand the other, one does not need to annex him but become his guest. The 'exogamic' character of language can only be realized by using the Right to Asylum: *dakhīlak*.[55]

[54] Massignon speaks of *taḍmīn* and *takhrīj* in terms that recall Jn 12.24, as well as the life awarded to those who are 'killed' by desire in al-Ḥallāj's poem cited above: 'Le *tadmin* veut dire : « Enfouir en terre un germe pour qu'il pousse hors de terre. » [. . .] [L]e *tadmin* n'est que l'éclosion du germe spirituel enclose dans la coque mortelle du sens littéral, et n'en est pas séparable. En sémitique, le symbole surgit de la lettre, vivant sa vie dans l'obéissance à la lettre.' *EM*, 2:270.

[55] 'J'ai rêvé parfois d'écrire, sur ces quatre bases, une introduction "du dedans" à l'étude de l'arabe, une « Fatima, ou l'arabe à travers son voile d'exil » à la manière de S. Reinach, dans « Cornélie, ou le latin sans pleurs. » – Pour que les lecteurs « expatrient » leur désir de comprendre hors de leurs normes ; en le décentrant, comme Copernic son univers ptoléméen, en passant, comme le géomètre transforme son système de coordonnées cartésiennes en système de coordonnées polaires réaxés sur le centre axial de l'autre. – Pour comprendre l'autre, il ne faut pas se l'annexer, mais devenir son hôte. Le caractère « exogamique » du langage n'est réalisable qu'en usant du Droit d'Asile : « *dakhīlak* ».'

The term also carries connotations of vulnerability and suspicion: in addition to 'your guest' or 'your refugee', *dakhīlak* might also be translated by 'your intruder'. Like the duality in the French word *hôte*, the *dakhīl* can be either a friend or an enemy. Cf. Emile Benveniste, *Vocabulaire des institutions indo-européennes* (Paris: Minuit, 1969), 1:87–101.

Massignon's argument is best approached as a series of displacements and substitutions. The proposed title of Massignon's Arabic grammar is a calque on a Latin primer that was indeed published by the classicist Salomon Reinach in 1912 and went through multiple editions: *Cornélie, ou le latin sans pleurs* (*Cornelia, or Latin without Tears*). Massignon considers expatriation to be a key part of understanding in general and learning Arabic in particular. It is not enough to learn from a textbook: the student of Arabic will have to travel, and risk never returning from the voyage into the Arabic language and Arabic culture. This is, of course, what happened to Massignon himself, and the term expatriation has, as we have seen, been particularly important in explaining the operation of his and al-Ḥallāj's ideas. Furthermore, Massignon never forgot the fact that it was as a guest of the Arabs, in Iraq, that he was not only saved from physical danger but that he was brought back to himself spiritually. In 1961, a year before his death, he wrote: 'I must say, it is the Arabs who taught me this religion of hospitality forty years ago when I was under arrest and in danger of death having been denounced as a colonialist (spy). But I was their guest and I was safe; released after three days out of respect for God, for the Guest.'[56] Massignon therefore proposes something more serious than a mid-century Arabic primer. What he is getting at is the importance of completely decentring oneself in order to prepare for the arrival of the other; or indeed to abandon oneself to the other's desire. Learning a language depends on the same mechanisms that brought al-Ḥallāj to God.

Massignon relies on two figures to convey this particular sort of displacement: co-ordinate transformations and the narrative of the Copernican revolution. This particular image complex recurs with

[56] 'Je dois le dire, ce sont les Arabes qui m'ont appris cette religion de l'hospitalité, il y a quarante ans de cela, arrêté, en danger de mort, dénoncé comme colonialiste. Mais j'étais l'hôte et j'ai été sauvé ; après trois jours relâché par respecte de Dieu, de l'Hôte.' 'Le Problème des réfugiés et son incidence sur le Proche-Orient,' *Politique étrangère* 14, no. 3 (1949): 231, https://www.persee.fr/doc/polit_0032-342x_1949_num_14_3_2806.

some frequency chez Massignon, and often in relation to al-Ḥallāj's statement, *Anā al-Ḥaqq*. The link between hospitality, decentring and compassion appears in the preface to his *Passion of Ḥallāj* in a passage that uses one of Massignon's structural keywords, *involution*:

> The Hallājian method leads to an involution of reason in its object, which is the pure essence, and not the contingent: God, entirely alone [. . .] Hallāj teaches us that one must unite with a thing not in us, but in the thing itself (*Stf.*, No 84); the world, for example, by means of a transfiguring compassion with the suffering of the world.[57]

The parenthetical reference (*Stf.*84) refers to a key moment in an important commentary on the Qur'ān by Muḥammad b. al-Ḥusayn al-Sulamī, an early Sufi hagiographer whose exegesis contains a great deal of material attributed to al-Ḥallāj. *Ad* Q18:78–81, al-Ḥallāj formulates his principle regarding the relationship between subject and object across the principle of *qurb* (proximity, understood as proximity to God in the first instance): 'Approaching things with the self is distancing [from those things], and approaching them in themselves is proximity.'[58] Just what this might mean is explained in Massignon's *Essay* on the vocabulary of Sufism, where he spells out the implication that *qurb* is effectively substitution:

> In the fragment Stf [Sulamī's *Tafsīr*] 84, Hallāj explains that true 'closeness' (*qurb*) is achieved by a mental 'approach.' Which is not external annexation of the object by gradual analysis of its differentials but internal substitution of oneself for the object, by being transported unto the midst of it in a mental decentring

57 *Passion English*, 1:lvi. 'Le procédé hallagien aboutit à une involution de la raison en son objet, qui est l'essence pure, et non le contingent : Dieu, tout esseulé. [. . .] Ḥallāj enseigne qu'il faut nous rapprocher d'une chose non en nous, mais en elle (*Stf.*, no. 84) : du monde, par exemple, au moyen d'une compassion transfigurante à la souffrance du monde.' *Passion*, 1:21.

58 القرب من الشيء بالنفوس هو البعد والقرب منها بها هو القرب
Massignon, *Essai*, 378.

> analogous to the Copernican decentring of Ptolemy's system of understanding the world. This method is the basis of all of Hallāj's parables […] It is not an intellectualization detached from the experience of love's ecstasy; it is a conversion from a system of rectangular coordinates to one of polar coordinates.[59]

Massignon wrote these lines in 1922. But he repeats the point in the late 1950s and early 1960s in a pattern that attests to the ethical, intellectual and spiritual importance of the ideas involved.

> Ḥallāj used to say: To understand something is not to *annex* it to oneself, but rather to transfer oneself to the very centre of the other; it is like what happened when we substituted the system of Copernicus for that of Ptolemy; we thought we were the centre of the world on earth, he operated a *decentring*. The essence of Language must be a kind of decentring, we cannot make ourselves understood unless we enter into the system of the other, as Péguy used to say: 'He who loves enters into the dependency of the beloved.' Christ came to serve.[60]

The practice that most frequently invokes and re-enacts these substitutions and decentrings is the salutation of the stranger. In that same essay, Massignon emphasizes the intercultural relationship in the contact with the other, explicitly bridging the gap between hosting the divine as formulated by al-Ḥallāj and being a guest of the other in a more worldly context:

59 Massignon, *Essay*, 32 n. 'Ḥallāj explique que la vraie 'proximité' (*qurb*) se réalise par un "rapprochement" mental. Qui ne consiste pas à s'annexer l'objet du dehors, en analysant graduellement ses différentielles, mais à s'y substituer du dedans, en se transportant en son centre par un décentrement mental; analogue au décentrement copernicien du système de Ptolémée… Ce n'est pas une "intellectualisation" *ex eventu* de l'extase amoureuse, c'est une transformation en coordonnées polaires d'un système de coordonnées rectangulaires.' *Essai*, 43 n.

60 'Hallāj le disait: Comprendre quelque chose d'autre ce n'est pas *s'annexer* la chose, c'est se transférer au centre même de l'autre ; c'est comme dans le système de Copernic, quand on l'a substitué au système de Ptolomée ; nous nous croyions le centre du monde sur terre, il a fait un *décentrement*. L'essence du Langage doit être une espèce de décentrement, nous ne pouvons nous faire comprendre qu'en entrant dans le système de l'autre, comme disait Péguy : « Celui qui aime entre dans la dépendance de celui qui est aimé. » Le Christ est venu pour servir.' *EM*, 2:268.

> Salutation is the very beginning of language. Language is exogamic, as Lévi-Strauss put it very profoundly [. . .] In Salutation, the first thing is that we salute the *stranger*, the other, which is something *immense*. This is the entire issue of hospitality. It is the thing that has attached me to the Arabs since it [i.e. hospitality] saved me in their lands.[61]

What is at work in Massignon's ethics of intercultural contact would thus seem to be something more intense than merely being 'open' or 'tolerant' of others. The invocation of Lévi-Strauss is not innocent, nor are the citations from Péguy, the mention of Christ and use of the language of salutation and hailing. The sort of openness to the other implied here is what might usefully be called an openness of the messianic variety: we become compassionate guests of the other by risking, indeed sacrificing ourselves for their sake, in their territory. Let us also note the consequences of what Massignon means by *involution*: if al-Ḥallāj says 'I am God' it is because he has de-centred himself, transformed himself, transferred himself to the axis of the Other, who is God. Openness to the other thus entails turning oneself inside out, just as the operation of semitic languages involves a turning of the root inside out to generate the verbal forms that constitute the linguistic and cultural spaces of Arabic and Hebrew (*inter alia*) as idioms of hospitality and truth. [62]

Having prescribed expatriation as the *a priori* condition of learning another language, and specifically the Arabic language, Massignon declares that the rules of asylum must ground the appearance of the

[61] 'La Salutation, c'est tout le commencement du langage. Le langage est exogamique, comme l'a dit très profondément Lévi-Strauss [. . .] Dans la Salutation, c'est la première chose : nous saluons *l'étranger*, l'autre, ce qui est une chose *énorme*. C'est tout le problème de l'hospitalité. C'est la chose qui m'a attaché aux Arabes depuis que j'ai été sauvé chez eux par elle.' *EM*, 2:263.

[62] The importance of Arabic as a medium of hospitality is emphasized elsewhere by Massignon: 'C'est de ce texte fondamental [the Qur᾿ān] que l'Islam a déduit le principe de l'*Iqra* (*dakhâla, jiwâr*), droit d'hospitalité ; d'*ikrâm al-dayf, respect sacré de la personne humaine* de l'hôte envoyé par Dieu.' *EM*, 1:789.

exogamic character of language. Lévi-Strauss defines exogamy as the necessary first step of creating group cohesion, of avoiding the fission and segmentation which consanguineous marriages would bring about.[63] Exogamy enables exchange, and exchange is socially valuable in and of itself, providing means of superimposing alliances and treaties governed by rule on the natural links of kinship. He also enumerates the social permutations of kinship in terms that prefigure what Massignon does with semitic languages in terms of their conception as structures and differential characteristics. In his conclusion Lévi-Strauss goes still further, developing the well-known equivalence between linguistics and anthropology.[64] Massignon foregrounds the role of language in enabling social integration with others. If we are to be well integrated with others, Massignon is saying, it can only be by being hospitable: by granting them, and allowing them to grant us, asylum in our respective linguistic and cultural spaces. The importance of the other in this process comes out in another intervention by Massignon on intercultural contact, where he anticipates and rejects the terminology that would become current some thirty years after his death in the work of Samuel Huntington.[65] Massignon dismisses the inevitability of a conflictual relationship between cultures with a majestic sweep of the hand in the name of hospitality:

> I do not share the Cartesian conception of a 'clash' of cultures opposing a modern, technical culture to one that is outdated and

[63] Claude Lévi-Strauss, *Les Structures élémentaires de la parenté*, Second edn (Berlin: Mouton de Gruyter, 2002; repr., 2002), 550–551.

[64] Lévi-Strauss quotes William Isaac Thomas: 'exogamy and language [...] have fundamentally the same function – communication and integration with others.' Lévi-Strauss, *Structures*, 565; William Isaac Thomas, *Primitive Behavior: An Introduction to the Social Sciences* (New York: McGraw-Hill, 1937), 182.

[65] Although the phrase 'clash of civilizations' is most frequently associated with Samuel Huntington, Richard Bulliet has identified an earlier instance that might have inspired Massignon's use of the word 'clash'; namely Basil Mathews's *Young Islam on Trek: A Study in the Clash of Civilisations* (1926). Richard W. Bulliet, *The Case for Islamo-Christian Civilization* (New York: Columbia University Press, 2004), 1–4.

> non-technical [. . .] The first contact between two civilizations, both primitive and hostile, is the principle of hospitality. Hospitality is supposing that the stranger, the enemy, nonetheless has something good to offer.[66]

The First World War, which saw multiple instances of strangeness and enmity, was especially significant in underlining the importance of hospitalanguage for Massignon. By 1914 he had been mobilized and gained some serious front-line experience of war in the 1st Zouave and 56th Colonial Infantry regiments, earning a medal in 1916 for his reconnaissance activities during the Dardanelles campaign of 1915. Due to his expertise in Arabic, Turkish, Persian and Middle Eastern affairs more generally, he was assigned to François-Georges Picot as an adviser on the Sykes–Picot accord in 1917, taking part in negotiations with Prince Faisal and King Hussein in May of that year, eventually meeting T.E. Lawrence and joining him in the triumphant entry of the Entente forces under Allenby into Jerusalem in December. We might mention in passing that Massignon had a much better relationship with Sir Mark Sykes, who, in his opinion, 'got' something about the Arab world that other Entente and colonial leaders including Picot missed completely and disastrously.[67] Massignon's account of that experience and of Lawrence in particular is telling, as much by what is said as by the implied contrast between Lawrence and himself. It is as if Lawrence were stuck in the place that Massignon was in when he had his crisis: unsafe, insecure, inarticulate. By 1917, Massignon had mastered

[66] 'Je ne partage pas la conception cartésienne de « clash » des cultures opposant une culture moderne technique à une culture périmée non technique [. . .] Le premier contact entre deux civilisations, primitives et hostiles, c'est le principe de l'hospitalité. L'hospitalité, c'est de supposer que l'étranger, l'ennemi, a quelque chose de bon, tout de même, à nous donner.' *Opera minora*, ed. Youakim Moubarac, 3 vols (Beirut: Dar Al-Maaref, 1963), 1:209–213.

[67] Louis Massignon, 'In Memoriam Sir Mark Sykes: Remarks on the Present Disruption of British Policy in the Near East,' *Revue du Monde Musulman* 37 (1918–1919).

multiple languages in addition to Arabic, was exact to a fault, and, having overcome his crisis, became quite officer-like despite his aversion to what he called the officer's mentality (i.e. their cowardice and corruption). Lawrence, on the other hand, combined a wild, savage personality with what Massignon calls 'a young girl's shyness [*des timidités de jeune fille*]' and, to Massignon's amazement, a poor grasp of Arabic language and Islamic Law.[68] This difference in approach to the other – roughly what one might call the scholarly approach and the adventurer's approach – leads to a disturbing conclusion: 'I felt that Lawrence avoided any effort to be close. "You like the Arabs more than I do," he concluded.'[69] Whereas Massignon might have thought that his responsibility as an advisor to Sykes-Picot and a collaborator with Lawrence would be to construct a Middle East in which people could live together, in a hospitable post-Ottoman paradise,[70] Lawrence prefers the monastic solitude of the desert. Massignon's account on this point is striking by the profusion of ascetic terms:

> He talked, not of a future to be built with others, but of a kind of solitary space for two in a strange detachment from the world. He brought to mind a kind of elemental freedom forged out of an

[68] The full passage brings out the vast difference between Massignon and Lawrence when it comes to speaking Arabic: 'Nous nous tâtâmes; lui me répondait dans un dialectal dépouillé, véhément, pas très correct, heurté.' Lawrence tried to confide in Massignon the Hashemite plan to have King Hussein declared the Imām, rather than the Caliph, of the Muslim *umma*, but Massignon adds: 'Mais c'etait là le bout de sa science en « Usûl al-Fiqh ».' *EM*, 1:564.

[69] *Testimonies*, 34. 'Je sentis que Lawrence se déroberait à toute tentative de vie commune; « vous aimez les arabes plus que moi » conclut-il.' *EM*, 1:564.

[70] Nor was this his idea alone, as witness Alfred Le Châtelier's article on the 'United States of the Orient' as a possible future configuration of the Ottoman Empire. Alfred Le Châtelier, 'États-Unis d'Orient,' *Revue du Monde Musulman* 36 (1918–1919). It bears pointing out that Massignon was officially appointed *suppléant* to Le Châtelier's Chair in Muslim Sociology at the Collège de France in 1919, that his name is listed as *directeur* of the *Revue du Monde Musulman* on the journal's masthead as of this year, and, finally, that in this particular volume Le Châtelier's article is followed immediately by Massignon's eulogy for Mark Sykes. All of this attests to the intellectual and personal esteem attached to Massignon by this time.

> asceticism so utterly withdrawn that my own naked faith was shocked by the presence of his *no man's land*.[71]

Lawrence seems to outdo Massignon on the terrain of asceticism, except that it is applied to an undertaking where it cannot possibly thrive; namely international affairs. The ability to imagine a common international and interreligious future – a sort of everyone's land, as opposed to Lawrence's no man's land – is the mark of Massignon's self-overcoming, as well as the foundation for his postwar political vision for a new Middle East policy based on hospitalanguage. Massignon's superior grasp of Arabic enables, in his mind, a better future for the postwar world than Lawrence's broken and as it were faithless Arabic; a dialect for a moribund world without a future.[72]

The story of Massignon's and Lawrence's involvement in the Sykes-Picot accords does not end well: as they listened to Allenby proclaim martial law in Jerusalem they realized that they were betrayed by the British government, as they would be by the French government after the battle of Meissaloun in 1920.[73] Again, Massignon's account of this appalling turn of events revolves around the question of language and hospitality:

> Lawrence stayed close to me; his defeat was equal to mine, or even worse, and his innate nobility made him open his heart to me. Charged with assuring King Hussein that the Holy City would be

71 *Testimonies*, 35. The original is striking by the ascetic/mystical terminologies it employs: 'C'est lui qui parla, non pas d'un avenir à construire ensemble, mais dans une espèce **d'esseulement** à deux, dans un étrange **détachement** du monde; il me fit penser à une sorte de **liberté essentielle**, faite d'une **ascèse si renoncée** que toute ma foi dépouillée s'y aheurtait: en *no man's land*.' *EM*, 1:564; emphasis mine.

72 An earlier version of the Massignon-Lawrence encounter, published in Massignon's short introduction to a French translation of Lawrence's letters (1949), shows that initially the narrative was biased towards a love of the language rather than its speakers: 'Lawrence a-t-il écrit une seule [lettre] à Fayçal en arabe? Il m'a dit ne pas aimer autant que moi cette langue, il s'y était forgé un dialectal heurté, sarcastique et hautain, langue de chef de bande; était-ce par pudeur ? Dieu le sait.' *EM*, 1:567.

73 Henry Laurens, *La Question de Palestine. Tome premier: 1799–1922, l'invention de la Terre sainte* (Paris: Fayard, 1999), 314–375.

> entrusted to him, Lawrence had just learned about the negotiations of Lord Balfour with Lord Rothschild for a Jewish homeland. His country had entrusted him with the task of betraying his host, and Lawrence felt it was a sacrilege committed in violation of a promise given to an Arab, just as I had felt earlier at Meissaloun. Our entry into the Holy City occurred under this sign of this desecration.[74]

Every speech act in this passage relates to hospitality as a sacred duty with very real political consequences. The situation itself is striking: two queer men, assigned to help their respective colonial governments carve up what is left of the Ottoman Empire in the Middle East in recognition of their expertise, both 'sexual outlaws' in a no man's land, are both betrayed by the very governments that they served. One had excellent classical Arabic, while the other extended his rebellion even to the study of language and just picked up whatever spoken nomadic Arabic he could. As a result, one survived the experience of betrayal while the other seems to have been broken by it. If the 'religion' of hospitality can protect, it is only through the hospitalanguage complex, which dictates fidelity to language as well as to the guest.

After the war, and for the rest of his life, Massignon was relentless in calling for this hospitable and linguistic reconstruction of the Middle East. In a talk that he gave in 1921 and subsequently published in 1922, Massignon lays out the programme that will stay with him until his death, and which gives rise to some of the statements that we saw today. Massignon begins by reminding his audience that the key players in the *nahḍa* were predominantly Arab Christians who saw

[74] *Testimonies*, 37. Again, the vocabulary of the original emphasizes Massignon's outrage and sadness at the position he shared with Lawrence: 'Lawrence resta près de moi, sa défaite était égale à la mienne, et même pire, et sa noblesse innée m'ouvrit alors son cœur; chargé de **faire croire** au roi Hussein qu'on lui confierait la Ville sainte, Lawrence venait d'apprendre les tractations de Lord Balfour avec Lord Rothschild pour le Foyer juif. Son pays l'avait chargé de **tromper son hôte**, et Lawrence ressentait **le sacrilège commis contre la parole donnée à un Arabe**, comme je devais la ressentir à mon tour lors de Meïssaloun. Notre entrée dans la Ville sainte s'était faite sous le signe de la **désécration.**' *EM*, 1:566; emphasis mine.

themselves as Arabs first and Christians second. And their work in the formation of an Arab identity revolved around the reinvention and reconstitution of the Arabic language. Massignon makes parallels with the various European and Asian nationalisms of the nineteenth century, all of whom were boosted if not driven by the rediscovery and republication of ancient texts in their respective languages. The Arabic language had a different history, of course – it never quite disappeared in the way that ancient Greek did, but was eclipsed both from without (by Persian, Turkish, European imperial languages) and from within (by the spoken Arabic dialects). Nevertheless, for Massignon the key principle is that the language operates as something that brings people together. The Ottoman authorities were not blind to the danger that this posed: between 1890 and 1920, for instance, they did not allow the publication of a single book in Arabic in Aleppo, and enforced Turkish in Damascus by methods that Massignon describes as being 'purement germaniques.'[75] The importance of the language and its speakers as the basis for a postwar political configuration can be heard in the phrase that Massignon attributes to King Hussein: 'I am an Arab *before* being a Muslim' [Je suis arabe *avant* d'être musulman.][76] Massignon says that there is something that he only understood by speaking Arabic, and that thing, in sum, is the religion of hospitality, now seen as something which, like the Arabic language, operates as a common denominator wherever Arabic is spoken:

> There are among the Arabs certain everyday virtues that we do not often find among those who claim to be civilized. Yes, they shot at me in the desert, as a precaution or with premeditation, but I also experienced what is called *ḍiāfa*, hospitality, this thing which is,

[75] *EM*, 1:545.

[76] *EM*, 1:548. Massignon had cited this phrase as early as 1919, in his eulogy for Mark Sykes, which underlines its importance for his political outlook. 'In Memoriam Sir Mark Sykes,' 17.

> alas, disappearing in our Western countries; a disinterested hospitality, not the commercial Anglo-Saxon variety that always seeks something in return, but the hospitality of those who know that they will probably never see their guests again.[77]

Hospitality thus takes precedence over any other sort of social or economic intercourse. When Massignon advises the colonial and mandate authorities to encourage the teaching and speaking of Arabic, be it in Syria or Algeria, he is actually encouraging the propagation of hospitalanguage.

From *Anā al-Ḥaqq* to *Satyagraha*

The nexus of hospitality and the emergence of the truth is also evident in Massignon's relationship to another important contemporary; namely, Gandhi. As early as 1921, Massignon made a point of introducing Gandhi's ideas to the francophone public.[78] Foremost among them was *Satyagraha*,[79] the avowed 'defence' or holding fast to the truth that brings Gandhi close to al-Ḥallāj; a relationship that Massignon consistently foregrounded in his later writings where the independence of colonial states occupies an ever-larger space.[80] For Massignon, the nexus between God, the Truth (*al-Ḥaqq*, *satya*) and hospitality becomes the basis for a spiritual programme of political

77 '[I]l y a chez les Arabes [...] certaines vertus usuelles que l'on ne rencontre pas fréquemment chez nos civilisés. Certes l'on m'a tiré dessus au désert, par précaution ou avec préméditation, mais j'y ai connu aussi ce que l'on appelle *diafa*, l'hospitalité, cette chose qui, hélas, dans nos pays occidentaux, disparaît de plus en plus, une hospitalité désintéressée, non pas l'hospitalité commerciale anglo-saxonne du donnant donnant, mais l'hospitalité de celui qui sait qu'il ne reverra probablement jamais son obligé.' *EM*, 1:560.

78 'Documents sur la situation sociale dans l'Inde,' *Revue du monde musulman* 44–45 (1921): 55–63.

79 Massignon offers multiple definitions of *Satyagraha* :' « défense de la vérité » par un vœu, une parole donnée'; 'la revendication civique du vrai' and, in a piece written in English, 'steadfastness in keeping a hold on truth.' *EM*, 2:807, 2:799; *Testimonies*, 140.

80 *EM*, 1:412; 2:799–819; *Testimonies*, 149.

liberation and justice. As a devout Catholic, Massignon persistently felt that something was lacking in what he called the 'materialist' approach of the world's leading powers after the Second World War. Without an opening to the intervention of the sacred, neither communism nor capitalism could work. Without a degree of respect for the human based in the value of honour and made manifest in the keeping of promises and vows, no political configuration could succeed. The texts that he wrote in the 1940s and 1950s echo this increasingly strident anticolonial position, based on restituting the place of the truth – understood as *al-Ḥaqq*, both God and truth – within the space of human affairs.

Massignon's reading of Gandhi traces a straight line between the cardinal virtues of hospitality and *Satyagraha* on one hand, and political action on the other. Unity is the value that presides over this process: unity between the divine and the human (as seen through the case of al-Ḥallāj) and unity between people, as seen through Gandhi's efforts for the creation of a united India.[81] The question of unity gives rise to one of the most curious comparisons in Massignon's *œuvre*: the mirror of the betrothed (*miraye Bibi Meryem*: the mirror of Our Lady Mary) as a metaphor for the gaze that we should train on the guest. This custom, observed in Persia, India and Afghanistan, stands for a unity in alterity: when they first meet, the betrothed couple do not look directly at each other, but rather see each other in a mirror. They thus see themselves as God sees them – 'decentred' or expatriated – and have a common vision of the truth that they are:

> Let us not cast our gaze upon this Guest. Let us regard the Guest first in what is called the 'mirror of the betrothed' or 'mirror of Bibi Meryem' [i.e. the Virgin Mary] [. . .] They (the betrothed) look first at the far end of the room, and it is there, in the mirror, that they see each other in a corrected position, *mutaqābilīn* (Q37:43, 56:16), as

[81] *EM*, 2:796.

> they will when they face each other in Paradise, and as God, hidden deep in their hearts, sees them, decentred, outside their reciprocal egoisms.[82]

This unity in truth is something to which the other invites us, just as we invite the other into our space. Elsewhere, Massignon argues that this particular perspective, where one encounters the other face to face (*mutaqābilīn*) as a figure for a common vision of justice as seen through the other.[83] Seeing oneself in the mirror, seeing oneself as another alongside the other, becomes a necessary condition for solidarity.

These figures of unity buttress the institution of hospitality. For Massignon, the guest is not merely a figure of God: the guest *is* God. As such the visitation of the stranger is an occasion for showing openness to the divine rather than distrust and contempt. In the case of Gandhi, this translates into the dissolution of the boundaries of caste and religion in favour of real unity on all fronts:

> Above the banal intellectual syncretism of ordinary Hinduism, Gandhi pushed his passion for Unity as far as this realization of unity with the Stranger that is hospitality, and which is the consummation of the 'works of mercy', because it contains them all, abolishing the untouchable status of the Pariahs, sacrificing caste privilege for the sake of the Pariahs; he received in exchange the right to participate in the salvific rites from which the Islamic monotheisms are exempt.
>
> [. . .]
>
> In the last analysis, there are not multiple (eight, they say) works of mercy; there is only one: sacred hospitality, which trusts the

[82] 'Et ne lançons pas notre regard directement sur cet Hôte, regardons-le d'abord dans ce qu'on appelle, en Perse, aux Indes et en Afghanistan, le « miroir des fiancés », ou le « miroir de Bibi Meryem » [. . .] Ils regardent d'abord au fond du salon, et c'est dans le miroir qu'ils s'aperçoivent en position redressée, *mutaqâbilîn* (Coran 37, 43 ; 56, 16); l'œil droite à droite, l'œil gauche à gauche, comme dans le face-à-face du Paradis, tels que Dieu les voit, caché au fond de leurs cœurs, décentrés hors de leurs égoïsmes réciproques.' *EM*, 2:801.

[83] *EM*, 2:344.

> Guest, this mysterious stranger, this unknown person who is God, disarmed, placing Himself at our mercy.[84]

The punctuation and vocabulary in these passages (passion, Unity) stress the importance of uniting with the stranger and the passage across religious gaps: just as al-Ḥallāj's cry *Anā al-Ḥaqq* made him the *Christ coranique* in Massignon's eyes, so is Gandhi's full (i.e. spiritual) participation in Muslim rites licensed by his welcome to the other. This is what defines the message of the Congress Party for Massignon, over against the separatism of Jinnah and the idea of Pakistan.[85]

Massignon's treatment of hospitality brings us to a closely related question: the feminine. Although he was far from being a feminist, the key concept of hospitality in his work is bound inextricably with women in general and two exemplary women – Mary and Fāṭima – in particular.[86] Hospitality is naturally inscribed in the process of conception; in the acceptance of an other within the body and the self in a way that determines, and subverts, one's being. Massignon repeatedly cites the *fiat* of Mary, her consent to the divine will and Word, as an exemplary instance of hospitality. Femininity names the capacity for receiving the divine guest. In the essay on Gandhi, Massignon goes further still by generalizing this principle and linking it to his own spiritual conversion:

> In the life of man, woman represents the visitation of the Stranger, of the sacred. She is the sign of hospitality, she substitutes cognatic

[84] 'Plus haut que le syncrétisme intellectualiste banal de l'hindouisme ordinaire, Gandhi poussa sa passion de l'Unité jusqu'à cette réalisation de l'unité avec l'Étranger qui s'appelle l'hospitalité, qui est la consommation des « œuvres de miséricorde », parce qu'elle les contient toutes, abolissant l'intouchabilité des parias; sacrifiant ses privilèges de caste aux parias; il reçut en échange participation aux rites de salut dont les monothéismes islamiques ont eu dispensation.

[…]

Il n'y a pas, au fond, plusieurs (huit, dit-on) œuvres de miséricorde, il n'y en a qu'une, c'est l'hospitalité sacrée, qui fait foi à l'Hôte, à cet étranger mystérieux, cet inconnu qui est Dieu même venant se mettre à notre merci, désarmé.' *EM*, 2:798–800.

[85] *EM*, 2:799.

[86] Laude, *Pathways*, 103–112.

> kinship for the masculine kinship of the agnates, she suspends this legal kinship four times in the legal genealogy of the Messiah (Tamar, Rahab, Ruth, Bathsheba) before abolishing it in the virgin conception, with Mary.[87]

The feminine as the sign of hospitality operates by substituting a spiritual, matrilineal genealogy for the patrilineal, carnal genealogy that often furnishes the legal norm. The Virgin Birth takes this principle to its summit, thereby expanding this mode of conception to all of humanity and making it universal. This nexus of hospitality, universalism and spiritual genealogy is especially important for Massignon as it provides the basis for his reading of the Muslim recognition of the mission of Jesus.[88] This notion of universalism based on hospitality also extends to Massignon's reading of al-Ḥallāj, who did not shy away from using a multitude of figurative and symbolic idioms and modes to bear witness of God as Host and source of all difference in His Creation.[89] Hospitality is the mode of being and unity between divine and human nature. The guest, who is always divine for Massignon, opens up unexpected futures, while at the same time embodying the reminder of the value of the human insofar as the latter houses and protects the soul. Hospitality makes us superhuman by keeping the sacred core of our world alive and ever-present.[90]

[87] 'La femme, dans la vie de l'homme, représente la visitation de l'Étranger, du sacré. Elle est le signe de l'hospitalité, elle substitue la parenté cognatique à la parenté généalogique mâle des agnats, elle suspend cette parenté légale, quatre fois, dans la généalogie légale du Messie (Thamar, Rahab, Ruth, Bethsabée), avant de la supprimer dans la conception virginale, avec Marie.' *EM*, 2:796.

[88] 'Or, l'essentiel du message monothéiste rigoureux de Muhammad, s'exilant à Médine, dans un milieu biblique israélite, a été de proclamer, à propos du Messie, le secret virginal de la transcendance intacte de la gloire de Dieu, le secret des cœurs que les Anges ne peuvent deviner, l'Élection, cela que ce Messie doit révéler en revenant pour le Jugement Dernier.' *EM*, 1:214–215. Given Massignon's belief in the divinity of Christ, this passage sheds further light on his claim that saying the *basmala* accords the right of asylum to God.

[89] Massignon, *Passion*, 1:237–249; *Passion English*, 1:192–204.

[90] 'Il faut dans l'hospitalité (c'est elle, non la parenté charnelle, qui est la base de la société définitive), percer jusqu'à sa signification essentielle, d'apparentement de la nature divine à notre nature humaine, leur unité, cette « passion de l'être ».

Witness and Human Rights

Massignon's semiotics of gender include one further opposition that recurs repeatedly within his *œuvre*; one between men who speak and bear witness and women who are silent and conceive: 'The man attests, while the woman conceives. The *shahāda* (bearing witness that God is one) becomes, for women, a *dhikr khafī* (memorial of the heart).'[91] Far from being a lesser form of devotion, this is precisely what brings women spiritually closer to God in Massignon's universe, and what defines their place alongside Gandhi in his struggle for *Satyagraha*.

Nor is this all. The structure of witnessing (*shahāda*) is, as we have seen, central to the dignity of the human being in Islam, and the source of a key problem in the politics of imperialism and postcolonialism, where the repeatedly broken promises of the imperial powers operating in Muslim lands has given rise to enmity and rage. The importance of the ability to testify in everyday legal, social and commercial situations and in the Ḥallājian space of bearing witness to the Truth, *al-Ḥaqq* that is God, ultimately founds the status of the *shāhid ānnī*, the witness in a given present moment to God's being as *al-Ḥaqq*.[92] If hospitality works in Massignon's scheme, it is only as a result of this primordial moment of human witness to the divine, and the recognition that every stranger, every guest, is a divine emissary: that the guest is the guest of God, *ḍayf Allah*. Accordingly, 'we only

[. . .]

Le sacré [. . .] est une prise de contact, une proposition, à notre adresse, de structures mentales nouvelles, inattendues; notre Hôte nous propose des réalités « en devenir », des futurs libres, des finalités potentielles regorgeant d'intelligibilité, qui s'objectiveront: indéfiniment « ouvertes », et pour toujours, dans le sens de la recherche la plus infinie, et de l'espérance la plus théologale. Par l'hospitalité, nous trouvons le sacré au centre du mystère de nos destinées, comme une aumône furtive, et divine, dont aucune assurance, sociale ou autre, ne nous dispensera jamais.' *EM*, 2:802.

91 'L'homme atteste, tandis que la femme conçoit. La *shahâda* (attestation que Dieu est Un) devient chez la femme un *dhikr khafî* (mémorial du cœur).' *EM*, 2:796–797. This opposition resurfaces in Massignon's aforementioned essay on the elementary structures of the Arabic language in relation to a South Tunisian aphorism reported by Gilbert Boris: masculine silence is refusal, while feminine silence is consent. *EM*, 2:247.

92 *EM*, 1:782.

have access to the mystical, above all in Semitic cultures, through perfect hospitality, the right of asylum, *ikrām al-ḍayf*, philoxenia.'[93] Bearing witness enables philoxenia, which in itself reinforces the faith of the witness, opening up the prospect of a universal right of asylum: 'Abraham's hospitality foretells the final consummation of all nations, blessed by Abraham, and assembled in this Holy Land that must not be monopolized by any of them.'[94]

That, at least, is how things *should* work. In the imperial scenario things unfold in a more detrimental direction. The desacralization – indeed, the denigration – of the institution of hospitality renders enmity inevitable. The ceremonies that frame hospitality – preamble, salutation, prophylactic rites, polite conversation – are meant to operate as an 'embryonic' version of social relations more generally.[95] The stranger, the guest, is understood to be a divine emissary bearing a priceless treasure, in which the hopes of the host are invested. The imperial European stranger, on the other hand, has no such intention. If he or she (usually he) participates in the rituals of hospitality, it is as a game that must be played the better to enable the exploitation of the host. Nothing of cultural or spiritual value can be gained from interaction with the host. The only thing that matters is the pillaging of natural resources through superior technology and the 'management' of local labour. This asymmetry of values and practices effectively destroys (Massignon uses the term 'sterilizes') whatever

93 'On n'accède à la mystique, surtout chez les Sémites, que par l'hospitalité parfaite, le droit d'asile, *l'ikrâm al-dayf*, la philoxénie.' *EM*, 1:642–643. Cf. Massignon's description of the ethical value of this outlook, which eschews exploitation in favour of hospitality: '[L]e vrai prix de la vie sociale, qui n'est pas d'exploiter la simplicité du prochain pour s'enrichir, mais d'accueillir l'hôte étranger, *Dayf Allah*, en poussant la générosité jusqu'au sacrifice ; la vertu sémitique, qui n'est pas le médiocre « méson » aristotélicien entre deux excès, mais une tension héroïque d'un seul côté, vers le « Dieu d'Abraham, non des savants ».' *EM*, 1:656.

94 'L'hospitalité d'Abraham est un signe annonciateur de la consommation finale du rassemblement de toutes les nations, bénies en Abraham, dans cette Terre Sainte qui ne doit être monopolisée par aucune.' *EM*, 1:788.

95 *EM*, 1:787.

offering of peace may have been contained in the host's salutation and offer of hospitality. What was, for the (Muslim) host, a religiously ordained duty of salutation and protection (*salām*, *amān*), becomes for the European invader a curious and inconsequential local custom in a moment of catastrophic forgetting of the Abrahamic genealogy of the institution of hospitality (Gen. 18.1–33):

> The 'clash' of cultures between the European colonizer and the *Muslim* colonized creates a psychic wound in the latter and a far more serious disagreement; for the European has, in order to start the relationship, participated in a ceremony of salutation and hospitality, in which he sees nothing but a primitive and prophylactic magic ritual, whereas for the Muslim host the *Salām*, the *Amān* (safety), are canonical acts of his monotheistic Abrahamic religion. In making light of all this, the European shows that he has forgotten the Bible, and the imprint of the vocation of Abraham (to which the circumcision of Muslims and Jews still bear witness) on the Semitic peoples like a divine pact. He [the European] no longer understands that the heroic manner in which Abraham practised hospitality earned him not only the heritage of the Holy Land, but also the entrance into it of all the foreign guests who were 'blessed' by his hospitality.[96]

Massignon's allusion to Abraham's hospitality is especially telling: in his view, terrestrial sovereignty is more easily and properly acquired through obedience to divine precepts (as in Abraham hosting

[96] 'Le « *clash* » de cultures entre le colonisateur européen et le colonisé *musulman* aboutit chez ce dernier à une blessure psychique et une mésentente encore plus grave, car l'Européen a participé, pour entrer en rélations, à un cérémonial de salutations et d'hospitalité, ou il n'a vu que le rite de magie prophylactique du primitif, alors que le Salâm, l'Amân, chez l'hôte musulman, est un des actes canoniques de sa religion monothéiste abrahamique. En le traitant légèrement, l'Européen montre qu'il a oublié la Bible, et l'empreinte que la vocation d'Abraham a imprimée (la circoncision des Juifs et des Musulmans l'atteste encore) – sur les races sémitiques comme un pacte divin. Il ne comprend plus que la manière héroïque dont Abraham a pratiqué la vertu d'hospitalité ne lui a pas seulement valu d'avoir la Terre Sainte en héritage, mais d'y faire entrer tous les hôtes étrangers que son hospitalité a « bénis ».' *EM*, 1:788.

the three angels in Mamre and receiving the Holy Land in return) than through the violent dispossession of the other. It is the link to the divine that creates legitimate worldly power and sovereignty. Indeed, one of the most important lessons of al-Ḥallāj's life is that community is not created through war, but through prayer and ascetic sacrifice.[97] Massignon's aim, as it was of his spiritual mentor Charles de Foucauld, is the creation of a spiritual basis that would unite all of humanity.[98] As Massignon argues in a forceful defence of Palestinian refugees in 1951, the Biblical stranger (*ger*; גר; cf. Gen. 15.13, 17.8, 28.4) is paradigmatic of their situation, and the only possible redemption of their condition is the granting of this universal right of asylum.[99]

Massignon often described the Holy Land (he used the term *Terre Sainte*) as the *kindergarten* of a reconciled humanity, a foretaste of paradise rather than a war prize to be divided among privileged conquerors.[100] He also proposed that Jerusalem have the status of a world metropolis and be designated the seat of the UN. Massignon was vehemently opposed to the partition of Palestine, calling instead for a place based on the idea of hospitality that could act as a 'seamless tunic' that sheltered and reconciled all the world's strangers, and a place where intimacy is the order of the day, starting with the children of Abraham, who have more reasons to love than to hate each other.[101] This synthesis of Biblical narrative and institution, this rejection of division and segregation, creates something truly democratic: a space

[97] *Parole donnée* (Paris: Union Générale d'Editions, 1970), 64–65.

[98] Jean-François Six, 'Louis Massignon Prophète du dialogue entre Orient-Occident,' in *Louis Massignon*, ed. Jean-François Six, Cahiers de l'Herne (Paris: L'Herne, 1970), 260–261.

[99] *EM*, 1:776–778. Cf. Derrida, 'Hostipitality,' 400–402.

[100] *EM*, 1:719. Cf. *Trois prières*, 136; *Testimonies*, 8.

[101] '[C]ette Terre sainte qui ne devrait pas être un objet de partage entre privilégiés, mais la tunique sans couture de la réconciliation mondiale, un lieu d'intime mélange entre tous, et, pour commencer, entre ceux qui ont tout de même plus de raisons de s'unir que de se haïr.' *EM*, 1:736.

that is always open to and actively welcomes unwanted others, a space where the sexual aliveness of the inhabitants vindicates the *Ḥaqq* of humanity as a whole.[102]

Conclusion

One point worth pondering is why Massignon did not convert to Islam, despite the many other conversions that punctuated his life. It is clear that, for Massignon, Arabic was the language of the Truth, but that the doctrine that delivered that Truth was Christian first and foremost. Similarly, his ambivalence with respect to the idea of *ḥulūl* in al-Ḥallāj speaks to another commitment and devotion. The garden of reconciled humanity that he proposed would be a mosaic, not a melting pot. The desire for hospitality and total self-expatriation depends on the maintenance of differences, rather than fusions that abolish them altogether. The Truth (*al-Ḥaqq*) depends on these differences – between human and divine, male and female, Muslim and Christian, cross and crescent. The mysticism of substitution depends on the absolute irreplaceability of those being substituted. The preservation of conviction, born of the visits of many strangers, each of whom initiates a cycle of subversion and reconciliation, depends on and propagates the impossibility of absolute certainty. The question that was asked during the Visitation of the Stranger – 'Which of us two is the lover?' – necessarily remains open. It will be up to Massignon's student, Corbin, to resolve it through a merger of the believer and the observer.

[102] Massignon opposes the postwar strategy of *westphalisation* and the partition of land along religious lines (*cujus regio ejus religio*) to his vision of the Holy Land as seamless tunic and the one place on the planet where the alignment of religion and state should not apply: 'Au lieu de persévérer dans la *westphalisation* des rapports internationaux, il faut bien avouer que s'il y a un pays ou le temporal doit s'incliner devant le spirituel pour réaliser nos besoins d'unité mondiale, c'est bien la Palestine'. *EM*, 1:737.

2

Henry Corbin: A Certain Vision

For Henry Corbin, the esoteric operates as self-cure for a lifelong search for certainty. This search is inscribed in a very Cartesian register, which is to say that the locus of certainty for Corbin is necessarily individual (as opposed to collective), internal (as opposed to social), personal (as opposed to institutional), and spiritual (as opposed to historical and material). The source of the truth cannot come from outside oneself: it can only be a personally and spiritually ascertained and enacted reality.

Corbin's concern is with the internal and spiritual first and foremost, pursued through the currents that guide the believer there: Sufism, Shīʿism, Illuminationism (*Ishrāqī* philosophy) and Gnosticism – the latter understood as a world religion with offshoots everywhere in the Abrahamic monotheisms.[1] These currents often overlap: Corbin was fond of the saying that Shīʿism contains Sufism, and the Sufi is merely a Shīʿī who does not know it.[2] In both Sufism and Shīʿism, the personal spiritual aspect of Islam corresponds to Corbin's reading of what is most urgent and pressing about Protestantism: Luther's re-working of the four levels of reading into a new hermeneutic that operates through the *significatio passiva*, the demand that the believer or seeker be realized or extantiated through a properly oriented reading of the sacred text.[3] This fusion of the personal and spiritual marks the beginning of an answer to the question that drives Corbin's *œuvre*: is any treaty negotiable between an internally oriented, spiritual

1 Henry Corbin, *Avicenne et le récit visionnaire* (Lagrasse: Verdier, 1999), 24–25.
2 *EII*, 1:xi, 83–85, 129–131.
3 *EII*, 1:160–193.

hermeneutics and the rigours of reasoned method, and if so, where might certainty be located?[4]

The work of Henry Corbin is dominated by the language and vocabulary of vision. It is no accident that one of his last papers is entitled 'Eyes of Flesh, Eyes of Fire.' Nor is it coincidental that in one of his earliest publications, an op-ed piece for the short-lived newspaper *La Tribune indochinoise* published under the pseudonym Trong-Ni, he described what the West could learn from Eastern thought in the following terms: 'What illumination, what enrichment, what certainty on the profound nature and behaviour of the human mind do we receive from there?'[5] One part of the answer would have to be Corbin's monumental contribution to the study of Shihāb al-Dīn Yaḥya ibn Ḥabash al-Suhrawardī, the twelfth-century philosopher whose name is most frequently associated with the Ishrāqī school of thought. Corbin's authoritative editions and translations of al-Suhrawardī's work, including *Ḥikmat al-Ishrāq* – a title that he translated as *La Sagesse orientale* (*Oriental Wisdom*)[6] – have definitively changed our understanding of Islamic thought.[7] The noun sequence in Corbin's

[4] *EII*, 1:159.

[5] 'Quelle illumination, quel enrichissement, quelle **certitude** sur la nature profonde et les démarches de l'esprit humain, en recevons-nous ?' Henry Corbin, 'Regards vers l'Orient,' *La Tribune indochinoise* (Paris), 15 August 1927, 4; emphasis mine. Another telling indication of the significance of *certitude* in relation to the Orient may be seen from the note that Corbin wrote after meeting the curator of the Musée Guimet, Joseph Hackin, in 1926, to discuss the possibility of completing an advanced degree in East Asian Studies and, again, bridging the gap between his understanding of the East and West: 'Depuis que j'ai vu Hackin au Musée Guimet je me sens envahi par une **certitude** joyeuse . . . Lorsqu'il m'eut instruit de ce que je devais faire pour passer à l'École française d'Extrême-Orient . . . ce fut la joie. . . je voyais le lien entre mes études de la philosophie médiévale et la métaphysique hindoue.' Christian Jambet, 'Repères biographiques,' in *Henry Corbin*, ed. Christian Jambet, Cahiers de l'Herne (Paris: L'Herne, 1981), 16; emphasis mine.

[6] Although this is the title under which Corbin's translation was eventually published, it bears pointing out that he frequently used the term *Théosophie orientale* to translate the title *Ḥikmat al-Ishrāq* as well. *Face de Dieu, face de l'homme: Herméneutique et soufisme* (Paris: Entrelacs, 2008), 180.

[7] Corbin's readings of al-Suhrawardī are both authoritative and unique. Some more recent work has taken its distance from his insistence on seeing in Ishrāqī philosophy as a survival of the pre-Islamic religions of Iran. John Walbridge reads al-Suhrawardī as a Hellenizing philosopher first and foremost. John Walbridge, *The Leaven of the Ancients: Suhrawardī and the Heritage of the Greeks* (Albany, NY: State University of New York

question cited above – illumination, (intellectual, spiritual) enrichment, certainty – could stand as a summary of Corbin's entire intellectual programme, starting from visual illumination to an insightful understanding of the movement of the mind and spirit idealised as the pilgrimage of the soul to the source of light, to the Orient, where certainty and vision go together.[8] Christian Jambet eloquently describes Corbin's project as a re-orientation, literal and figurative, of perception, thought, and being.[9] The voyage to the Orient is none other than the return to the self.[10] Corbin describes this personal Orient thus:

> It concerns the *Orient* that is the origin (*oriens/origo*) of being as light, and of the succession of *Orients* to which every order of beings is raised according to its rank: the *Major Orient* of the cherubinic intelligences (the world of the *Jabarūt*), the *Minor Orient* of the angels or celestial souls (the world of *malakūt*) and the *Middle Orient* of the *imaginal world* or Hūrqalyā.[11]

This Suhrawardian hierarchy of Orients and lights shapes the overall topography of Corbin's thought and work.

Press, 1999), 7, 223–224; John Walbridge, *The Wisdom of the Mystic East: Suhrawardī and Platonic Orientalism* (Albany, NY: State University of New York Press, 2001), 13–16.

8 Not coincidentally we find a comparable progression from vision to understanding and self-understanding in *Sein und Zeit*, which was also published in 1927, specifically when Heidegger presents his first definition of *Dasein*: 'Hinsehen auf, Verstehen, und Begreifen von, Wählen, Zugang zu sind konstitutive Verhaltungen des Fragens und so selbst Seinsmodi eines bestimmten Seienden, *des* Seienden, das wir, die Fragenden, je selbst sind. Ausarbeitung der Seinsfrage besagt demnach: Durchsichtigmachen eines Seienden – des fragenden – in seinem Sein.' *Gesamtausgabe: I Abteilung: Veröffentlichte Schriften, 1910–1976* (Frankfurt am Main: Klostermann, 1975), 2:9–10. [i.e. *Sein und Zeit* §2] The most accurate translation of the sort of vision Heidegger intends here is Joan Stambaugh's: 'regarding.' *Being and Time*, trans. Joan Stambaugh, SUNY Series in Contemporary Continental Philosophy revised ed. (Albany, NY: SUNY Press, 2010), 6. We will return to the relationship between seeing, understanding and the 'transparency' of the inquirer below.

9 Jambet, 'Philosophie angélique,' 100–103.

10 *Avicenne*, 63.

11 'Il s'agit de l'*Orient* qui est l'origine (*oriens/origo*) de l'être comme lumière, et de la succession des *Orients* auxquels se lève, à leur rang respectif, chaque ordre des Lumières d'entre les hiérarchies des êtres de Lumière: *Orient majeur* des intelligences chérubiniques (monde du *Jabarût*), *Orient mineur* des Anges ou Âmes célestes (le monde du *malakût*), *Orient moyen* du monde *imaginal* ou monde de Hûrqalyâ.' *Face de Dieu*, 179.

The following chapter will therefore treat the question of vision in this universe of light over four stages. The first will go over Corbin's early translations from Heidegger. The second will explore in detail the operation of the language of vision in Corbin's work in and around Ibn ʾArabî. The third part of our exposé will explore Corbin's Sufi/Shīʿī inspired spiritual hermeneutics, and the last will describe his ethics of spiritual chivalry.

Corbin Translates Heidegger

It would be difficult to overstate Heidegger's importance for Corbin. Ethan Kleinberg explains Heidegger's popularity among French intellectuals of the interwar years through the fact that the German philosopher was seen as the only one whose work was adequate to the hardship of concrete existence, providing a radical exit from the crises of neo-Kantianism and Bergsonian spiritualism into which French philosophy had fallen.[12] For Corbin, however, there was more at stake. In an interview where he explains common interest in Heidegger in addition to Sufism and *Ishrāqī* philosophies, Corbin says the following:

> Now, there is a term current in mystical theosophy (*ʿirfān*), so current that it has become the title of more than one book. This term is *Kashf al-maḥjūb*, meaning precisely: 'the unveiling of that which is hidden.' Is this not precisely the method of the

[12] Ethan Kleinberg, *Generation Existential: Heidegger's Philosophy in France, 1927–1961* (Ithaca, NY and London: Cornell University Press, 2005), 5–10. One idea of the reception of Heidegger in France can be gleaned from the terms that Alexandre Koyré used to present Corbin's first translation of *Was ist Metaphysik?* in *Bifur*. Heidegger is not just another star in the firmament, Koyré tells his readers, but rather, according to some (i.e. Friedrich Heinrich Heinemann, author of *Neue Wege der Philosophie*), 'un soleil nouveau qui se lève et qui de sa lumière éclipse tous ces contemporains.' Henry Corbin, 'Qu'est-ce que la métaphysique?', [Was ist Metaphysik?] Translation, *Bifur* 8 (June 1931): 5. Far from proposing a reconciliation between dominant philosophical trends of the early twentieth century – a goal that Koyré finds 'ridiculously pedantic' – Heidegger treats questions that are urgently posed by the age in which he lives. 'Qu'est-ce que la métaphysique?', 6.

> phenomenologist; that method which, in unveiling and making manifest the meaning hidden, covered over by the apparent, under the phenomenon, fulfils in its way the programme of Greek science: *sozein ta phainomena* (saving phenomena)? *Kashf* is the unveiling (*Enthüllung, Entdecken*) that makes manifest the truth covered over by the apparent, the *phainomenon* (let us remember all that Heidegger says about the concept of *alētheia*, truth).[13]

'Saving phenomena' thus takes on a particular meaning for Corbin: the revelation of hidden meanings becomes a way of ascertaining the truth of the apparent, phenomenal meaning. By inscribing phenomenology in a framework that combines ancient Greek philosophy and science alongside Sufism, Corbin's statement summarizes his own situation during the 1930s, a period during which, as his publications show, he was constantly oscillating between Heidegger, hermeneutics and mysticisms both Christian and Muslim. Far from marking a 'break' in his phenomenological interests, Corbin's lifelong work on Sufism, Shīʿism and Ishrāqī thinkers now emerges as a way of deepening them and taking them to their logical end-point, even if the latter belongs to a culture deemed different (though for Corbin this difference was minimal – what mattered was how much

13 'Or, il est un terme d'un usage courant en théosophie mystique ('*erfan*), si courant même qu'il sert de titre à plus d'un livre. C'est le terme *Kashf al-mahjub*, signifiant exactement: « dévoilement de ce qui est caché ». N'est-ce pas exactement la démarche du phénoménologue, la démarche qui, en dévoilant et en faisant se manifester le sens caché, occulté, sous l'apparent, sous le phénomène, remplit à sa façon le programme de la Science grecque: *sozein ta phainomena* (sauver les phénomènes)? *Kashf*, c'est le dévoilement (*Enthüllung, Entdecken*) amenant à se manifester la vérité occultée sous l'apparent, le *phainomenon* (pensons à tout ce que Heidegger a dit à propos du concept d'*aletheia*, vérité).' Henry Corbin, 'De Heidegger à Sohravardî: Entretien avec Philippe Némo,' in *Henry Corbin*, ed. Christian Jambet, Cahiers de l'Herne (Paris: L'Herne, 1981), 27. Elsewhere, Corbin explains what he means by *sozein ta phainomena* as the definitive procedure of phenomenology; the process of encountering phenomena wherever they occur: '« Sauver les phénomènes, » c'est les rencontrer là où ils *ont lieu* et où ils ont *leur lieu*.' *EII*, 1:xix. Elsewhere, in his treatment of sympathetic union and prayer, he writes: '[J]amais les états visibles, apparents, extérieurs, les phénomènes, ne peuvent êtres causes pour d'autres phénomènes. Ce qui agit, c'est l'invisible, l'immatériel.' *Imagination créatrice*, 138. Saving phenomena is being alert to the sympathetic action shared by the Creator and the creature.

Shīʿī gnosis, Greek philosophy and Sufism had in common). Even if references to Heidegger disappear from Corbin's *œuvre* after the 1940s, there is no gainsaying the German philosopher's importance as a springboard for a large body of philosophical reflection.[14]

During this phase, along with numerous articles and reviews dealing with Lutheran philosophy, the philosophy of existence and the question of history,[15] Corbin published translations of several texts by Heidegger, all of which were published in book form by Gallimard as *Qu'est-ce que la métaphysique ?* in 1937. Two of the texts translated in this collection – *Was ist Metaphysik?* and *Vom Wesen des Grundes* – are still in print today and operate as a key part of the presentation of Heidegger's philosophy to the francophone public in Heidegger's *Questions I et II*. Ethan Kleinberg has explored the ways in which Corbin's translation of the word *Dasein* as *réalité-humaine* misled Heidegger's early readers in France, despite the fact that it met with Heidegger's approval.[16] Corbin himself explains that he uses this term in order to take some distance vis-à-vis the traditional language of the philosophy of existence, thereby further emphasising the

[14] If nothing else, Corbin's legacy with the historical Zarathustra should give pause to those who are quick to proclaim the irrelevance of Heidegger and Nietzsche to his later work.

[15] Maria Soster, 'Henry Corbin pendant les années trente' (Première journée Henry Corbin, EPHE, Paris, www.amiscorbin.com, 17 December 2005).

[16] Kleinberg, *Generation Existential: Heidegger's Philosophy in France, 1927–1961*, 70–71, 130–132. Kleinberg argues that the term *réalité-humaine* 'does not convey the spatial character of *Dasein*, which displaces the subject as the localizable site of being.' *Generation Existential: Heidegger's Philosophy in France, 1927–1961*, 70. This issue is, however, further complicated by Heidegger's later assertion, in a dialogue with his student Karl Löwith, that *Dasein* has no 'there' (*Da*) ('L'être n'a pas de *là*' – alluding to what he considered Sartre's faulty translation of *Dasein* as *être-là*). See Laurence Hemming's treatment of this question in Laurence Paul Hemming, *Heidegger's Atheism: The Refusal of a Theological Voice* (Notre Dame, IN: University of Notre Dame Press, 2002), 5–6. Although Heidegger's French readers and interlocutors took serious issue with the term – as recently as 2001, Janicaud called it 'execrable', Dominique Janicaud, *Heidegger en France*, 2 vols. (Paris: Albin Michel, 2001), 1:46. He also cites Beaufret's joke that translating *Dasein* as *réalité-humaine* is like calling a cat *réalité-féline*. *Heidegger en France*, 1:47 n. – the fact remains that *réalité-humaine* continued to circulate among them. Despite his misgivings, Beaufret himself cites Corbin's translation extensively. See Jean Beaufret, *Introduction aux philosophies de l'existence. De Kierkegaard à Heidegger* (Paris: Denoël/Gonthier, 1971), 16–26.

radical nature of Heidegger's ontology.[17] It might therefore be worth asking how Corbin decided to use this particular term, despite its limitations.

Corbin's first translation of a text by Heidegger was in 1931, when he published the first version of *Was ist Metaphysik?* in the final issue of the avant-garde and anticolonial journal, *Bifur*. Although Corbin himself later disavowed the translation, probably because of the terms that he used to render Heidegger's strange vocabulary, it is instructive insofar as it yields indicators of how the final version of his translation took shape. What is immediately striking about the 1931 translation is the absence of the term *réalité-humaine*. Instead Corbin uses the term *existence* to designate *Dasein*.[18] Consider the following passage from the last part of the lecture ('The Response to the Question'):

> Nur auf dem Grunde der ursprünglichen Offenbarkeit des Nichts kann das Dasein des Menschen aud Seiendes zugehen und eingehen. Sofern aber das Dasein seinem Wesen nach zu Seiendem,

[17] Martin Heidegger, *Qu'est-ce que la métaphysique? : Suivi d'extraits sur l'Être et le temps et d'une conférence sur Hölderlin*, ed. and trans. Henry Corbin (Paris: Gallimard, 1938), 13–14.

[18] There are occasional departures from this practice depending on Heidegger's tone. Thus 'das reine Da-sein' becomes 'le simple fait d'être présent (*Da-sein*)' and 'die Verwandlung des Menschen in sein Da-sein' becomes 'la présence de l'homme dans le monde (*Da-sein*)'. *GA*, 9:112–113; 'Qu'est-ce que la métaphysique?,' 17–18. The latter instance of the word *Dasein* is especially significant as Corbin chose to translate it by 'présence réelle' in the later translation. *Qu'est-ce que la métaphysique?*, 32. Needless to say these are not the only variations: Corbin's correspondence with Heidegger in the early 1930s demonstrates not only that the German philosopher was closely involved in the preparation of *Qu'est-ce que la metaphysique?*, but that he read and commented on both translations of *Was ist Metaphysik?* carefully before giving the final version his blessing. Sylvain Camilleri and Daniel Proulx, 'Martin Heidegger et Henry Corbin; lettres et documents (1930–1941),' *Bulletin heideggérien* 4 (2014): 25–30, http://www.amiscorbin.com/wp-content/plugins/pdf-viewer-for-wordpress/web/viewer.php?file=http://www.amiscorbin.com/wp-content/uploads/2012/06/Camilleri-Proulx-Corbin-Heidegger-Lettres_et_documents.pdf. By the time that Corbin produced his translation of the entirety of *Sein und Zeit* in the 1940s, he had opted for the more intuitively obvious terms 'Présence-humaine' and 'être-présence' as equivalents for *Dasein*, which suggests that the use of *réalité-humaine* marks an important transition in his thinking related to the definitive departure for the Middle East after 1939. Camilleri and Proulx, 'Martin Heidegger et Henry Corbin,' 40.

> das es nicht und das es selbst ist, sich verhält, kommt an als solches Dasein je schon aus dem offenbaren Nichts her.
>
> Da-sein heißt: Hineingehaltenheit in das Nichts. [19]

In David Farrel Krell's elegant translation this reads:

> Only on the ground of the original manifestness of the nothing can human Dasein approach and penetrate beings. But since Dasein in its essence adopts a stance toward beings – those which it is not and that which it is – it emerges as such existence in each case from the nothing already manifest.
>
> Da-sein means: being held out into the nothing.[20]

In 1931, Corbin translated this passage thus:

> C'est sur la base de la manifestation primordiale du néant que l'existence humain peut arriver et avoir accès à l'existant. Mais en tant que l'existence est, de par son essence, en rapport avec l'Etre, celui qu'elle n'est pas et celui qu'elle est elle-même, son origine provient toujours, du néant devenu manifeste. Exister-en-fait (*Da-sein*) revient à ceci : se trouver maintenu dedans (*Hineingehaltenheit*) le néant.[21]

The version published in 1938 reads as follows:

> C'est uniquement en raison de la manifestation originelle du Néant que la réalité-humaine de l'homme peut aller *vers* l'existant et pénétrer *en* lui. Mais pour autant que chaque réalité-humaine, de par son essence, est en rapport avec l'existant, avec celui qu'elle n'est pas et avec celui qu'elle est elle-même, déjà, étant telle parce que réalité-humaine, elle pro-cède du Néant révélé.
>
> *Réaliser* une *réalité-humaine* (Da-sein) signifie: *se trouver retenu à l'intérieur du Néant.*[22]

[19] Heidegger, *GA*, 9:114–115.

[20] Martin Heidegger, *Basic Writings: From Being and Time (1927) to The Task of Thinking (1964)*, ed. and trans. David Farrell Krell, Second edn (San Francisco, CA: HarperSanFrancisco, 1993), 103.

[21] Corbin, 'Qu'est-ce que la métaphysique?', 20.

[22] Heidegger, *Qu'est-ce que la métaphysique?*, 34.

Quite apart from the greater fluidity and fidelity to Heidegger proposed by the later translation, the use of the noun *réalité* and the verb *réaliser* imply a reading of Dasein as an activity rather than mere phenomenon. What made Corbin decide to go from *existence* to *réalité-humaine*, and from *exister* to *réaliser une réalité-humaine*? Why, moreover, did he further emphasize *Dasein*'s activity as something that proceeds from a revealed Nothingness, rather than something whose origin continuously emerges from that Nothingness?

Corbin's understanding of *Dasein* was inflected by his reading of Protestant thought, Sufism and mysticism more generally. As Corbin himself points out in a late autobiographical text (1978), he was completing his training as an orientalist in the late 1920s.[23] His discovery of Heidegger and esoteric Islam were therefore almost simultaneous; indeed he had discovered al-Suhrawardī, thanks to Massignon, *before* he started his many regular trips to Germany in the 1930s.[24] There is probably no better indicator of the simultaneity in Corbin's mind of Sufi/Ishrāqī thought and Heidegger's than the many Arabic marginal notes and glosses that Corbin made in his personal copy of *Sein und Zeit*.[25] Instead of going in one direction from Heidegger to esoteric Islam, Corbin's *œuvre* might be better described as a conjugation of the two paths.[26] One clue regarding the equivalence that Corbin proposes between Dasein and the truth comes from a later stage in his engagement with Heidegger; namely his project of translating *Sein und Zeit* in its entirety. Although he completed this translation during the time he spent in Istanbul (1939–1945), it was never published. Nevertheless, one of his translator's notes to *Sein und*

23 'Post-Scriptum à un entretien philosophique,' 38–43.

24 'De Heidegger. . .,' 23–24. Although it is difficult to establish with absolute certainty just when Corbin decided to read and translate Heidegger, Sylvain Camilleri and Daniel Proulx provide some useful details and hypotheses about Corbin's first encounter with and approach to Heidegger's thought. Camilleri and Proulx, 'Martin Heidegger et Henry Corbin,' 4–13.

25 Camilleri and Proulx, 'Martin Heidegger et Henry Corbin,' 9.

26 'Post-scriptum,' 38.

Zeit §18 shines an interesting light on the relationship between *Dasein* and *réalité-humaine*. The note seems to refer to the following sentence in Heidegger's text: 'Das Sein des Zuhandenen hat die Struktur der Verweisung – heißt: es hat an ihm selbst den Charakter der *Verwiesenheit*.'[27] Later in this chapter Heidegger explains that this character of referredness (*Verwiesenheit*) is what links things at hand (*Zuhanden*) to *Dasein*. The complexity of Heidegger's *Verwiesenheit* drives Corbin to reflect on the difficulty of expressing, in a unique and univocal French term,

> *[T]he state of the subject that has experienced the action of the verb* of the subject by which and through which the *reality* of this action is made real ([the truths] الحقيقة [to realize, materialize, verify] تحقق) what ancient logic called *significatio passiva*.[28] The word *referredness* must here be understood in this passive sense (*Verwiesenheit*), a state which consists of being referred (not referring) and in which the ontological difference is realized.[29]

27 *GA*, 2:112. In Joan Stambaugh's translation this reads: 'The fact that the being of things at hand has the structure of reference means that they have in themselves the character of *being referred*.' *Being and Time*, 82.

28 *Significatio passiva* is an especially important notion for Corbin, who used it as the basis for his reading of Hamann in his courses at the École Pratique des Hautes Études in 1938–1940. In an account of his course for the year 1939, Corbin returns to Luther's reading of the notion of justification in Rom. 3. Corbin concludes that the 'justification of God by man is always already a justification of man by God, *opus Dei*, it is a becoming, a history and a community between God and man.' ['La justification de Dieu par l'homme est d'ores et déjà la justification de l'homme par Dieu, *opus Dei*, et c'est bien un devenir, une histoire et une communauté entre Dieu et l'homme.'] 'Conférence temporaire : « Recherches sur l'herméneutique luthérienne »,' *Annuaire de l'École Pratique des Hautes Études, Section des Sciences Religieuses 1939–1940* (1939): 102, http://www.persee.fr/web/revues/home/prescript/article/ephe_0000-0002_1938_num_52_48_17452. Cf. Martin Luther, *Lectures on Romans*, ed. and trans. Wilhelm Pauck (Louisville, KY: Westminster John Knox Press, 2006), 77–79. *Ad* Ps. 31.2 (*In Justitia tua libera me*), Luther's insight led him to understand that this is a prayer for God's justice by which we become just, a process that Corbin compares to Ibn al-ʿArabī's insistence we impute attributes to God insofar as we experience them in ourselves. *Imagination créatrice*, 307 n. See also Corbin's comparison of the *significatio passiva* to the Arabic *amr mafʿūlī*. 'De Heidegger . . .,' 25; *EII*, 1:192–193.

29 'Comme toujours, nous nous heurtons ici à la difficulté d'imprimer en français par un terme unique et univoque (c'est-à-dire qui ne soit pas à la fois actif *et* passif) *l'état du sujet qui a subi l'action exprimée* par le verbe du sujet par quoi et en quoi se *réalise* la *réalité* de cette action ([les vérités] الحقيقة [concrétiser, matérialiser, vérifier] تحقق), ce que la logique

The use of the Arabic term *ḥaqīqa* – a constant in Sufi literature – strikes the reader as much by its presence in the text as by its use. If we were to expand all the brackets in Corbin's note, what emerges is an equivalence between realizing a reality (cf. the phrase 'réaliser une réalité-humaine' above) and the Arabic phrase *taḥaqquq al-ḥaqīqa* (the realization of reality/the truth). In other words, Corbin is pleading for a reading of *Dasein* along the lines of the *significatio passiva*: the locus of *Dasein* is the process of verification, of realizing the real, and of being realized as a result. *Dasein* thus emerges as the reality (*haqīqa*) that accompanies being. What Corbin intends by *réaliser une réalité-humaine* is thus the *significatio passiva* of the verb *Da-sein*. We are not far here from Corbin's arguments about the subject's self-creation through an individual act of conscience: being is an *act* for Corbin, and conscience is determined less by the external world than by the internal factors.[30] The various translations of *Dasein* that he produced during the 1930s and 1940s thus trace the development of Corbin's argument in relation to these questions, culminating in a position that is far from Heideggerian.[31]

ancienne appelait *significatio passiva*. Il faut prendre ici le mot de *reportation* avec ce sens passif (*Verwiesenheit*), état qui consiste à être reporté (non pas à reporter) et dans lequel se concrétise la référence ontologique.' Camilleri and Proulx, 'Martin Heidegger et Henry Corbin,' 54. The remainder of this particular footnote is significant given the political context of the Second World War and Heidegger's affiliation with the Nazi party (though he had long since been expelled by the time that Corbin was in Istanbul, and in any case the text follows the publication of *Sein und Zeit* by several years). Corbin comments on the resonances between *reportation/Verwiesenheit* and *Verweisung*: '*cf.* déportation: l'allemand *Verweisung* contient aussi bien précisément ce sens de bannissement, de relégation, d'exil, que celui, immédiat, de renvoie et de référence.' It is possible, though difficult to prove conclusively, that Corbin is proposing here a connection between the structure of being referred that characterizes things-to-hand and the atrocious history of displacement, migration and death that constituted so much of the history of the twentieth century.

30 The 'act of being' is developed extensively by Mullā Ṣadrā. Corbin, *EII*, 4:77–81. See also chapter 3 below.

31 Tom Cheetham provides a good introduction to these questions. Cheetham, *World*, 3–15. See also Pierre Lory's eloquent summary of the stakes and differences between Corbin and Heidegger in his review of Cheetham's work. 'Note sur l'ouvrage de Tom Cheetham, The World Turned Inside Out: Henry Corbin and Islamic Mysticism,' www.amiscorbin.com, 2005, accessed 8 August 2015, http://www.amiscorbin.com/note-sur-l-ouvrage-de-tom-cheetham-the-world-turned-inside-out-henry-corbin-and-islamic-mysticism/.

Another aspect of Heidegger's thinking that must be addressed here is his work on truth, especially in its relation to un-covering. In the passage cited above, Corbin's eloquent response to his interviewer places in apposition un-covering (*Entdeckung, Enthüllung*) and truth as *alētheia*. The opening of Heidegger's foreword to Corbin's volume of his work is striking by the recurrence of the word truth (*Wahrheit*; *vérité*). In particular the question of truth as un-covering becomes fundamental to metaphysics:

> In the latter [i.e. the fundamental question of metaphysics], the question asked about Being becomes first of all, and necessarily at the same time, the question of the being [*Wesen*] of the truth, which means unveiling [*Enthüllung*] as such; an unveiling by reason of which we find ourselves fundamentally and generally able to come into a manifest reality.[32]

For Corbin, this un-covering is neither spontaneous nor impersonal: it has everything to do with the individual conscience for whom a given reality becomes manifest. Indeed, this manifestation itself, construed as a theophanic vision, depends on the spiritual effort made by the seeker or researcher. Un-covering, the lifting of the veil, only occurs in the presence of those who earn this event. A significant part of this earning – process of reaching the stage where reality can be un-covered – has to do with the discipline of one's spiritual being.

Corbin's subsequent formulations of truth and reality unfold as a synthesis of his engagements of Heidegger, Hamann (on whom he

[32] 'Dans cette dernière [la question fondamentale de la métaphysique], la question posée sur l'Être devient tout d'abord, en même temps et nécessairement, la question de l'essence de la vérité, c'est-à-dire du dévoilement [*Enthüllung*] comme tel, dévoilement en raison duquel nous venons à nous trouver préalablement et en général dans une réalité manifestée.' *Qu'est-ce que la métaphysique?*, 7. Heidegger's original text reads: 'In dieser [die Grundfrage der Metaphysik] wird die Frage nach dem Wesen der Wahrheit d.h. der Enthüllung überhaupt, auf deren Grund wir erst und überhaupt in ein Offenes zu stehen kommen.' Camilleri and Proulx, 'Martin Heidegger et Henry Corbin,' 25.

lectured at the EPHE in the 1930s), Luther[33] and al-Suhrawardī. Finding the truth about being involves, as Heidegger puts it, a 'making-transparent' (*Durchsichtigmachen*) of the seeker/philosopher.[34] In §31 of *Sein und Zeit, Das Da-sein als Verstand* [Da-sein as Understanding], Heidegger equates transparency with self-knowledge:

> We shall call the sight which is primarily and as a whole related to existence *transparency* [*Durchsichtigkeit*]. We choose this term in order to designate correctly understood 'self-knowledge' in order to indicate that it is not a matter here of perceptually finding and gazing at a point which is the self, but of grasping and understanding the full disclosedness of being-in-the-world *throughout all* its essential constitutive factors.[35]

At this point in the text of his copy of *Sein und Zeit*, Corbin's marginalia draw an explicit parallel between *Durchsichtigkeit* and theophany:

> διαφαίνω (θέος!) diaphanous presence, to appear to oneself through oneself (middle voice: phenomenology = epiphany of the phenomenon to oneself). Cf. in the Orphic Theogonies φαινης.[36]

There is nothing in *Sein und Zeit* to suggest this jump to Orphic Theogony. What seems to be going through Corbin's mind is the association between φαινης as the luminous first-born of the Orphic

[33] Luther occurs regularly in Corbin's marginal annotations to *Sein und Zeit*. To take one example, he identifies Heidegger's *das Man* ('the they', specifically *ad Sein und Zeit* §27, p. 29, *GA*, 2:171–172) with Luther's Herr Omnes.

[34] *GA*, 2:10.

[35] *Being and Time*, 142. 'Die Sicht, die sich primär und im ganzen auf die Existenz bezieht, nennen wir die *Durchsichtigkeit*. Wir wählen diesen Terminus zur Beziehung der wohlverstandenen »Selbsterkenntnis«, um anzuzeigen, daß es sich bei ihr nicht um das wahrnemende Aufspüren und Beschauen eines Selbstpunktes handelt, sondern um ein verstehendes Ergreifen der vollen Erschlossenheit des In-der-Welt-seins *durch* seine wesenhaften Verfassungsmomente *hindurch*.' *GA*, 2:195.

[36] 'διαφαίνω (θέος!) présence diaphanique, s'apparaître à soi-même à travers soi-même (voie moyenne : phénoménologie = épiphanie de phénomène à soi-même). Cf. dans les Théogonies orphiques φαινης.' Camilleri and Proulx, 'Martin Heidegger et Henry Corbin,' 55.

deities and Intelligence as the first created entity in al-Suhrawardī's thought.[37] Corbin's unpacking of *Durchsichtigkeit* as a transparency to oneself that enables the perception of epiphanies (and therefore, by extension, all phenomenology), is much closer to the ethics of Aḥsāʾī and Mullā Ṣadrā insofar as it depends on a certain spiritual training that will eventually allow the seeker to see realities that would otherwise remain unrevealed. For Corbin (via Mullā Ṣadrā, it is a question of thinking, or understanding, existence as Presence, and Presence as a unique fusion of knowing subject and known object.[38] Reaching this state of transparency to oneself involves a profound level of commitment and belief. In 'Phänomenologie und Theologie' – a text that Heidegger discusses in his correspondence with Corbin[39] – Heidegger stresses the fact that revelation only occurs (reveals itself) to faith, recalling as he does so Luther's definition of faith:

> The occurrence of revelation, which is handed over to faith and accordingly occurs in faithfulness itself, un-covers itself only to faith. Luther says: 'Faith is allowing ourselves to be seized [literally, surrendering ourselves as prisoners: *Sichgefangengeben*] by those things that we do not see.'[40]

37 Further examples of this link are not lacking, either in the marginalia to Corbin's draft translation of *Sein und Zeit* or elsewhere in Corbin's work. Consider the opening lines of Suhrawardī's *Muʾnis al-ʿUshshāq* (*The Lovers' Companion*), which Corbin translated as 'Le Familier des amants' in 1933: 'La première chose que Dieu créa fut une essence lumineuse, dont le nom est Intelligence, car selon la tradition, « ce que Dieu créa d'abord, ce fut l'Intelligence ».' 'Pour l'anthropologie philosophique : un traité persan inédit de Suhrawardî d'Alep,' *Recherches philosophiques* 2 (1933): 397.

38 'L'existence comme Présence, et la Présence comme union *sui generis* du sujet connaissant et de l'objet connu.' *EII*, 4:81. Cf. *Face de Dieu*, 193–195. See also Massignon's remarks about al-Ḥallāj's method and the 'involution' of reason in its object. *Passion*, 1:21.

39 Camilleri and Proulx, 'Martin Heidegger et Henry Corbin,' 19.

40 Martin Heidegger, *Pathmarks*, ed. and trans. William McNeill (Cambridge; New York: Cambridge University Press, 1998), 44, translation slightly modified. 'Das Offenbarungsgeschehen, das sich dem Glauben überliefert und demgemäß in der Gläubligkeit selbst geschieht, *enthüllt sich* nur dem Glauben. Luther sagt: »Glaube ist das Sichgefanengeben in den Sachen, die wir nicht sehen.«' *GA*, 9:53, emphasis mine. This anticipates Heidegger's definition of the fundamental task of philosophy as 'being gripped' by concepts [*Ergriffenheit*] in the *Grundbegriffe der Metaphysik*. *GA*, 29/30:9. Cf. Michael Ehrmantraut, *Heidegger's Philosophic Pedagogy* (London; New York: Continuum, 2010), 58–60.

What, we might ask, does someone who is gripped by the invisible see?

Lessons in Vision

'Everything is only revelation; there can only be re-velation.'[41] Revelation is all there is, and all there can be. Thus does Corbin open an early (1932) theological fragment that sums up his vision of the universe. The fact that all is revelation, however, does not mean that all is easily seen and known: 'Now, revelation comes from the Spirit, and there is no knowledge of the Spirit.'[42] The mind must be taught to see, to perceive what is revealed, and, possibly in doing so, to know itself. Perhaps the first and most important lesson is that the sort of theophanic seeing that interests Corbin is not the immediate variety, but rather the one that comes with faith and spiritual effort (what the Sufis called *himma*).[43] If seeing is believing, then belief must take precedence insofar as it makes seeing possible. Things must be believed to be seen.

The most extensive statement of Corbin's theories about spiritual (in)sight comes in his study of Ibn al-ʿArabī, though as is often the case there are significant prefigurations in his work on Avicenna.[44] The title of *L'Imagination créatrice dans le soufisme d'Ibn ʾArabî* indicates Corbin's priority: what matters in his presentation of Ibn

[41] 'Tout n'est que révélation; il ne peut y avoir que ré-vélation.' Corbin, 'Théologie au bord du lac,' 62.

[42] 'Or la révélation vient de l'Esprit, et il n'y a point de connaissance de l'Esprit.' 'Théologie,' 62.

[43] We might see here a parallel with Derek Attridge's ideas about responsibility and opening up to the other in the literary register: 'Attentiveness to what is outside the familiar requires effort, even if it is the effort of resisting effortful behaviour, of emptying out the too full, excessively goal-oriented consciousness.' Derek Attridge, *The Singularity of Literature* (London and New York: Routledge, 2004), 122.

[44] It bears pointing out that Corbin's reading of Ibn ʾArabî is unique and, by some accounts, idiosyncratic. William C. Chittick, *The Sufi Path of Knowledge: Ibn Al-Arabi's Metaphysics of Imagination* (Albany, NY: State University of New York Press, 1989), xx.

al-ʿArabī's Sufism is the Sufi thinker as a theoretician of vision. Central to this endeavour is the concept of what Corbin calls the creative, or active, imagination, and the world to which it enables access; namely the imaginal world, or *mundus imaginalis*. The latter, probably one of the most intellectually and spiritually demanding concepts in the history of Islamic thought, bears witness to Corbin's taste for intermediacy.[45] The *mundus imaginalis* (in Arabic, *ʿālam al-mithāl* or the world of images), that suprasensible world that exists in between the perceptible and the imaginary, is home to the spiritual revelations and theophanies that are the seeker's aim.[46] The faculty that opens the door to this world is the creative imagination: creative because it participates in the production of the world that it reveals to the seeker, and, moreover, because that world is real (if invisible to the uninitiated) rather than imaginary.[47] The creative imagination goes beyond mere theoretical introspection: it is not a theory, but rather an initiation into the art of vision and a penetration into the world thus perceived.[48] In the case of Ibn al-ʿArabī, Corbin asserts that all creation is essentially an un-covering; *tajallī*. Although this term might normally

[45] Christian Jambet, *Henry Corbin et Louis Massignon* (Paris: www.amiscorbin.com, 2011).

[46] Corbin's use of this concept is foundational, influential – it recurs in places as diverse as works by specialists of Islamic philosophy working in his wake and Lacan's Seminar VII – and unique. Lacan, *Séminaire VII*, 177–178. Van Lit has recently demonstrated that the conceptual topography of the idea of the world of images as Corbin understands it owes much more to al-Shahrazūrī than, as Corbin would have it, al-Suhrawardī, and that the faculty of imagination is more passive than active. *The World of Image in Islamic Philosophy: Ibn Sīnā, Suhrawardī, Shahrazūrī, and Beyond* (Edinburgh: Edinburgh University Press, 2017), 65–67, 92–103.

[47] Corbin, *Face de Dieu*, 41–47. This idea has wide currency outside Islamic philosophy as well: there are parallels with certain strands of early modern thought, as in Boehme, Paracelsus, Swedenborg (to whom Corbin dedicated several publications) among others. Corbin cites Koyré on these thinkers: 'La notion de l'imagination, intermédiaire magique entre la pensée et l'être, incarnation de la pensée dans l'image et position de l'image dans l'être, est une conception de la plus haute importance qui joue un rôle de premier plan dans la philosophie de la Renaissance et qu'on retrouve dans celle du Romantisme.' Alexandre Koyré, *Mystiques, spirituels, alchimistes du XVIe siècle allemand*, Collection Idées, (Paris: Gallimard, 1971), qtd. Corbin, *Imagination créatrice*, 193. It is not just the intermediate and productive nature of the creative imagination that matters for Corbin; it is also the mutual interpenetration between being and thinking that links imagination to reality.

[48] Corbin, *Imagination créatrice*, 114.

be translated as 'revelation' or even, in the present context, 'uncovering', Corbin prefers the term *théophanie* in a passage worth quoting at length:

> The initial idea of Ibn ʿArabi's mystic theosophy and of all related theosophies is that Creation is essentially a *theophany* (*tajallī*). As such, creation is an act of the divine imaginative power: this divine creative Imagination is essentially a theophanic Imagination [i.e. the being of that Imagination is theophanic]. The Active Imagination in the gnostic is likewise a theophanic Imagination; the beings that it 'creates' subsist with an independent existence *sui generis* in the intermediate world which pertains to this mode of existence. The God whom it 'creates', far from being an unreal product of our fantasy, is also a theophany, for man's Active Imagination is merely the organ of the absolute theophanic Imagination (*takhayyul muṭlaq*). Prayer is a theophany par excellence; as such, it is 'creative'; but the very God to whom it is addressed because it 'creates' Him is precisely the God who reveals Himself to Prayer in this Creation, and this Creation, at this moment, is one among the theophanies whose real Subject is the Godhead revealing Himself to Himself.[49]

A first approach to this difficult passage would focus on the repeated use of the word 'essentially' (*essentiellement*). Given the long shadow cast by Heidegger, it would make more sense to think of this adverb as an index of being: the *being* of the creative imagination in Ibn al-ʿArabī's (and to a very large extent Corbin's) thought *is* theophany.

[49] Corbin, *Alone*, 182–183. '[L]'idée initiale de la théosophie mystique d'Ibn ʾArabî et de toutes celles qui lui sont apparentées, c'est que la Création est essentiellement une *théophanie* (*tajallî*). Comme telle, la création est un acte de la puissance imaginative divine: cette Imagination divine créatrice est essentiellement Imagination théophanique; les êtres qu'elle « crée » subsistent d'une existence indépendante, *sui generis*, dans le monde intermédiaire qui lui est propre. Le Dieu qu'elle « crée », loin d'être l'irréel de notre fantaisie, est lui aussi une théophanie, car l'Imagination active de l'être humain n'est que l'organe de l'Imagination théophanique absolue (*takhayyol motlaq*). La Prière est une théophanie par excellence; à ce titre elle est « créatrice »; mais précisément le Dieu qu'elle prie parce qu'elle le « crée », c'est le Dieu qui se révèle à elle dans cette Création, et cette Création, dans l'instant, est une d'entre les théophanies dont le Sujet réel est la divinité se révélant à elle-même.' Corbin, *Imagination créatrice*, 196–197.

Similarly, the being of the divine Creative Imagination is theophany. Both variants of creative imagination are revealed in and as theophany. This is thus a universe in which there is no emptiness and no contingency: everything is theophany, everything visible is God's self-revelation to Himself; God's Being is in everything and theophany is how we see this omnipresence.

Corbin's early work on Avicenna (Ibn Sīnā) advances the idea of an initiatory narrative that, interpreted correctly, enables the reader (or listener) to experience a theophanic vision that literally and figuratively re-orients his/her being.[50] A similar framework surrounds his reading of al-Suhrawardī's allegorical narratives: a correct interpretation opens up the possibility of theophanic vision, and much else.[51] Needless to say, this correct interpretation calls for the self-transparency of the interpreter that Corbin describes through his reading of Heidegger. Corbin's study of Ibn al-ʿArabī adds a new element to this process: the mutual interdependence of the two visions and two creative imaginations; namely God's and the seeker's. Corbin cites *De sacrificio*, Proclus's short treatise on the priestly art, as a means of understanding the rapprochement between Creator and creation.[52] Proclus stresses sympathy (we might say desire) and prayer as the means by which the soul of the creature makes its way towards God. Proclus also cites the phrase that Aristotle had attributed to Thales: 'All things are full of gods,' in much the same way that Ibn al-ʿArabī asserts that all things turn out to be theophanies.[53] Everything 'prays

[50] *Avicenne*, 34–48.

[51] *EII*, 2:186–188; *L'Homme & son ange: initiation et chevalerie spirituelle* (Paris: Fayard, 2016), 34.

[52] *Imagination créatrice*, 125–131.

[53] Brian Copenhaver, 'Hermes Trismegistus, Proclus, and the Question of a Philosophy of Magic in the Renaissance,' in *Hermeticism and the Renaissance: Intellectual History and the Occult in Early Modern Europe*, ed. Ingrid Merkel and Allen G. Debus, Folger Institute Symposia (Washington, DC; London: Folger Shakespeare Library; Associated University Presses, 1988), 104; Jean Trouillard, *L'Un et l'âme selon Proclos* (Paris: Les Belles Lettres, 1972), 183–184.

and sings hymns' to the deity to which it is related by bonds of sympathy and desire. The priestly art consists of using these relationships and correspondences in such a way as to bring about the descent of the gods towards 'their' creatures and the ascent of the latter towards their deities and creators. Similarly, in Ibn al-ʿArabī's universe, prayer both functions as and brings about theophany. In both cases, the relationship between the human and the divine begins with divine action that invites prayer, which in turn invites theophany, leading to an ongoing, open-ended process of communication between the human and the divine.[54]

In short, it is prayer that teaches us to see. In Corbin's reading of Ibn al-ʿArabī, prayer emerges as the highest stage and 'culminating act' of creative imagination.[55] The model at work here is that of desire moving in two directions, from the divine to the human and vice versa, as it does in Proclus's model of sympathetic theurgy. Corbin refers to the union of mystic and deity as an *unio sympathetica*, seeing in Proclus's example of the sunflower following (worshipping) the sun a model for Ibn al-ʿArabī's (and his own) theophanic spirituality.[56] This sympathy between the divine and the human springs from a two-way oscillation of desire: a desire to be revealed and known by God, and a desire to see and know in the heart of the believer. The responsibility for revealing God's divine Being is thus shared between them. According to one tradition, God says 'I was a hidden Treasure and I desired to be known,' and accordingly, this theophanic knowledge occurs during the ritual of prayer in the heart and mind of the believer. The recitation of the *Fātiḥa* (Q1) during prayer re-enacts this bi-directional plea that reveals God and makes the believer what s/he is.[57] To sum up:

[54] Trouillard, *L'Un et l'âme selon Proclos*, 177–178; Corbin, *Imagination créatrice*, 258–268.
[55] *Imagination créatrice*, 260.
[56] *Imagination créatrice*, 118–119.
[57] *Imagination créatrice*, 264–268.

> The Divine Being needs His faithful [*fidèle*] in order to manifest Himself; reciprocally, the believer needs the Divine Being in order to be invested with existence. In this sense, his Prayer [. . .] is his very *being*, his very capacity for being; it is the being of his hexeity [*heccéité*] demanding full realization; and this prayer [*demande*] implies its fulfilment since it is nothing other than the desire expressed by the Godhead still hidden in the solitude of His unknownness: 'I was a hidden Treasure, and I wanted to be known.'[58]

God creates in order to be known, or, as Corbin translates this desire, 'in order to become the object of knowledge among His creatures.'[59] The end-point of this process is that the human subject, the believer, becomes a *tajallī*, becomes a revelation of this God who desires to reveal Himself and be known. In this way, we return to the nexus of ontology and epistemology, of being and meaning.

This process paves the way for another tradition: 'He who knows himself, knows his Lord' (*man ʿarafa nafsahu ʿarafa rabbah*), which takes us back to the relationship between epistemology and ontology with which we started. Once again, this knowledge (or gnosis, *ʿirfān*) is intensely personal. Ibn al-ʿArabī's God is,

> [A] God whose secret is sadness, nostalgia, aspiration to know Himself in the beings who manifest his Being. A passionate God, because it is in the *passion* that his *fidèle d'amour* feels for Him, in the theopathy of his *fidèle*, that He is revealed to Himself. And this always individually, in an 'alone with the alone,' which is something very different from universal logic or from a collective participation,

58 Corbin, *Alone*, 257. 'L'Être Divin a besoin de son fidèle pour se manifester; réciproquement, ce dernier a besoin de lui pour être investi de l'existence. En ce sens, c'est son *être* même, la capacité même de son être, qui *est* sa Prière (*duʿāʾ bi-l-istiʿdād*), l'être de son haeccéité demandant l'actuation plénière, intégrale; or cette demande implique son exaucement même, puisqu'elle n'est rien d'autre que le vœu exprimé par la Divinité encore cachée dans sa solitude d'inconnaissance: « J'étais un Trésor caché, j'ai aspiré à être connu. »' *Imagination créatrice*, 268.

59 *Imagination créatrice*, 132.

> because only the knowledge which the *fedele* has of his Lord is the knowledge which this personal Lord has of him.[60]

If we had to give an answer about why Corbin went to the East, it would have to be something like 'to know God', personally and certainly, to enact his own personal version of a Sufi pilgrimage, and perhaps to find evidence of a kind of universal Protestantism that unites all adherents of the Abrahamic faiths. This ecumenical Protestantism differs significantly from Massignon's garden of a reconciled humanity in important ways. Understanding that difference entails a detour through Corbin's readings of al-Suhrawardī.

Visionary Hermeneutics I: Initiations

Corbin situates the need for initiation tales in the literary and spiritual history of Iran:

> Why did classical Persian literature not produce any novels in the modern sense of the term? Because in order to produce such novels, it is necessary not to see the world 'in a mirror.' The story (*hikaya*) that interests the Irani gnostic is the novel of initiation. It is this very interest that is seen in the passage from the heroic epic to the spiritual epic. This is the most important fact of Iran's spiritual culture. We will see this expressed in the work of al-Suhrawardī.[61]

[60] Corbin, *Alone*, 94; translation slightly modified. '[U]n Dieu dont le secret est tristesse, nostalgie, aspiration à se connaître soi-même dans les êtres qui manifestent son être, les êtres de son être. Dieu *pathétique*, parce que c'est dans la *passion* que son fidèle d'amour éprouve de lui, dans la *théopathie* de son fidèle, qu'il se révèle à soi-même. Et cela dans un *chaque fois*, un « seul avec le seul », qui diffère tout autant de l'universel logique que du partage communautaire, parce que la seule connaissance que le fidèle a de son Seigneur est précisément la connaissance que ce seigneur personnel a de lui.' *Imagination créatrice*, 115.

[61] 'Pourquoi la littérature persane classique n'a-t-elle pas produit de romans, au sens que nous donnons à ce mot? C'est que, pour produire ce genre de romans, il ne faut pas percevoir le monde "dans un miroir". Le récit (la *hikâyat*) qui intéresse le gnostique iranien, c'est le roman d'initiation. Mais précisément cet interêt manifesté dans le passage de l'épopée héroïque à l'épopée mystique, et c'est là un fait capital de la culture spirituelle de l'Iran. Nous verrons le fait s'annoncer dans l'œuvre de Sohrawardi.' *EII*, 1:xxii.

Corbin is of course right to identify the initiation narrative as being at the heart of medieval Persian literary production, as it constitutes a significant proportion of Arabic and South Asian literature from this and later periods. The initiation narrative holds the mirror up to the reader, or rather is itself the mirror in which readers see themselves reflected.[62]

Al-Suhrawardī's 'Tale of Western Exile' ('Qiṣṣat al-Ghurbā al-Gharbiyya') exemplifies the operation of the initiatory narrative as theorised by Corbin. The plot follows the soul's trajectory from the inside to the outside of the world, and then back in and then back out again. In doing so, the narrative falls in line with much theurgic literature of the variety discussed above, where the 'lesson' imparted during the initiation is really that of inducing the soul's departure from the body before the death of the latter. This injunction translates into a saying of the Prophet Muammad that is much beloved by Sufis and Ishrāqīs alike: 'Die before you die' – die, that is, to your material self, that your spiritual self may live and grow.[63]

The tale is framed by a prelude:[64] al-Suhrawardī tells us that he will explain what is meant by 'the great disaster' [*al-ṭāmma al-kubrā*], a term taken from the Qur'an (Q79:34) and read in most commentaries as meaning the Day of Resurrection. The tale itself narrates the experience of a young man who goes in the company of his brother on a bird-hunting trip. They reach the Tunisian city of Qayrawān

[62] It would nonetheless be a mistake to assert a complete divorce between the history of the Western novel and the initiation tale. Thomas Pavel has demonstrated the importance of the latter as a starting point for the development of the novel, with particular emphasis on Heliodorus. Thomas Pavel, *La Pensée du roman* (Paris: Gallimard, 2003), 56–68. Corbin himself connects *Theagenes and Chariclea* to the novel of initiation as well, citing Merkelbach's study of novels and mysteries in antiquity and according to which Chariclea plays the part of the soul returning to its origin. *EII*, 2:240–241.

[63] *EII*, 2:44–45.

[64] For the Arabic text I have followed Corbin's edition, including paragraph numbers. Yaḥyā ibn Ḥabash Shihāb al-Dīn al-Suhrawardī, *Œuvres philosophiques et mystiques II. 1. Le Livre de la théosophie orientale 2. Le Symbole de foi des philosophes 3. Le Récit de l'exil occidental*, Second ed., ed. Henry Corbin, Bibliothèque iranienne. Nouvelle série (Tehran; Paris: Académie Impériale Iranienne de Philosophie; A. Maisonneuve, 1977), 274–297.

(which operates in this context as a kind of Ishrāqī Sodom), where they are there taken prisoner. They are thrown into a deep dark well, over which is situated a grand castle. Their captors tell them that they are allowed to go up into the castle at night, but that they must return to the well by day. One day, in the castle, they receive a message from their father brought by a hoopoe (*hudhud*; cf. Q27:20). The message informs the protagonist that if he wants to be saved, he must stop wasting time and embark on a journey. Additional, and seemingly paradoxical, travel directions involve killing his wives and people (*ahl*). This he does, starting the trip and ridding himself of all loved ones, until he reaches the fountain of life and a mysterious mountain, identified with Mount Sinai, which happens to be where his father lives. The protagonist's father congratulates him on his return from the West, but tells him that he must go back to his imprisonment and the well, adding to comfort him that he will be able to return to this mountain and see his father whenever he likes. Finally, he informs the protagonist that above him there are other fathers, other ancestors, going all the way up to the supreme ancestor, who is light upon light. The story ends with a postlude in which the narrator explains that the story is about him, and a prayer for deliverance from the prison of nature and the shackles of matter (*al-qayd al-hayūlī*).

Needless to say, this is not a realist text. Corbin's reading provides the key to al-Suhrawardī's strong figurative language. The story of 'Western Exile' is the story of the Gnostic soul. Given the framework of al-Suhrawardī's philosophy, and his championing of the Orient (the source of light) as the figurative locus of wisdom, it is inevitable that any estrangement from wisdom or gnosis would take the form of an exile in the land of the Occident. From the standpoint of Iran or Syria, Tunisia and al-Qayrawān look very much like the far (and wild) West. Hence the title: Occidental exile. The theme of the soul 'thrown' into a material or corporeal universe from which it tries to extract itself to return to the one, or God, will be familiar to readers of Gnostic literature, as will the motifs of the letter from the parents and the self or body as a garment, all of which bear a strong resemblance to the 'Hymn of the Pearl' in the *Acts of Thomas*.[65] The ascendance into the castle at night translates into the vision of intelligible forms in dreams, while during the day when quotidian business takes over, no such contemplation is possible. Finally, the father that he meets at the end of the tale is none other than his celestial self, the 'Man of Light' of the *Acts of Thomas* or the *Insān Kāmil* (perfect, fully-developed person) of Sufi tradition: a perfect version of the self withal.[66] In al-Suhrawardī's neoplatonic framework, this entity is identified with the archangel Gabriel, who occupies the lowest of ten degrees of archangels, a chain leading all the way up to the divine paternal intellect, the *nous patrikos* of the Chaldean Oracles.[67] However we identify this sage whose sight amazes the narrator, we should remember that in structural terms their encounter constitutes the moment of self-knowledge, here overlaid with a markedly Muslim wrapper, taken from the tradition about knowing oneself and knowing one's Lord. Knowing the Lord or meeting the Lord is here translated into this personal vision of the archangel. Thus, the soul's journey in the 'Tale of Western Exile' is a story about the soul getting to know itself.

A key part of that self-knowledge is the recitation of the Qur'an. One of the things that makes this text particularly difficult to translate is the fact that every other word or phrase is taken from the Qur'an and woven seamlessly into the fabric of the story. In another short treatise entitled 'Kitāb Kalimat al-taṣawwuf' [The Book of the Word of Sufism], al-Suhrawardī enjoins the reader to read or recite the Qur'an

[65] Hans Jonas, *The Gnostic Religion: The Message of the Alien God and the Beginnings of Christianity*, Second, enlarged ed. (Boston, MA: Beacon Press, 1963), 112–129; *EII*, 2:265–267.

[66] *EII*, 2:294–296. On the multiple meanings and connotations of the term across various Muslim traditions, see also Roger Arnaldez, 'al-Insān al-Kāmil', *EI2*.

[67] *EII*, 2:283–284; Helmut Seng, *Un livre sacré de l'Antiquité tardive: les Oracles Chaldaïques* (Turnhout: Brepols, 2016), 42–47, 66–67.

'as if it had been revealed to you alone.'[68] Every step of the Ishrāqī mystic's return to his father's house is troped through an episode from the life of a Qur'anic prophet or other: he receives the message from his father through a hoopoe – a bird that plays a key part in the Qur'anic version of the Solomon story – he takes the trip in a vessel identified with Noah's ark, his ridding himself of corporeal qualities and vices is mapped onto the destruction of Lot's people (hence the injunction to 'kill your people'), he goes to Sinai like Moses and so on. In other words, the narrator re-enacts the key chapters of the Qur'an and the lives of the Qur'anic prophets through his person – he *is* successively Noah, Lot, Moses, Solomon – thereby reciting it as if it had been revealed for him alone.[69] This recital is a key part of the aforementioned dialectic whereby the spiritual initiate makes the Qur'an his own. This appropriation of the Qur'an depends on interpretation – *ta'wīl* – understood as a combination of recital and hermeneutic, an *Aufhebung* of theoretical certainties into lived, existential certainties which form a key part of the adept's spiritual development.[70] In this framework, interpretation is lived experience at levels historical and personal.

The initiate receives certainty from the encounter with the angelic, celestial self.[71] Knowledge of the celestial self generates both a new form of self-knowledge and a new basis for certainty: all that is known now descends from this celestial self (the Lord/*rabb* of the self) rather than being the product of individual reasoning alone. The production of certainty depends on a personal and epistemological orientation towards this second self. At the same time, the account of this encounter must occur not only as a tale to be narrated, but as an event

[68] Yaḥyā ibn Ḥabash Shihāb al-Dīn al-Suhrawardī, *L'Archange empourpré. Quinze traités et récits mystiques traduits du persan et de l'arabe*, ed. and trans. Henry Corbin (Paris: Fayard, 1976), 172; *EII*, 2:209.

[69] *EII*, 2:279.

[70] *EII*, 2:259.

[71] *EII*, 2:264.

to be experienced. Hence the particularity of stories like the 'Tale of Western Exile': these are not allegories; they are ways of translating doctrine into real events that take place in the celestial realm (*malakūt*); the sphere of angels, souls, and immutable spiritual truths.[72] Corbin details the story's movement between levels of certainty in the reader's/believer's mind in a passage that deserves to be quoted at length:

> A) There is theoretical certainty (*ʿilm al-yaqīn*); knowing, for example, that fire exists, and having heard of what fire is. B) There is visual certainty (*ʿayn al-yaqīn*); for example, seeing fire with one's own eyes, being witness to fire. C) There is personally realized certainty (*haqq al-yaqīn*); being burned by the flame, becoming fire oneself. The distance from *A* to *B* is the distance between theoretical doctrine and doctrine experienced as personal event. In the current context, we would say that level *A* is learning what the 'Orient' is from al-Suhrawardī's *Oriental Theosophy* [*Ḥikmat al-Ishrāq*]. Level *B*, where doctrine becomes event, is the one where we become witnesses to this 'Orient' because we are 'taken' by the *narrative*, and by what only the *narrative* form makes possible. But then reaching level *C* is not just re-descending to level *A* in order to discover the theoretical esoteric meaning of the narrative. On the contrary, it is taking everything that is said at level *A* and raising it to level *B*, so that, once doctrine becomes event, the pilgrim awakens to the consciousness of this event as something personally experienced, and whose reality and truth are personified in that pilgrim's self.[73]

72 Cf. Louis Gardet's description of this sphere: 'It is the world of immutable spiritual truths, and hence of the angelic beings, to which are added the *entia* of Islamic tradition, the Preserved Table, the Pen, and the Scales [...] and often also the Ḳur ʾān. The spiritual reality (*rūḥ*) which is in man belongs to it. So too do the separated intellects, and hence the human ʿaḳl which partakes of them.' Gardet, 'ʿĀlam', *EI2*.

73 'A) Il y a la certitude théorique (*ʿilm al-yaqīn*); c'est savoir, par exemple, que le feu existe, avoir entendu dire ce que c'est que le feu. *B*) Il y a la certitude oculaire (*ʿayn al-yaqīn*); c'est, par exemple, voir le feu de ses propres yeux, en être le témoin. *C*) Il y a la certitude personnellement réalisée (*haqq al-yaqīn*); c'est être brûlé par la flamme, devenir soi-même le feu. Du niveau *A* au niveau *B* la distance est celle qu'il y a entre la doctrine théorique et la doctrine devenu événement personnel. Dans le cas présent, nous dirons que le niveau *A*, c'est apprendre du livre de la « Théosophie orientale » de Sohravardî ce

The initiation of the reader, who personally embodies the reality of the narrative, is paralleled by the metamorphosis of the heroic epic into a mystical one. Corbin thinks through this metamorphosis through the relationship between al-Suhrawardī's stories and the Grail legend; a synthesis that paves the way for the idea of spiritual chivalry that occupied Corbin's later years. Both Ishrāqī narratives and the Grail legend centre on ideas of return and restoration, modulated through the soul's return to its home and the restitution of a cosmic spiritual order. They also operate as a self-cure for Corbin's rejection of the Buddhist ethical doctrine of renunciation during his youth. He narrates this part of his biography as follows:

> At the time, I studied Sanskrit for two years. Under the supervision of the eminent scholar Alfred Foucher, we explained the *shlokas* from Bergaigne's manual. I still remember one, which I will never forget: *Tena adhîtaṃ, shrutaṃ tena, tena sarvam anuṣṭhitam* … (I cite and transcribe from memory some forty years later): 'He who finds rest in the abandonment of all hope has heard and understood everything.' I remember the protest that took root in the heart of the young philosopher that I was: *Non possum, non possum*, I cannot accept that.[74]

Corbin rejects despair to make way for an ethics of perpetual spiritual rejuvenation: it is no accident that the term *futuwwa/fotowwat* and

que c'est que « l'Orient ». Le niveau *B*, c'est celui où la doctrine devient *événement*; c'est être fait le témoin de cet « Orient », parce que l'on « est pris » dans le *récit*, dans ce que seule la forme du *récit* permet de dire. Mais alors le niveau *C*, ce n'est pas du tout redescendre tout simplement au niveau *A* pour découvrir le sens ésotérique théorique du récit; c'est tout au contraire prendre tout ce qui est dit au niveau *A* et l'exhausser au niveau *B*, de telle manière que, la doctrine étant devenue événement, le pèlerin s'éveille alors à la conscience de cet événement comme de quelque chose qui lui arrive à lui, et dont il est en sa personne la réalité et la vérité.' *EII*, 2:191.

74 'Je fis alors du Sanskrit pendant deux ans. Sous la direction de l'éminent maître Alfred Foucher, nous expliquions à l'époque les *çlokas* du manuel de Bergaigne. Je me rappelle encore l'un deux, car je n'oublierai de ma vie. *Tena adhîtaṃ, çrutaṃ tena, tena sarvam anuṣṭhitam* … (je cite et transcris de mémoire plus de quarante ans après). « Il a tout compris, il a tout entendu, il a tout expérimenté, celui qui, tournant le dos à l'espérance, a trouvé le repos dans l'abandon de tout espoir. » Je me rappelle quelle protestation il y avait au cœur du jeune philosophe que j'étais: *Non possum, non possum*. Je ne peux pas accepter cela.' *L'Homme & son ange*, 244.

javanmardî – the Sufi code of honour which he translates as spiritual chivalry – occurs with increasing frequency during the last decade of his life. Corbin calls *futuwwa* the supreme ethical category and the basis for all professional associations of shared values, not least in relation to craft guilds.[75] Corbin's rejection of the ethics of despair is also symptomatic of his commitment to a polemical cosmogony based on a dualist belief in a universe of light and darkness, good and evil. For Corbin, suffering can only be a necessary step in the cosmic battle between light and darkness. Once again, visibility, now seen as confrontation, is the key to the ethics that he calls for: 'It is not about giving up or resigning oneself, it is about **facing**.'[76]

Visionary Hermeneutics II: Spiritual Chivalry

Despite Corbin's lifelong commitment to foregrounding the personal aspect of spiritual belief and practice, the formulation of his ideas on spiritual chivalry comes close to valorizing the institutional, conceived through a transcultural pleroma of spiritually elite characters who might be considered collective versions of the celestial self seen in the 'Tale of Western Exile' – the twelve Shīʿī Imāms, the Knights of the Round Table, the Joachimites, the Johannites of Strasbourg, the *Gottesfreunde* – who protect the certainties established through spiritual practice and lead humanity to its fulfilment by hastening the Parousia and the next life.[77] This is not to say that Corbin advances a

[75] *L'Homme & son ange*, 208. The core value of *futuwwa* is not only youth but honour and the commitment to a vision of social justice. See Massignon's treatment of *futuwwa* as a *pacte d'honneur artisanal* as well as Jambet's introductory comments. Massignon, *EM*, 2:613–639.

[76] 'Il ne s'agit pas de renoncer, de se résigner, il s'agit de faire **face**.' *L'Homme & son ange*, 244; emphasis mine.

[77] The importance of these comparisons may be seen from the fact that they constitute the core of the final chapter of Corbin's *En Islam iranien*. *EII*, 4:390–460. On the question of spiritual elitism, see *EII*, 4:446. See, too, the central role played by the Grail legend throughout the second volume of *En Islam iranien*, especially the central chapters. *EII*, 2:141–210.

syncretic view that proposes an equivalence between the twelver Shīʿism and the Grail legend, but he does imply a degree of isomorphism between them. The central factor in this isomorphism is the idea of the Grail as the self: the quest for one is the quest for the other.

The first step towards the pleroma is the aforementioned encounter with the celestial, angelic self, which functions as a first principle of transcendent individuality. Vision enables individuality. This encounter activates and is activated by the creative imagination; leading to a revelation that initiates the seer into the real order of things. This is also the start of a lifetime of voyages to the very beginning of existence, away from material existence and towards the light; a spiritual maturity that leads to a state of eternal youth (*Puer aeternus*).[78] The initiate's creative imagination also depends on the construction of a personal hermeneutics (as in 'recite the Qur'an as if it were revealed to you alone') that must, if it is to function properly, itself lead to a collective understanding that supports the object of the seer's quest – the Grail in the Grail legend, the twelfth (invisible) Imām in twelver Shīʿism. This encounter with the celestial self, which Corbin calls *unio mystica*, also modifies the task of philosophy, which now finds itself re-oriented along an axis that changes the philosopher into a *théosophe* and *chevalier*:

> This type of philosopher, the 'wise man of God' or *theosophos*, fully reveals his way of being and his cosmic spiritual function in the work of al-Suhrawardī and the Ishrāqīs [...] The central axis of this metaphysics, and of the anthropology that it governs, is oriented towards the union of the human intellect – and thereby of the whole interior spiritual person – towards what the philosophers call the 'active intellect' and which they identify with the Holy Spirit, the Angel Gabriel of the revelation, the Angel of humanity

[78] *L'Homme & son ange*, 13–14.

> [...] and finally of the Imām as personal guide. Now, it is precisely thanks to this *unio mystica*, however we explain or represent it, that the channels of communication between the superior world of the *Malakūt* and ours stay open, and *eo ipso* that humanity perseveres in being. And it is that *eo ipso* that defines the chivalrous service of the philosopher as 'sage of God', and which makes him a *javānmard par excellence*. This is the philosopher as conceived by the Ishrāqīs and the Shī'ī theosophists.[79]

What the angelic or celestial self communicates to the *théosophe* is not only the reality of the order of things, but also, and more significantly, the nature of the esoteric meaning of the revealed text. As such, the task of all theosophy becomes that of a prophetic philosophy: understanding both the sacred law as it is revealed in a literal sense, but also of its hidden meanings that are always in danger of disappearing. The most important revelation is that of the forgotten origin, made visible through contact with the active intellect. Thus does the process of rejuvenation begin. Just as the self is returned to the *nous patrikos* in the 'Tale of Western Exile', so is the universe brought back to its originary beauty:

> The meaning of this rejuvenation is that we do not turn our backs on our origin, but rather are led back to the origin, to the *apokastasis*, to the restoration of all things in their novelty, in their original beauty [...] The more we progress, the more we approach the point

[79] 'Ce type de philosophe comme « sage de Dieu », *theosophos*, révèle pleinement son mode d'être et sa fonction spirituelle cosmique chez Sohrawardî et les *Ishrâqiyûn* [...] L'axe de cette métaphysique et de l'anthropologie qu'elle gouverne, est orienté dans le sens de l'union de l'intellect de l'homme, mais par là-même de tout l'homme intérieur, de tout son être spirituel, avec celle que les philosophes désignent comme l' « Intelligence agente » et qu'ils identifient avec l'Esprit-Saint, l'Ange Gabriel de la révélation, Ange de l'humanité [...] et finalement sous l'aspect de l'Imâm comme guide personnel. Or, cette *unio mystica*, de quelque manière qu'on l'explique ou qu'on se la représente, c'est justement grâce à elle que se maintient la communication entre le monde supérieur du *Malakût* et notre monde, grâce à elle *eo ipso* que l'humanité persévère dans l'être. Et c'est cela *eo ipso* qui définit le service chevaleresque du philosophe comme « sage de Dieu », et qui fait de lui un *javânmard* par excellence. C'est le philosophe tel que l'ont conçu les *Ishrâqîyûn* et les théosophes shî'ites.' *EII*, 4:418.

> from which we left. I think the best comparison is to what is known as the 'miracle of the octave' in music. We depart from a fundamental sound, and it is always to that sound, to the octave, that we progress.[80]

There follows an initiation into a new interpretive and historical system that reads the history of humanity as a series of prophetic (*nubuwwa/nobowwat*) and mystical (*walāya/walāyat*) cycles. The history of the prophets, from Adam to Muhammad, is coupled with the history of the *awliyā*ʾ; the bearers of the esoteric counterpart to the exoteric (and usually legislative) revelation of the prophets. Corbin describes the fate of the Abrahamic monotheisms as the tragedy of the lost word (*le drame de la « Parole perdue »*), in light of the fact that as belief systems they revolve around the revelation of a sacred book, and the meanings contained therein.[81] What is lost is the esoteric. The recovery of the lost word depends on the adoption of an enabling hermeneutics; one that foregrounds the esoteric as the true meaning of the revealed text.[82] The core procedure of this hermeneutics, like the encounter with the celestial self, is restitution: returning meanings to their origins (*taʾwīl*).[83] At the origin, we find the Imām, who guides the hermeneutic process and embodies the meaning of history. After the Occultation of the twelfth Imām, however, a community of interpretation is needed to keep this meaning alive. It is this that renders *futuwwa* necessary and meaningful; for everyone must become a knight in the service of the Imām, with the ultimate aim of making the hidden Imām visible, with hastening his appearance:

80 'Le sens de cette réjuvénation est de non pas tourner le dos à l'origine, mais de nous ramener à l'origine, à l'*apokastasis*, à la restauration de toutes choses en leur fraîcheur, en leur beauté originelle [. . .] Plus nous progressons, plus nous nous approchons de ce dont nous étions partis. Je crois que la meilleure comparaison que nous puissions proposer, c'est ce qu'en musique on a appelé le « miracle de l'octave ». À partir du son fondamental quel que soit le sens dans lequel nous progressions, c'est toujours vers ce même son fondamental, à l'octave que nous progressons.' *L'Homme & son ange*, 232.

81 *L'Homme & son ange*, 81.

82 *L'Homme & son ange*, 84.

83 *EII*, 1:xx, 188.

> *Futuwwa* is really the characteristic ethos, the manifestation *par excellence*, of *walāya*. This is because *futuwwa* consists in everyone, wherever they are, being the knight of the Imām, and the companion of the twelfth Imām. This ethics makes everyone responsible for the coming of the *Parousia*, which will not just happen, one fine day, without preparation. The *Parousia* takes place in the interior of every knight, in every one of the *javānmardan*. The entire cycle of *walāya* is accomplished not only in the cycle of sacred history; it is accomplished inside every believer, inside every *fidèle*.[84]

Not for nothing does al-Suhrawardī describe the *awliyā*ʾ as God's eyes on the world ('les yeux par lesquels Dieu regarde encore le monde'[85]): only they have the hidden Imām permanently in view, and only they can prepare his return to visibility. The vocation of the *waliyy* is precisely to be God's eye on the world. This, moreover, is no superfluous privilege; for it alone enables the continued existence of the world. The parousia can only take place when the efficacy of the *ta*ʾ*wīl* has been made plain for the entire world to see as a result of the internal transformation that occurs within the heart of each *fidèle*. The idea of spiritual chivalry is built around a universal palingenesis[86] made possible by a collective grounding in this restorative hermeneutics.[87]

84 'La *fotowwat* est vraiment l'éthos caractéristique, la manifestation par excellence, de la *walâyat*. Car la *fotowwat* consiste en ce que chacun, là même où il est, soit le chevalier de l'Imâm, le compagnon du XIIe Imâm. Cette éthique rend chacun responsable de l'avenir de la parousie, qui n'est pas quelque chose qui surgira un beau jour, de l'extérieur, sans que rien ne l'ait préparé. La parousie s'accomplit à l'intérieur de chacun des chevaliers, chacun des *javânmardân*. Tout ce cycle de la *walâyat* ne s'accomplit pas seulement dans la hiérohistoire totale; il s'accomplit d'abord à l'intérieur de chaque croyant, à l'intérieur de chaque fidèle.' *L'Homme & son ange*, 222–223.

85 *EII*, 4:402.

86 Corbin stresses the parallels between joining the tradition of spiritual chivalry, thereby helping to maintain an uninterrupted chain of gnosis and understanding built around the Imām from generation to generation, and entering the kingdom of God (*Malakūt*): '[C]ette tradition est tout le contraire d'un cortège funèbre, elle est une perpétuelle renaissance. Y prendre rang, c'est entrer dans le *Malakût*, et comme le dit une sentence directement venue de l'Évangile de Jean que nos théosophes citent avec prédilection: « Ne peut entrer dans le *Malakût* quiconque n'est pas né une seconde fois. »' *EII*, 4:435. cf. Jn. 3.3.

87 *EII*, 4:435.

Not only does this restorative hermeneutics restore the hidden Imām to visibility; it fulfils the terms of the pledge (*amāna*) that binds God and humanity.[88] This pledge is not only about bearing witness to the unity and uniqueness of God for eternity, nor is it limited to attesting the reality of the Imām; it is also about maintaining the place of the human in relation to the divine. Corbin adds to the many versions of spiritual chivalry mentioned above the characters who populate Goethe's epic verse fragment, *Die Geheimnisse*, emphasizing as he does so the parallels between Goethe's twelve knights and the twelve Imāms, and above all the cosmic role played by the figure at the centre of Goethe's text; namely the enigmatic *Humanus*, the Perfect Man (*Insān Kāmil*), and the transhistorical figure of the Imām as a universal mediator that unites all religions and belief systems.[89] Being a *fatā* or a Sufi, in Corbin's estimation, means doing justice to God's covenant with creation and returning the *amāna* that was placed in trust with

[88] As described in Q7:172 and Q33:72. The first of these two verses is the standard reference for the so-called doctrine of *alast* ('Am I not?'): 'Remember when your Lord took away from Adam's children the seeds from their loins, and made them witness upon themselves: "Am I not your Lord?" They answered: "Yes, we witness."' Q33:27 is the *amāna* (trust) verse: 'We offered the Trust to the heavens, the earth and the mountains, but they declined to carry it and were afraid of it, but man [*al-insān*] carried it – and he has ever been unjust, intemperate.' See Corbin's analysis of the central place of these two verses in esoteric Muslim thought. *EII*, 1:94–110; 3:192.

[89] *EII*, 4:405–409; Johann Wolfgang von Goethe, *Sämtliche Werke nach Epochen seines Schaffens, Münchner Ausgabe*, ed. Herbert Georg Göpfert et al. (Munich: Hanser, 1985), 2.2:339–348. Verses 245–248 of *Die Geheimnisse* are particularly resonant with Corbin's concerns:

> *Humanus* heißt der Heilige, der Weise,
> Der beste Mann [cf. *Insān kāmil*], den ich mit Augen sah:
> Und sein Geschlecht, wie es die Fürsten nennen,
> Sollst du zugleich mit seinen Ahnen kennen.

It is worthy of note that Corbin does not invoke the Goethe of the *West-östlicher Divan*, and who arguably comes closer to Corbin's literary interest in Iran. Furthermore, Corbin's reading of *Die Geheimnisse* does not deviate significantly from Goethe's own commentary on the poem, seeing in Humanus 'l'homme pleinement HUMAIN comme centre d'une constellation d'individualités typiques, que leurs aspirations rassemblent autour de lui en raison de leur affinité, et qui ne peuvent trouver leur épanouissement total qu'en se rassemblant ainsi autour de lui.' *EII*, 4:405. Cf. *Goethe MA*, 2.2:838–841; Hartmut Reinhardt, 'Geheime Wege der Aufklärung. Goethe, die Illuminatenorden, und das Epos-Fragment ›Die Geheimnisse‹,' in *Die Weimarer Klassik und ihre Geheimbünde*, ed. Walter Müller-Seidel and Wolfgang Riedel (Würzburg: Königshausen & Neumann, 2002), 171–176. I am deeply indebted to Matthew Bell for these references.

humanity, thereby fulfilling humanity's promise.[90] This process is described in Ḥusayn Vā'iz Kāshifī's *Futuwwat nāma-yi Sultānī* via an imagined dialogue between Moses and God. In response to the question 'What is *futuwwa*?', God replies that it is to return the pure, immaculate soul that every person receives as a sacred deposit.[91] Quite apart from the neoplatonic resonance of this statement, caring for the *amāna* in the Shī'ī tradition also means bearing witness to the mission of the Imāms, their *walāya*, and the entire doctrine of the esoteric *Bāṭin*.[92]

The many pleromas that populate Corbin's late works, be they Eastern or Western, operate as a chain of institutional guarantors of the certainty that he so ardently sought. Each one acts as a custodian of a system of interpretation and meaning, which allows the world to 'persevere in being' (*persévérer dans l'être*). The permanence of these hermeneutic practices enables a continuity of community and belief, as well as a preservation of the vision – indeed, a safeguarding of the phenomena – that animates them. Corbin once proposed replacing the idea of a permanent revolution with permanent hermeneutics, less as a means of exhaustive interpretation than as a way of creating a perpetually renewed encounter between image and idea.[93] This permanence also constitutes the key moment in the thought of Corbin's most important student, Christian Jambet, who will be the subject of the next chapter.

90 Typically, Corbin underplays the social and political aspects of *futuwwa* in favour of the spiritual and the visionary. Lloyd Ridgeon provides a fuller historical account of those aspects, as well as a socially grounded reading of Kāshifī's *Futuwwat nāma*. Lloyd V. J. Ridgeon, *Morals and Mysticism in Persian Sufism: A History of Sufi-futuwwat in Iran* (London: Routledge, 2010), 99–108.

91 'C'est remettre à Dieu l'âme pure et immaculée, telle que l'homme la reçut en dépôt.' *EII*, 4:412.

92 'En très bref, il y a ce que les Imâms ont répété dans les *hadîth*: « Ce secret, c'était notre *walâyat*. » Or, la *walâyat* est elle-même le membre d'une triade constituée par un triple acquiescement: à l'Unité de l'Unique (*tawhîd*), à la mission exotérique des prophètes (*nobowwat*), à la mission ésotérique des Amis de Dieu (*walâyat*). Le poids dont l'homme se chargea, est le poids de cette triple Attestation (*shahâdat*).' *EII*, 1:98.

93 '[D]e même que d'autres ont parlé de la nécessité d'une « révolution permanente », je prônerais la nécessité d'une « herméneutique permanente » [...] [L]'herméneutique permanente n'altère aucun mot de la Tradition, chaque mot est à conserver, car il concourt à une nouvelle rencontre fulgurante entre l'Image et l'Idée.' 'De Heidegger. . .,' 36.

3

Christian Jambet's Resurrections

Will there ever be a time when Iranian names routinely sit alongside those of Western philosophers? When the mutual ignorance of the lands of metaphysics will come to an end? What an ideal for reason![1]

Beginnings

Philosophy begins with an event, preferably apocalyptic: one bright medieval August day, in a mountain town in Central Asia, the governor calls all inhabitants for an important announcement; namely, that the world has come to an end, and that the great resurrection that they have all been waiting for has arrived. What, we might ask, should they do? How should people behave at the end?

*

Christian Jambet was born in Algiers in 1949. His family was expelled during the war of independence, and like many other *pieds noirs* he settled in France. Jambet quickly excelled in his studies. Like many of his generation, he was drawn to Mao Zedong's Cultural Revolution, and in 1969 was one of a small number of French Maoists selected to go on an official visit to Mao's China, where he took part in rallies which he considered a mystical experience.[2] A big part of the mystical

1 'Le temps viendra-t-il jamais, où des noms iraniens voisineront couramment avec ceux des philosophes occidentaux? Où les pays de la métaphysique cesseront de s'ignorer? Quel idéal pour la raison!' Christian Jambet, *La Logique des Orientaux. Henry Corbin et la science des formes* (Paris: Seuil, 1983), 13.

2 Christophe Bourseiller, *Les Maoïstes. La Folle histoire des gardes rouges français*, Points (Paris: Seuil, 2008), 167.

dimension had to do with Jambet's sense of belonging with the revolutionary masses *and* with the visibility of Mao in the rallies that he attended in Tian An Men. As we will see, revelation and participation are processes that will be repeated in other revolutionary mechanisms that interest Jambet.

Jambet was also a founding member of the Gauche Prolétarienne (GP) activist group, and remained a member until its dissolution in 1973. Thereupon he had what might be called a conversion experience in the wake of revelations about the Gulag, as well as the appalling consequences of the Great Leap Forward and the Cultural Revolution, though he did try to remain faithful to aspects of his Maoist ideals. This has not protected him from repeated attacks from all quarters, some of which continue to this day.[3] With another former member of the GP, Guy Lardreau, he sat down and re-read all of Western philosophy, from the pre-Socratics onwards. He also enrolled in courses in Arabic and Persian, and started studying Islamic philosophy under the supervision of Henry Corbin. In a very short time, Jambet had mastered a vast body of work. Although he insisted, in an interview in 1978, that his first love was literature, he maintains that he cannot comment on philosophy without the company of (mostly Modernist) literary monuments like Baudelaire, Blanchot, T.S. Eliot, Yeats, and Genet, and that the bulk of his work from then on was about philosophy, with a focus on Sufism, Illuminationism and Shīʿism. Christian Jambet taught in French secondary schools for decades before being named to a Chair at the EPHE, from which he recently retired.

As was the case with his predecessors, Jambet interests us precisely due to what might be called a lack of objective, neutral, 'scientific'

[3] As in the attack on the legacy of the GP in works like Jean Birnbaum's *Les Maoccidents* (2009), where Jambet, Lardreau, Milner and plenty of former GP-istes are dismissed as closet neoconservatives. *Les Maoccidents: un néoconservatisme à la française* (Paris: Stock, 2009), 85–98.

distance between himself and his subjects. Needless to say, this tends to irritate observers from other academic traditions, as witness the savage review of Jambet's *Qu'est-ce que la philosophie islamique ?* penned by Dmitri Gutas.[4] Whereas Massignon used Sufism and the story of al-Ḥallāj to think through desire, and whereas Corbin found certainty in the vision of the Sufi and Shīʿī, Christian Jambet uses the esoteric to think through questions of eschatology and resurrection, both of which he treats as immediate concerns rather than matters that will only happen in a dim, distant future. It is only in death, he argues, that the desiring subject finds certainty.[5] In particular, Jambet seems to want to be delivered from doubt around questions of being and freedom – not only being free, but the freedom to be. As we shall see, much of this has to do with his conception of philosophy. In arguments that echo Foucault and Hadot, Jambet argues that all philosophy is liberation and self-transformation; that philosophy is the care of the self and the art of existence.[6] The resulting freedom is founded on a belief in eschatology and the next life. Sages like Socrates and Jesus who valorize the internal law and scoff at exteriorities embody wisdom and freedom.[7] Philosophy thus prepares us for an afterlife. Furthermore, the aim of philosophy is to allow a complete participation of human and divine intellect. Therefore, philosophy is itself resurrection.[8]

If we were to articulate one question the answer to which would generate Jambet's *œuvre*, it would be this: Where is freedom in Islamic

4 Dimitri Gutas, 'Forward to the Past,' review of Christian Jambet: *Qu'est-ce que la philosophie islamique ?*, *Philosophy East and West* 64, no. 4 (2014), https://doi.org/10.1353/pew.2014.0068. A more measured and informative account of Jambet's book is found in Julien Cavagnis, 'Corbin, Hadot, Foucault. Mise en dialogue de *Qu'est-ce que la philosophie islamique?* de Christian Jambet,' *Cahiers Philosophiques*, no. 1 (2012), https://www.cairn.info/load_pdf.php?ID_ARTICLE=CAPH_128_0111.

5 'C'est dans la mort que le sujet parvient à la certitude de soi.' *Le Monde. Réponse à la question, Qu'est-ce que les droits de l'homme?* (Paris: Grasset, 1978), 181.

6 *Qu'est-ce que la philosophie islamique ?*, Folio Essais (Paris: Gallimard, 2011), 124.

7 *Philosophie islamique*, 156.

8 *Philosophie islamique*, 162.

philosophy? Is there a properly Islamic philosophy of freedom? Jambet uses the esoteric, be it in the form of Shīʿī thought or Mullā Ṣadrā's philosophy, as a way of exploring what he calls the 'creative freedom of the real' ['la liberté créatrice du réel'].[9] This exploration revolves around two foci: the idea of freedom and the phenomenon of order. Jambet's interrogation of metaphysical forms in Islamic philosophy is linked to its generally neoplatonic bent. Here freedom is not expressed in terms of necessity and free will. Instead, the founding principle of freedom finds its home in being. Being is necessity, and, ipso facto, freedom. Freedom is being itself, in its autarchy, independence, and truth.[10] This holds for being insofar as there exists, above being, the figure of the One, seen as a source of flux, emanation, and creative spontaneity. Al-Suhrawardī's metaphysics of light, and Mullā Ṣadrā's doctrine of movement, are two among many forms of metaphysical freedom found in a literary and philosophical space far removed from Kant, who stands for notions of autonomy under which we still labour today. This space is, moreover, determined by its link to a revelation and system of belief that accords such freedom to God alone.

This ontologico-theological space is spanned by the pervasiveness of order and the theme of manifestation. Jambet compares what he finds in the philosophies that interest him something akin to the proliferation of concepts in service of order in Leibniz.[11] The word

[9] This section of the chapter owes a great deal to an unpublished personal interview generously accorded by Christian Jambet on 10 July 2018. This interview will only be cited where necessary in the case of a direct quotation and for the sake of clarification.

[10] Jambet's statement is more complete: 'Concevoir la liberté comme l'être lui-même, dans son autarcie, son indépendance complète, et dans sa donation libre de nécessité d'être et de vérité. C'est ça qui me parait être central chez les auteurs que je travaille.' Interview with Christian Jambet, by Ziad Elmarsafy, 10 July 2018.

[11] 'Une folle invention de concepts au service de l'ordre.' Jambet, Interview. Despite the differences that separate their readings of Leibniz (on which see below), Jambet is here alluding playfully to Deleuze's account of Leibniz. Cf. Gilles Deleuze, *Le Pli: Leibniz et le baroque* (Paris: Minuit, 1988), 58–59. Citing Ortega y Gasset, Deleuze refers to a proliferation of principles rather than concepts.

'order' should be understood as both an imperative (*al-amr*, as in the imperative *kun!; Be!*) and hierarchical configuration of being (*al-tarattub*; *tartīb al-wujūd*). This order of the universe constitutes a set of metaphysical topographies that varies by author and philosopher – topographies ordered around light for al-Suhrawardī, around movement for Mullā Ṣadrā – but which consistently bespeaks the prevalence of space over time. This prevalence enables the construction of vast *tableaux* of reality centred on the ineffable principle of being as a source of creative freedom. The total and infinite order of these constructions has as its *telos* the human, framed by a number of determinant models and images. Hence the importance of manifestation as the mechanism that makes order apparent and credible: everything in the universe is modelled on a superior entity, and acts as a model for an inferior existent.[12] Everything that exists is a theophany; a revelation and manifestation of the divine.[13] The philosopher's task is to observe and interpret these manifestations and visions, in a manner not unlike the development of a photograph.[14]

This specular and spectacular hierarchy of being differs radically from the ontologies that developed from the same sources (Plato, Plotinus, Aristotle) in the West. One of the greatest differences is that what is proposed is a universal totality with no division between inside and outside. In Jambet's account of Islamic philosophy, there is only the created world, which forms the object of knowledge and understanding. Furthermore, this knowledge and understanding can only proceed by presentation rather than re-presentation. To think is to grasp (*idrāk*), and to understand is to assimilate a concept to oneself

[12] As in Ibn al-ʿArabī's great chain of being, whereby the divine names act as models for Platonic forms, which themselves are the models of the natural existents etc. Cf. *Philosophie islamique*, 303–306.

[13] *Le Caché et l'Apparent*, Mythes et religions (Paris: L'Herne, 2003), 43–44.

[14] Here we see a marker of the methodological difference between Jambet and Corbin: the former lets the philosophical vision appear, while the latter proceeds through a logic of revelation and correspondences between various spiritual traditions.

(*istīʿāb*), or indeed to create a resemblance between the concept and oneself (*tashabbuh*). The mind becomes one with the object of its knowledge.[15] Philosophy proceeds through acts of presence and vision whereby the intelligible is seen, and the intellect is brought into the presence of the intelligible. Jambet's is an epistemology of immediacy.

It is also an epistemology that refuses to separate metaphysics from ontology. The metaphysics in question revolve around the question of the One – in other words, that of the unicity of God (*tawḥīd*). Not for nothing have generations of thinkers argued that only those who profess the exact *tawḥīd* will find salvation (*najāt*). The interpretation of Q102:1 (literally: 'Say He God One')[16] has driven centuries of intense metaphysical reflection around the questions of the being and place of the One within the ordered universe of the philosophers. The vocabulary of being and the vocabulary of the One are bound inextricably with each other. Jambet is especially drawn to those, like the Ismāʿīlīs and the Sufis, who radically abstract being from the One (i.e. argue that the One is not, or exists beyond being), and those who, like Naṣīr al-Dīn al-Ṭūsī, propose instead a dialectic internal to the One, leading to a key neologism in Jambet's *œuvre*: the paradoxical One (*l'Un paradoxal*), or the One that is *and* is not. This paradox – a way of saying what cannot be said – is the form taken by the pronouncement of the truth in Islamic philosophy, be it in the *shaṭaḥāt* (paradoxes) of the Sufis, such as al-Ḥallāj's 'I am the Truth', or in their underlying metaphysical henologies.

The conceptual map of Jambet's thought is framed by a stratified historicism. Jambet's point of departure is the by now common notion of the plurality of history: as is the case with the idea of freedom, revolution, and resurrection, Jambet adheres to the notion that there

[15] This does not mean that Jambet approaches these texts as an adept or disciple. He insists: 'Je suis tout sauf un mystique musulman!' Jambet, Interview.

[16] In the Khalidi translation, this reads: 'Say "He is God, Unique."'

is not one history; there are many; and, moreover, that there is much more to history than the myths forged by the victors. Over against the historical eschatologies of Hegel, Marx, and Mao (among others), Jambet argues instead for the course of heterogeneous histories running in parallel. The integration of these divergent historical modes yields a truer version of world history. His study of the Great Resurrection of Alamūt (on which more below) is conceived in this mode, aiming to foreground radical historical heterogeneity through the narrative of an event without archives and the fate of those on the losing side of history. This methodology leads Jambet repeatedly to truths that are not historically determined, which he describes as 'modes of truth that are independent of history, or in any case resistant to the course of history.'[17] The merit of the writers and thinkers that interest him is precisely that they have delayed, or at least contradicted, the way of the world.[18] Hence his interest in parts of the world that are particularly rich in messianic political upheaval, anti-triumphalist movements like the *malāmatiyya*, and resistance to the state as political configuration: it is here that this war between the course of world history and individual points of resistance is at its most intense.

*

This foregoing helps us to get past what might seem to be a curious break in Jambet's career, from Maoist activist to France's foremost specialist of Islam and heir to Corbin's mantle. This is only an illusion, however; for if his writing has changed, his concerns have not. Religion is a decisive factor in the study of all revolutions, cultural or otherwise. The arc traced by Jambet's works as a specialist of Islamic philosophy,

[17] 'Des modes de vérité indépendants de l'histoire, ou en tout cas résistants au cours de l'histoire.' Jambet, Interview.

[18] 'Ma conviction la plus profonde [...] c'est que le mérite des penseurs auxquels on fait allusion est d'avoir retardé, ou en tout cas contredit, si peu que ce soit, le cours du monde.' Jambet, Interview.

and especially of the seventeenth-century thinker Mullā Ṣadrā of Shirāz, goes from a preoccupation with revolution that still carries traces of his youthful activism in works like *La Grande Résurrection d'Alamût* (1990) to works that stare death and resurrection head-on such as *Mort et résurrection en Islam* (2008) and *La Fin de toute chose* (2017). Apart from their erudition and rigour, what is striking about this rich panoply of works and studies is the persistence of the themes and questions that we find in Jambet's earliest works: the *Apologie de Platon* (1976) and the two works that he co-authored with Guy Lardreau, *L'Ange* (1976) and *Le Monde* (1978). All these texts revolve around the foci of freedom and order.

Jambet's early work has been the object of some very thorough studies by specialists of post-1968 politics and theory. Julian Bourg's fine history of May '68 argues that Jambet became an ethicist, and described him, along with the other *nouveaux philosophes*, as a contemporary Jansenist of sorts following the failures of the *années 68*.[19] Peter Starr's remarkable *Logics of Failed Revolt* offers a still useful reading of the Lacanian overhang that informed so much of his early work, even as he decries the form and content of *L'Ange*, which he describes as 'an exceptionally dense and self-conscious piece of philosophical mysticism [. . .] two parts hysterical confession to one part hysterical overestimation of "The Master."'[20] Starr sees in the position of Jambet and Lardreau a reinvention of Hegel's beautiful soul paradigm under Lacan's influence:

> How does Lacan's privileging of psychotic miscognition serve to block the dialectical movement proper to Hegel's *schöne Seele* [beautiful soul] scenario, and so constitute the very 'dialectical

[19] Julian Bourg, *From Revolution to Ethics: May 1968 and Contemporary French Thought* (Montréal, Québec: McGill-Queen's University Press, 2007), 257–259.

[20] Peter Starr, *Logics of Failed Revolt: French Theory after May '68* (Stanford, CA: Stanford University Press, 1995), 88–89.

impasse' he finds characteristic of the revolutionary as a *belle âme*? And why would Jambet and Lardreau choose to reconceive cultural revolution precisely on the model of the beautiful soul?[21]

As brilliant as such analyses are, very few of them take any account of Jambet's later (post-1975) work. One notable exception to the pattern of recent work in Jambet is Andrew Gibson's *Intermittency* (2012). Taking his cue from Alain Badiou's theory of the event, Gibson presents a very thorough reading of Jambet's work as a counter to Kojève's reading of Hegel, a 'counter-phenomenology of the spirit' seen through the lens of the Great Resurrection of Alamūt.[22]

Apart from Corbin, the thinker most frequently associated with Jambet – in part due to the focus on his work in the 1970s – is Lacan. It would be incorrect, however, to approach Jambet as a Lacanian thinker. Indeed, Jambet himself considers that *L'Ange* was a book written with *and against* Lacan.[23] Jambet's ideas about the Real lie at some distance from Lacan's definition of the Real as the impossible (the latter being itself impossible in a conceptual universe with no outside) – indeed, he goes so far as to say that it is precisely the failure of Lacan's scheme of Real-Symbolic-Imaginary that enables him to read Avicenna.[24] Jambet's henology works against the logic of Lacan's pronouncements on the One ('Y a de l'Un'), where any sentence that places 'The One' in the position of the subject – i.e. the sort of sentence

[21] Starr, *Logics of Failed Revolt: French Theory after May '68*, 9.

[22] Andrew Gibson, *Intermittency: The Concept of Historical Reason in Recent French Philosophy* (Edinburgh: Edinburgh University Press, 2012), 12–13, 113–156. The following chapter covers some of the same questions as Gibson, but as the reader will quickly notice, I part company with him on several points, not least the place of ethics and eschatology in Jambet's thought. *Intermittency*, 141.

[23] Jambet, Interview.

[24] 'Le modèle qui m'était le plus cher [. . .] c'est-à-dire le réel-symbolique-imaginaire, m'a permis de comprendre Avicenne. *Chez Avicenne, il n'y a pas de réel au sens lacanien*. La modalité de l'impossible ne peut absolument pas définir ou pointer, pour parler comme Lacan, le réel, et il n'y a absolument aucune comparaison possible entre l'ineffable chez nos auteurs et le réel lacanien. Le réel lacanien, c'est le déchet, ce qui chute de la chaine.' Jambet, Interview, emphasis mine.

typical of the writers that Jambet studies – is rejected outright.[25] Another key point on which Jambet abandons Lacan is the latter's propositions regarding the relationship between knowledge and truth: for Lacan, truth is what knowledge lacks – a position diametrically opposed to that of Jambet's philosophers.[26] Jambet aims, on the contrary, to demonstrate that correspondence between knowledge and truth, or that knowledge is adequate to the truth. The idea that the truth is spoken by the prophets rules out the possibility of taking the Lacanian position that posits a disjunction between knowledge and truth.

The other thinker whose name looms large behind Jambet's work is Foucault. The key principle of *dualitude* operative in Jambet's thought owes much to Jambet's relationship with Foucault, who is seen as the thinker who went the farthest in working through the non-dialectisable opposition, or war, between the forces of submission and those of liberation.[27] At one point in the late 1970s Jambet had planned to write a book about Foucault entitled *Michel Foucault éducateur*, but Foucault's early death prevented its completion. It will be remembered

[25] A short history of Lacan's ideas about the One might begin with his reading of the *Parmenides* in Seminar 19 and their later development in Seminar 20. *Le Séminaire de Jacques Lacan. Livre XIX, . . . ou pire* (Paris: Seuil, 2011), 129–135; *Le Séminaire de Jacques Lacan. Livre XX. Encore*, Points, (Paris: Seuil, 1999), 86–90, 181–182. Jambet comments on this aspect of Lacan's thought as follows: 'It is Lacan who must be credited with the most radical dismissal of any theology of the one. Lacan distinguishes the imaginary thesis "the one is [*l'un est*]" (which he identifies with the thesis "everything is everything [*tout est tout*]," everything is whole, or all) from the thesis appropriate to the real of the subject: "there is one [*il y a de l'un*]" (itself a consequence of the thesis "nothing is everything [*rien n'est tout*]," nothing is whole or all).' 'Some Comments on the Question of the One,' *Angelaki* 8, no. 2 (2003): 36, https://doi.org/10.1080/0969725032000162558. Cf. Jacques Lacan, *Autres écrits* (Paris: Seuil, 2001), 440, 527.

[26] The necessary incompleteness of knowledge and the impossibility of saying 'the whole truth' feature repeatedly in the Lacanian corpus: *Écrits* (Paris: Seuil, 1966), 867–868; *Le Séminaire de Jacques Lacan. Livre XVIII. D'un discours qui ne serait pas du semblant* (Paris: Seuil, 2008), 14; *Séminaire XX*, 117–118, 149. This last passage is cited in Christian Jambet and Guy Lardreau, *L'Ange. Pour une cynégétique du semblant* (Paris: Grasset, 1976), 75.

[27] 'Some comments,' 37–38.

that Foucault was very much preoccupied by the 1979 revolution in Iran.[28] Foucault was, according to Jambet, one of the few who understood the spiritual politics of Shīʿī Islam and the concomitant transformation of dogma into political theology.[29] Foucault's writings about the 1979 revolution held exemplary value for Jambet.[30] Jambet was also an avid reader of the arguments made in the three (now four) volumes of the *History of Sexuality*. In an intervention that aired in 1991 on France Culture, Jambet elucidated Foucault's ideas at length. The aforementioned opposition between the hidden and the apparent is key to understanding Foucault's style of thought and writing:

> Foucault's style is descriptive. His concern is not to show structures or reveal hidden structures, but rather to see to it that what appears at the very surface of Greek or Roman language [*parole*] is recognized. There is no plumbing the depths of doctrine; instead, there is a search for what is most apparent and manifest. Consequently, all hermeneutics are rejected in favour of description. There is no search for a hidden meaning, but rather a

[28] Michel Foucault, *Dits et écrits: 1954–1988*, ed. Daniel Defert and François Ewald, 4 vols (Paris: Gallimard, 1994), 3:662–794.

[29] 'Retour sur l'insurrection iranienne,' in *Michel Foucault*, ed. Philippe Artières et al., Cahiers de l'Herne (Paris: L'Herne, 2011), 373–374.

[30] Jambet's account of Foucault's reading of Iran in the late 1970s makes clear the parallels with his own reading of Alamūt: 'Il s'agit, non de la politique d'un futur état, mais de l'essence d'un soulèvement, de la politique « spirituelle » qui le rend possible, et c'est, par conséquent, une interrogation « transcendantale » : à quelle condition une culture peut-elle déterminer une révolte à partir d'une espérance et une expérience scandées comme « événements dans le ciel » ? Ici, l'Orient n'est plus questionné comme un des noms forgés par l'Occident, mais comme le lieu d'une problématisation différente mais réelle, étrangère mais autonome, du pouvoir et de la liberté. M. Foucault voit, d'emblée, que l'histoire y est l'expression d'une méta-histoire, ou encore d'une hiéro-histoire, que la temporalisation des temps est suspendue à des événements messianiques dont le lieu d'être n'est pas le monde des phénomènes connu par la science. Il voit aussi qu'un certain type de subjectivité est dès lors rendu possible, assez éloignée du sujet de la science, du droit et de la morale, tels que la coupure galiléenne et cartésienne les a définitivement instaurés en Occident.' Christian Jambet, 'Constitution du sujet et pratique spirituelle. Remarques sur l'*Histoire de la sexualité*,' in *Michel Foucault philosophe. Rencontre internationale, Paris 9,10,11 janvier 1988*, ed. Association pour le Centre Michel Foucault, Des Travaux (Paris: Seuil, 1989), 272–273.

> search for an apparent meaning, which is, in reality, more hidden than the supposedly hidden meaning.[31]

This opposition leads Jambet to a reading of the uses of pleasure that effectively transcribes ethics onto a scale of being, from a maximum to a minimum of freedom. Jambet adds to this a correlation with the intensification of existence – the more free we are, the more intensely we exist. 'Aesthetics of Existence: all of the codes of conduct that regulate our existence, and our duties in particular, are not regulated by the opposition between what is permitted and what is forbidden, but by a "stylization of freedom." The subjects in the Greek city-state must not only know their freedom; they must also recognize it.'[32] This recognition is linked to 'the necessity of caring for oneself, which refers to *sophrosyne* (wisdom), which consists of choosing those *aphrodisia* (sources of pleasure) that liberate, and rejecting those that do not.'[33] In other words, the dyad between transgression and law is not eternal. The Greek experience of the self involves a struggle

31 'Le style de Foucault est un style descriptif. Il ne s'agit pas, pour lui, de montrer des structures ou de manifester des structures cachées, mais de faire que ce qu'il apparait à la surface même de la parole grecque ou romaine soit reconnu. On ne va pas chercher dans les profondeurs des doctrines, on cherche au contraire ce qu'il y a de plus apparent et de plus manifeste. Par conséquent, on refuse toute herméneutique au profit d'une description. On ne cherche pas le sens caché, mais on cherche plutôt le sens apparent, lequel est en réalité plus caché que le sens prétendument caché.' Christine Goémé and Judith d'Astier, *Michel Foucault, l'art de penser* (Paris: Institut National de l'Audiovisuel (INA), 1991), Sound Recording. It bears pointing out that Jambet's opposition between hermeneutics and description is unusual in light of Foucault's pronouncements and writings on the hermeneutics of the subject as a way into the question of the care of the self. See, for instance, Foucault's summary of his course on 'L'Hermenéutique du sujet.' *Dits et écrits*, 4:353–365.

32 'L'Esthétique de l'existence: l'ensemble des conduites tenues sur l'existence, et en particulier sur les devoirs, n'est pas régie par l'opposition du permis et de l'interdit, mais par une « stylisation de la liberté. » Le sujet dans les cités grecques doit non seulement connaître sa liberté mais il doit aussi la reconnaître.' Goémé and Astier, *Michel Foucault, l'art de penser*. Jambet alludes here to arguments presented by Foucault in the two middle volumes of the *Histoire de la sexualité*; namely *L'Usage des plaisirs* and *Le Souci de soi*. See also *Dits et écrits*, 4:539–561, 4:708–735.

33 '[L]a nécessité de s'occuper de soi-même, qui renvoie à une *sophrosyne* (une sagesse), qui consiste à choisir parmi les *aphrodisia*, les sources du plaisir, celles qui libèrent, et à ne pas choisir celles qui ne libèrent pas.' Goémé and Astier, *Michel Foucault, l'art de penser*.

(*combat*) for the self, rather than a repression of the self or part of the self, and the outcome of that struggle determines where the self falls in the scale of existence. This is also something that we see in Jambet's readings of al-Suhrawardī and Mullā Ṣadrā.

Jambet concludes his intervention with a view of Foucault as a thinker of freedom first and foremost (rather than, say, power or sexuality). In this respect Jambet is no different from many of his contemporaries.[34] Jambet's strongest investment here is in the nominalist argument: there is not one thing called freedom, there are freedoms, and therefore freedom must be thought in the plural. Foucault plays a soteriological role for Jambet, saving him from the tyranny of decidedly single-minded approaches to freedom that might be found in the thought of Mao Zedong or the GP. The engagement with Foucault also enables him to formulate some ideas about freedom that are a blessed relief from the version that has held sway all over the world in recent decades:

> I believe that there is in the ontology of oneself a nominalist approach to freedom. This means that the subject is existentially constituted every time, that is to say in the most real way possible, and that the subject is constitutive through action and discourse. The subject is therefore totally historical and real. We might say that the sovereignty over the self exercised by Greeks and Romans is not the version of free will to which we have grown accustomed since Erasmus, or even earlier, since the Augustinian problematic. There is therefore a form of freedom, and a form of the individual, that precedes the one to which Christianity accustoms us and which still dominates our problematization of freedom; namely, free will. But this Greco-Roman sovereignty is both constitutive [of the subject] and constituted [by the subject]: it is therefore entirely historic. The ontology of oneself, the ontology of the subject, is therefore in itself a nominalism. It is the expression of a series of

[34] Bourg, *From Revolution to Ethics*, 239–241.

historical experiences that are both discontinuous and real. Foucault does all he can to end the opposition between the historical and the real, that is to say between a historical that is mere appearance and a real that is firmly stationed in eternity.[35]

Let us note in passing the peculiarity, by contemporary standards, of Jambet's reading of Foucault: there is no reference to governmentality, for instance. Moreover, this habit of finding myriad forms of freedom in past societies is arguably more typical of Jambet's work than of Foucault's, as are the associated phenomena of struggling for the self to determine the intensity of existence, letting go of the law and the multiple ontologies of the self.

*

Jambet's and Lardreau's ideas about revolution in *L'Ange* are formulated against the backdrop of the waste land that was France in the 1970s.[36] The concept of angelic revolution defended by Lardreau and Jambet requires a renewed ontology rather than a political programme, since,

[35] 'Je crois qu'il y a dans l'ontologie de soi-même une approche nominaliste de la liberté. Cela signifie que le sujet est à chaque fois constitué dans l'existence, c'est-à-dire dans ce qu'il y a de plus réel, et qu'il est constituant dans ses actions et dans les discours qu'il peut tenir. Donc il est totalement historique et en même temps réel. On pourrait dire que la souveraineté qu'exerce sur soi le grec ou le romain n'est pas le libre arbitre auquel nous sommes accoutumés depuis Érasme et bien plus avant encore, depuis la problématique augustinienne. Il y a donc une forme de la liberté, et une forme de l'individu, qui est à la fois antérieure à ce que le christianisme nous accoutumera à adopter et qui est encore ce qui règne sur notre problématisation de la liberté – le libre arbitre. Mais cette souveraineté est à la fois constitutive, du sujet grec et romain, et en même temps elle est constituée : elle est entièrement historique. Donc l'ontologie de soi-même, l'ontologie du sujet, est en soi un nominalisme. Elle est l'expression de toute une série d'expériences historiques qui sont à la fois discontinues et réelles. Foucault fait tout pour que cesse l'opposition de l'historique et du réel, c'est-à-dire d'un historique qui ne serait qu'une apparence et d'un réel qui serait, lui, frappé au coin de l'éternité.' Goémé and Astier, *Michel Foucault, l'art de penser*.

[36] I allude to Eliot deliberately, not only because of the allusions to 'The Waste Land' that come early in *L'Ange* and under Lardreau's pen ('nous nous laverons les pieds in soda water, et nous écouterons les voix d'enfants chanter sous la coupole' *L'Ange*, 11), but also because Jambet underlines the extent to which Eliot's poem speaks for a world damaged by the absence of a politics of vision and manifestation, and which calls out for redemption and reparation.

they argue, it must entail a change of being rather than a return to some version of a pre-revolutionary order. This is the only way to end the reign of what they call *le Maître*, which is the name that they use for the process whereby opportunists and dictators manage to outwit even the cleverest of revolutionary vanguards to claim their place at the top of the body politic, and whereby world history alternates between revolution, reaction, and tyranny. 'Out of and against the deepest despair is born the idea that another world is possible, despite the domination exercised by all worldly powers. This possibility is designated by the figure of the Angel.'[37] The Angel is synonymous with cultural revolution, defined as a series of changes in a global framework rather than being limited to the GPCR.[38] In order to avoid repeating what they saw as the mistakes of the past, Jambet and Lardreau make the case for the rebel as the better version of the revolutionary. The latter, in their view, is still stuck in a line of thought dominated by *le Maître*. The rebel undertakes rebellion with other aims in mind. Like Jambet and Lardreau, the rebel is opposed to the *conception politique du monde*; namely that view that accepts the continued predominance of *le Maître* and a view of the world as a set of competing interests. In the *Apologie de Platon*, Jambet defines this political conception of the world thus: 'What is the political conception of the World? A way of seeing harmony where war reigns, enjoyment where there is misery, freedom where order is perfected, the rebel where the Master is upheld.'[39] Apart from setting out the optics

[37] 'Contre toutes les puissances et les dominations, maintenir l'espoir qu'un autre monde, malgré tout, est possible. A designer cette possibilité, nulle autre image ne s'imposa à nous que celle de l'Ange.' *L'Ange*, 10.

[38] *Apologie de Platon: Essais de métaphysique* (Paris: Grasset, 1976), 35.

[39] 'Qu'est-ce que la conception politique du Monde ? Une façon de voir l'harmonie où règne la guerre, la jouissance où règne le malheur, la libération où se parfait l'ordre, le rebelle où se maintient le Maître.' *Apologie*, 84. One of the more damning statements about the *conception politique du monde* is the following: 'L'Essence de la conception politique du monde, c'est de désirer un maître sans le savoir.' *Apologie*, 54. The parallel with Lacan's statements about the student revolutionaries of May '68 is obvious. What is less obvious, however, is that what Jambet finds reprehensible is less the desire for a master than the lack of awareness of that desire. As we will see below, the Alamūtīs clearly desire a master, and whole libraries of ink have been written on the proper way to recognize that master.

within which Jambet and Lardreau operate, and the toxic falsity of the *conception politique du monde* to which they stand opposed,[40] this statement also anticipates something central to Jambet's mode of thinking; namely the opposition between the hidden and the apparent (*le caché et l'apparent*), and the translation between them. The political conception of the world distorts our viewing, so that we think we are witnessing a revolution but are in fact merely seeing a new Master displace the old. In his later years, Jambet will map this opposition between the hidden and the apparent onto the two poles of Arabic hermeneutics; namely the apparent, exoteric, meaning, or *al-Ẓāhir*, and the hidden, esoteric meaning, or *al-Bāṭin*. The *conception politique du monde* covers over the esoteric *Bāṭin* (i.e. war) with harmony – or rather covers up the war that produces the appearance of harmony, the dictatorial servitude that produces the appearance of freedom, and generally produces the language of political expediency. And what interests Jambet are systems of thought that induce the *apparition* or un-covering of the *Bāṭin*.

According to Jambet, the *conception politique du monde* has dominated human history and thought from the outset: every revolution produces a reaction, and an even more atrocious version of the Master than the one it set out to overthrow. Plato's intelligence enabled him to think through the consequences, to realize just how high the price of political compromise really is, and to understand the difficulties associated with the politics and ethics of rebellion – which is why he, even more than Socrates, deserves an apology. Political community is the start of tyranny. The only effective opposition to all of this is through rebellion. The figure of the rebel that comes through the *Apologie* is of someone who rejects the politics of survival and the arts of the possible, who refuses to believe that the world is all there is,

[40] Jambet, Interview. During this interview, Jambet identified the *conception politique du monde* with Sartre's politics.

in favour of the immortality of the soul – which is the very mark of the desire for rebellion in the subject[41] – and life itself. Masters and slaves survive, but only rebels live, in outright opposition to corruption, inequality and injustice. The rebel's life has a name: the immortality of the soul.[42]

Socrates was therefore one of the earliest and most important rebels in this scheme. What makes Jambet's reading of rebellion striking, however, is the name that returns repeatedly both in the *Apologie de Platon* and in *L'Ange*; namely Lin Biao, who is seen as the rebel and philosopher-king who embodied the spirit of the Cultural Revolution, itself understood as a revolution that 'touches people to their very souls.'[43] It is this concern with the soul, taken literally and as a priority, and seen as the seat of rebellion, that sets Jambet apart: for him a cultural revolution will change every individual's deepest being and feeling rather than merely limiting itself to changing people's means of production and political behaviour.[44] Religion, as the most thoroughly developed idiom for thinking about the soul, is therefore

[41] 'L'âme n'est rien que la marque dans le sujet du désir de rébellion.' *Apologie*, 197.

[42] 'L'aristocrate survit, avantagé du jeu des forces, l'esclave survit, entre le ressentiment et la consolation. Le rebelle seul oppose cette vie qu'il aime tant à la décadence politique ou à l'atroce monotonie de l'inégalité et l'injustice. Cette vie, il l'appelle « immortalité de l'âme ».' *Apologie*, 93.

[43] See Mao's 'Sixteen Points on Cultural Revolution,' first published in the *Peking Review* on 12 August 1966, online at https://www.marxists.org/subject/china/peking-review/1966/PR1966-33g.htm. See also the accounts of this phase of the Cultural Revolution by Roderick MacFarquhar and Michael Schoenhals, *Mao's Last Revolution* (Cambridge, MA; London: Harvard University Press, 2008), 90–92; Maurice J. Meisner, *Mao Zedong: A Political and Intellectual Portrait* (Cambridge: Polity, 2007), 173–174. See also Julian Bourg's account of the French appropriation of Mao's ideas 'Principally Contradiction: The Flourishing of French Maoism,' in *Mao's Little Red Book: A Global History*, ed. Alexander C. Cook (Cambridge: Cambridge University Press, 2014). Apart from underlining the relationship between revolution and the soul (at least in the English translation), the phrase returns repeatedly as one that defines cultural revolution in Jambet's work and interviews.

[44] 'Si « révolution culturelle » signifie ce qui remet en cause l'homme en ce qu'il a de plus profond, non seulement ses façons de produire, ses façons de faire de la politique, mais aussi ses façons de sentir, ses façons de se lier aux autres, son âme bien plus que ses rapports sociaux, alors oui, c'est bien d'une révolution culturelle que je veux parler.' Jacques Paugam, *Génération perdue: ceux qui avaient vingt ans en 1968? ceux qui avaient vingt ans à la fin de la guerre d'Algérie? ou ni les uns ni les autres?* (Paris: R. Laffont, 1977), 46.

decisive in understanding the idea of cultural revolution as formulated by Jambet.

Jambet's investment in the soul is a marker of his renewed interest in metaphysics. Although he, like many thinkers of his own generation and indeed like his supervisor Corbin, knew the work of Heidegger well, Jambet does not accept the end of metaphysics as a given. Jambet and Lardreau (mostly Jambet) were adamant in their view that every revolution presupposed an ontology; a doctrine of being. In their view the most important thinkers on this count ('les trois qui comptent' according to the back cover of *L'Ange*), and the ones against whom they will argue that being is dual, not singular, are Hegel, Leibniz and Lacan.[45] Furthermore, their interest in the immortality of the soul stands in stark contrast to the ubiquitous references to death that are found in twentieth-century thought, not least in the work of Lacan. As Mikkel Borsch-Jacobsen points out, the term 'master' in Lacanian thought also refers to that which masters everyone and everything; namely death, the absolute master.[46] In seeking to defeat the Master in the space of philosophy as well as politics, in trying to create worlds where the Master shall have no dominion, Jambet seeks to defeat death itself. Hence the appeal of the Angel as a figure that stands for this world. Hence, too, his insistence in his later work on Mullā Ṣadrā's idea that death and resurrection are changes in being (*tabdīl fī-l-wujūd*) rather than the end of everything.[47]

[45] Jambet presents a critique of Leibniz's *Theodicy* as a paradigmatic case of the discourse of the Master relying on a discourse that argues for the fundamental absence of radical evil. *Apologie*, 70–84. Jambet's argument relies heavily on the *Theodicy*. The correspondence between individual soul and universal order in such texts as the *Discours de métaphysique* and *Monadologie* illustrates Jambet's arguments about a fundamental link between political order and ontology.

[46] Mikkel Borch-Jacobsen, *Lacan: le maître absolu* (Paris: Flammarion, 1990), 22–23.

[47] *Mort et résurrection en islam. L'Au-delà selon Mullâ Sadrâ* (Paris: Albin Michel, 2008), 161–162. There will be much to say about this below, but one line of continuity between the early and late Jambet begins in his analysis of the term *metabolē*, culminating in his citing with approval Plato's desire for a new sort of humanity, identified as philosopher-kings in the *Republic* 473d and *Apology* 113–123. Cf. *Theaetetus* 176d, where Socrates explains that there is no doing away with the problem of the existence of philosophers, who are always out of place in the world.

Jambet's idea of rebellion prioritizes neither mastery nor raw power, and is far removed from calling for the dictatorship of the proletariat, or indeed anyone else. Rather, it is about the possibility, realized in history, of social and political rebellion based on a personal transformation at the deepest level of the self – a change bolstered by and dependent on the immortality of the soul. Moreover, this realization situates its participants at the intersection of history and its exterior, along a vector that connects the history of the world to what Jambet, following Corbin, variously calls meta-history or hiero-history. The starting point of all rebellion is the rebellion against oneself.[48] Over against those who, like Zhou Enlai in 1972, criticized those who made the Cultural Revolution a matter of people's souls, Jambet maintains that cultural revolution is precisely a means of the perfecting the soul that is dedicated to justice.[49] This dedication to the soul under a revolutionary process is what makes a rigorous reading of Plato necessary. Jambet is nothing if not consistent: he founds his call for a cultural revolution on a metaphysics of being; namely Platonism.[50] The core of Jambet's Platonism postulates an irreducible opposition between cultural and ideological (or political) revolution. With this in mind, his apology for Plato insists on the repeated priority of the soul as the central concern of philosophy rather than wealth or power.[51] Hence the strong argument of the *Apologie*: the soul must change if the world is to change. Angelic revolution, and the concomitant victory of the good soul over the corrupt, must

[48] Paugam, *Génération perdue*, 58.

[49] '[L]a révolution culturelle n'est que le perfectionnement continu d'une âme vouée à la finitude d'une éternelle mémoire de l'oppression.' *Apologie*, 115.

[50] 'On a pu croire gratuite, ou de pure mode, la reprise du concept de « *révolution culturelle* ». En fait, dès que nous opposions la série des « *révolutions culturelles* » à la série des révolutions idéologiques, nous postulions une métaphysique de l'être, un platonisme.' *Apologie*, 212.

[51] See the fine analysis of Plato's city-soul analogy in G. R. F. Ferrari, *City and Soul in Plato's Republic* (Chicago: University of Chicago Press, 2005), 37–83. On Book Eight of the *Republic* in particular, see Heinrich Ryffel, *ΜΕΤΑΒΟΛΗ ΠΟΛΙΤΕΙΩΝ: Der Wandel der Staatsverfassungen*, Reprint ed. (New York: Arno Press, 1973), 88–110.

necessarily be experienced as palingenesis; as re-creation.[52] The *Apologie* thus marks the beginning of a long strand in Jambet's thought centred on rebirth, recreation, and resurrection.

The *Apologie* ends with an epilogue that deals with the most prominent exemplars of these rebellions of soul and body: the *malāmatiyya* Sufis, who behave in such a way as to attract blame as part of the struggle against egoism and vanity, and a version of the 'Tale of the Two Antiochenes' from the *Patrologia Orientalis*; namely, Theophilus and Mary, early Christians who rebel by abandoning wealth and worldliness.[53] In both instances, the mechanism of rebellion operates through a will to absolute humility, and an assault on an entire way of being (wealth, power, ease, vanity) as a means of liberating the soul: 'damner son être pour en arracher l'âme.'[54] In these instances, exemplified by al-Ḥallāj's wish to be killed, rather than adored, by his followers, and Abū Yazīd al-Bisṭāmī's desire to be the only resident of hell, all moments that lay bare the struggle against the philosophy of survival, selfishness and vanity, Jambet locates important avatars of the Cultural Revolution.[55] Mysticism and Sufism are thus the earliest indicators of the occurrence of a cultural revolution. This is what revolution has become, and what rebellion will henceforth be in Jambet's thought and work: processes that prioritize ethical change as a means towards the fairest possible order, working against the unjust and oppressive nature of the world, and ones that aim at living through the salvation of the soul rather than mere survival.[56] A cultural

52 *Apologie*, 117.

53 *Patrologia Orientalis*, ed. René Graffin and François Nau (Paris: Firmin-Didot, 1903–), 19:164–175.

54 *Apologie*, 226.

55 'Dans ces thèmes qui, plus ou moins mêlés, traversent une bonne part de la mystique musulmane, il est impossible de ne pas voir posé à vif le problème central de la lutte contre la philosophie de la survie, contre l'égoïsme, contre l'amour-propre, soit une des manifestations répétées de la révolution culturelle.' *Apologie*, 226.

56 Julian Bourg has described the entire political and intellectual history of France during and after 1968 as a passage, or indeed a 'transubstantiation' from revolution to ethics *From Revolution to Ethics*, 223 ff.

revolution is the only one capable of linking a way of life (not survival) to a system of thought.

This epilogue prefigures the role that will be played in Jambet's later years by Islam and the Abrahamic monotheisms as a framework for thinking about freedom and revolution. For Jambet, God makes everything possible:

> God is thus not the opposite of freedom but the name under which the unfounded act of freedom can be thought, at least when this latter is not thought as the simple empirical independence of an isolated entity or existent [. . .] In their improbable but real combination, the Platonic idea of *the one which is not* [cf. the *Parmenides*] and the Manichaean notion of the *foundational two*, which enter into both conflict and harmony in the metaphysics of Shi'ite Islam, have allowed me (within the framework of those messianic movements that punctuate, in cyclical fashion, the time of oriental Islam) to bring to light 'forms of freedom' that are also forms of servitude.[57]

Though published in 2003, this passage extends the ideas of Jambet's early work, where he describes the One of the first hypothesis of the *Parmenides* (137d–142a) as the only pagan Western idea to represent the Angel.[58] The first hypothesis of the *Parmenides* also provides the foundation of what Jambet calls Paradoxical One (*l'Un paradoxal*) – a paradox that exists due to the fundamentally dual nature of the One:

[57] 'Some comments,' 38–39. Let us note in passing that whereas for Corbin, Shīʿī Islam at its most esoteric was a source of certain and stable knowledge, for Jambet it really operates as the opposite – a universe constantly bursting with ideas of freedom and disruption. In my view Jambet's version comes much closer to the historical record.

[58] 'Le Un de la première hypothèse du *Parménide* est la seule pensée occidentale païenne à figurer l'Ange.' *Apologie*, 197. A key intermediary step in Jambet's arguments about the One is the identification of the One of the *Parmenides* with the One of Neoplatonism. Cf. E. R. Dodds, 'The Parmenides of Plato and the Origin of the Neoplatonic "One",' *The Classical Quarterly* 22, no. 3/4 (1928). A less heterodox summary and analysis of the first hypothesis of the *Parmenides* is found in Mitchell H. Miller, *Plato's Parmenides: The Conversion of the Soul*, Princeton Legacy Library, (Princeton, NJ: Princeton University Press, 2017), 80–91.

> If the One can symbolize the two, that is because its nature is irreducibly double. On the one hand, the One engenders the Two, and then the triad and the sequence of numbers. On the other hand, the One is opposed to the Two, thus engendering a superior Two that can neither be added to nor subtracted from any number; a Two that is not a number.[59]

The two is therefore fundamental. There are only two worlds, two desires, two paths. 'L'être est deux,' as Jambet and Lardreau insist in *L'Ange*. The two goes by many names – good and evil, nature and grace – but the key thing is that they are loathsome to each other ('ils se répugnent'), and that no reconciliation, synthesis, or treaty is negotiable between them.[60] The two is ontologically prior to the One, and the two are (is) irreducible to the One, be it through Hegelian synthesis or any other operation. Jambet sets out the stakes thus:

> [H]ow are we to recognise the demands of the two, of non-dialectisable duality [*dualitude*]? I have long shared the fairly common conviction that the general movement of German idealism since Kant, modern philosophy in other words, led to the erasure, the foreclosure, of such a duality [. . .] I take seriously that conjunction of the one, the real and the absolute which has been assumed by the various theologies, in order to ask myself how, on the basis of the one, identity and war, unity and radical duality, might be arranged in a constantly reversible pattern – one that allows us to think, alternately, both the nature of order and the process of tearing away from the world as it is.[61]

'Tearing oneself away from the world as it is' takes us back to the epilogue of the *Apologie de Platon*, with its messianism and ideas of

59 'Si l'Un peut symboliser le deux, c'est que sa nature est irréductiblement double. D'une part, l'Un engendre le Deux, puis la triade et la suite des nombres, d'autre part l'Un s'oppose au Deux, faisant ainsi naître un Deux supérieur, qui ne peut s'additionner ni se retrancher d'aucun nombre, un Deux qui n'est pas un nombre.' *Apologie*, 198.

60 *L'Ange*, 10.

61 'Some comments,' 38.

liberation founded, precisely, on *dualitude:* we tear ourselves away from this world as it is in order to join another world. Elsewhere, Jambet praises the idea of liberty as being identical with this *arrachement.*[62] There is not one world, there are two, and freedom consists of being torn away from one to start the passage to the other.

Alamūt

Jambet did not find the good revolution – the revolution that is good and makes us good, or angelic – in China or Cambodia, where the Khmers Rouges (whom he briefly supported) were doing their worst as he wrote *L'Ange.*[63] Where he *did* find the angelic revolution that he desired was in the events that occurred in Alamūt, a mountain fortress in what is today Northern Iran. Here on 8 August 1164 (=17 Ramadan 559), Hassan ibn Buzurg Ummīd, the leader of the Nizārī Ismāʿīlīs, proclaimed that the world had come to an end, and that the Resurrection had occurred.[64] Jambet uses this event to reflect on the forms of freedom in a framework informed by the aforementioned thinkers, entitled, tellingly, *La Grande Résurrection d'Alamût: les formes de la liberté dans le shi'isme ismaélien.* Freedom understood here, in part, as liberation from what Lacan called the absolute master; namely, death, understood now in both physical and spiritual terms,[65]

[62] *La Grande Résurrection d'Alamût. Les formes de la liberté dans le shiʾisme ismaélien* (Lagrasse: Verdier, 1990), 15.

[63] It is worthy of note, as Starr points out, that Jambet and Lardreau's argument in *L'Ange* was that they did not err, but rather that they did not go far enough in *Logics of Failed Revolt: French Theory after May '68*, 92–93. This contradicts the argument that Jambet presents in the *Apologie de Platon* that, 'Pour voir l'Un il faut, non pas avancer encore, mais changer radicalement de sens.' *Apologie*, 197.

[64] Jambet's account of the event of Alamūt combines versions by an Ismāʿīlī historian (al-Quhistānī) and a Sunni historian (al-Juvaynī), before launching his virtuoso analysis that stretches to several hundred pages. *Résurrection d'Alamût*, 35–43. Farhad Daftary presents a more detailed political history of the Alamūt period. Farhad Daftary, *The Isma'ilis: Their History and Doctrines*, Second ed. (Cambridge: Cambridge University Press, 2007), 302–402.

[65] *Résurrection d'Alamût*, 11.

but also, and more significantly, freedom as something endowed with many *forms*, forms whose multiplicity requires a renewed ontology.[66] It comes as no surprise that Jambet invokes Foucault very early in his study of Alamūt, inviting readers to see his work on Alamūt as being inspired by the last two volumes of the *History of Sexuality* and paying homage to Foucault as 'le philosophe de la joie dans la volonté de savoir.'[67] Furthermore, and as if to underline certain continuities with the spirit of May '68, Jambet describes the event of the Great Resurrection of Alamūt as 'une prise de parole.'[68] Finally, Jambet claims that the resurrected Nizārī Ismāʿīlīs of Alamūt have undertaken and executed a Platonic project: 'The community has taken on the task of accomplishing the essential desire of Platonism: converting the social link between its members into a relationship of pure love.'[69]

This historically heterogeneous experience of a community without law founded on an instance of creative spontaneity prefigures and announces others in the future. Not for nothing does Jambet describe *La Grande Résurrection d'Alamût* as a 'figurative' book and the Great Resurrection as a transhistorical event.[70] It goes without saying that

66 *Résurrection d'Alamût*, 13–14.

67 *Résurrection d'Alamût*, 16 n.

68 *Résurrection d'Alamût*, 38. Cf. Michel de Certeau's use of this term to describe the events of May '68 in Michel de Certeau *La Prise de parole et autres écrits politiques*, ed. Luce Giard, Points essais (Paris: Seuil, 1994), 40–41. For Certeau, as for Jambet, revolution consists of a re-appropriation, nay a storming, of the fortress of language: 'En mai dernier [i.e. May 1968] on a pris la parole comme on a pris la Bastille en 1798.' *La Prise de parole et autres écrits politiques*, 40.

69 '[L]a communauté s'est donné pour tâche d'accomplir l'essentiel désir du platonisme. Elle a voulu convertir le lien social en un pur lien d'amour.' *Résurrection d'Alamût*, 365.

70 Jambet, Interview. Jambet compares his use of the word *figuratif* to the use of the same term by Pascal and the thinkers of Port-Royal, adding that Jansenist literature was one of his sources in theorising the history of Alamūt. Cf. Auerbach's definition of *figura*: '[S]omething real and historical which announces something else that is also real and historical.' *Scenes from the Drama of European Literature*, trans. Ralph Manheim (Minneapolis, MN: University of Minnesota Press, 1984), 29. On Pascal and Port-Royal more widely, see David Wetsel, *L'Écriture et le reste: The Pensées of Pascal in the Exegetical Tradition of Port-Royal* (Columbus, OH: Ohio State University Press, 1981), 86–91, 176–182. The strongest *figure* of Pascal in Jambet's *œuvre* is the invocation of Pascal's wager in the 'Méditation sur le pari.' *L'Ange*, 55–68.

Jambet's own political experience is apparent just beneath the surface, as one of the many hidden (*Bātin*) mechanisms that move the argument forward. Jambet calls upon certain bodies of literature that propose a figurative reading of the world, including not only the literature of the Ismāʿīlīs themselves, but also those that speak for situations of being in the world but not of it: the Jansenists, T.S. Eliot, Yeats, Blanchot, Borges, and others. These literary figures are, for Jambet, 'summoned' (*convoqués*) by his reading of the events of Alamūt.[71] Poetry operates as the key that unlocks certain metaphysical questions even in the absence of any obvious historical relationship. Literature supplements history where there is an absence of a proper historical archive. In particular, Jambet relies on literary texts to describe broken worlds from which the face of the divine has withdrawn (as it did some three decades after the Great Resurrection of Alamūt), to point the way towards their restitution, and to underline the threat posed by the disappearance of theologies of apparition and manifestation of the hidden.

Jambet's investment in the radical heterogeneity of Alamūt and its transhistorical figuration also underlies the equivalence between revolution and resurrection. Revolution rehearses the resurrection: we rehearse, and recite, what the next world will be like. I speak of a 'next world' deliberately; not necessarily of an 'afterlife' – just another, better world. Thinking about that other world is not simply a matter of fantasizing beatitude and wish fulfillment, but actually a start in making that better world. Taking part in a revolution or even a strike is not just about marching or protesting or withholding labour – though clearly all three can be effective instruments of change – it is about charting an intellectual and spiritual path to that other world and laying its foundations. As we do so, we also become members of that other world, and our being changes in the process: for Jambet, as

71 Jambet, Interview.

for the many people he thinks through, resurrection is coupled with an intensification of existence, defined in both neoplatonic and social terms (return to the One in neoplatonic terms, and anti-anti-nomianism in Alamūt).

For Jambet, the Nizārī Ismāʿīlīs of Alamūt are the Maoists of the Middle Ages, enacting a revolution that touches their souls and makes justice a reality. To a certain extent, such apocalyptic thinking is a constant in Iran's cultural, political, and religious histories, as well as in Shīʿī history more generally.[72] The resurrectionary politics of Alamūt beckon towards the arrival of a deeply desired future and the advent of the Imām, in a manner comparable to Mao's hastening of history and impatience with the stages predicted by classical Marxism. In Ismāʿīlī thought, everything that happens is destined to be overcome, to be destroyed and replaced, to be *révolu*.[73] And the form that this revolution takes in Alamūt is precisely the Grand Resurrection. All revolutions confirm that worlds are destined to go under, that the real has a history of past states and forms, and that death as such must be recognized, confronted, and itself overcome. Similarly, Jambet's lengthy descriptions of the Alamūtīs wandering the earth are reminiscent of the scenes used to describe early monasticism in *L'Ange*. Like the gnostics and Desert Fathers – whom Jambet explicitly identifies as the perpetrators of a dualist cultural revolution[74] – the Alamūtīs are souls without a place in this world, and are therefore busy uniting their forms of life and thought in such a way as to maintain a proper distinction between their own spiritually lively world and the spiritually moribund world that surrounds them.

What, then, is life like after the resurrection? In general terms, this life is about the pleasures of revelation – the revelation of meanings

72 Daftary, *The Isma'ilis* 34–86. Abbas Amanat, *Apocalyptic Islam and Iranian Shi'ism* (London: I. B. Tauris, 2009), 21–72. I am especially grateful to Joanna de Groot for this reference.

73 *Résurrection d'Alamût*, 66–67.

74 *Apologie*, 45 n.

and practices kept secret for far too long. Here, two key aspects of Ismāʿīlī thought, namely time and interpretation (*taʾwīl*), come into play. The Resurrection is inscribed in a cyclical conception of time, according to which the world's ages alternate between periods of resurrection, or *Qiyāma*, and periods of hiding, or *Taqiyya*. Hiding is necessary because of the endless persecution of the Ismāʿīlīs by other Muslims and non-Muslims, while the resurrection enables Ismāʿīlīs – indeed all of humanity – to be revealed as itself to itself. That revelation begins with the visibility of the Imām, the leader of the community who must be witnessed by all Ismāʿīlīs. The central event of the *Qiyāma* revolves around interpretation: the revelation of the hidden meaning of the Qur'an and tradition is the object of much learning and lively speculation. In other words, the *Qiyāma*, the Resurrection, is the event of the translation of the *Bāṭin* into the *Ẓāhir*, of the esoteric into the exoteric. The task of interpretation is to proceed from the exoteric, apparent, meaning to the esoteric, originary, spiritual meaning and demonstrate the priority of the latter. This interpretation extends to the entire world, not just sacred texts.[75] The term that Jambet, like Corbin, uses to designate this sort of knowledge is gnosis, which is their version of the Arabic word *ʿirfān*. Both see this oscillation between concealment and revelation as being central to understanding Shīʿī thought. One Ismāʿīlī thinker, Abū Yaʿqūb al-Sijistānī, says in the appropriately entitled *Kashf al-Maḥjūb* [*The Revelation of Hidden Things*] that it is the task of humanity to become one with gnosis, to become inseparable from it as fire is from fire:

> The Friends of God [*awliyāʾ*] have no trouble in preserving gnosis, in that the teachings of esoteric exegesis (*taʾwīl*) are imprinted on their spiritual souls (*nufūs-i rūhānī*) and become consubstantial with their souls; for that which is consubstantial to a given substance

[75] *Résurrection d'Alamût*, 86.

> becomes forever inseparable from it, as the movement of fire is inseparable from fire itself.[76]

Elsewhere, al-Sijistānī defines interpretation (*ta'wīl*), the result of gnosis, as follows: 'Hermeneutics is the explication of pure forms and their engraving in the seekers' hearts.'[77]

One consequence of this emphasis on gnosis is the de-emphasis of the law – or in the outright disestablishment of the law in the time of Resurrection – in favour of esoteric truth and spiritual (as opposed to legal and practical) discipline. The power of interpretation is a faculty that anyone can develop, but it is the Imām, the leader of the community, who has mastery of the making-apparent, the *phainesthai*, of the hidden meanings of sacred texts, traditions, and signs. The Imām who successfully interprets all of this data into a call for the resurrection acquires the title of the Imām of the Resurrection, or the Imām-Qāyim. Given the centrality of the Imām to Shīʿī and Ismāʿīlī thought, we must recognize that all Imāms including the Imām-Qāyim, are but embodiments of an eternal transhistorical Imām. In this sense, Jambet adds, the Imām *is* the Resurrection: his being is exemplary insofar as it is the being of the spiritual awakening and liberation that took place in Alamūt, which complete all preceding awakenings and are destined to take place again.[78]

[76] 'Les Amis de Dieu n'éprouvent aucune peine à conserver la gnose, en ce sens que les enseignements de l'exégèse ésotérique (*ta'wîl*) moulent de leur empreinte leurs âmes spirituelles (*nûfûs-e rûhânî*) et deviennent consubstantiels à la substance de leur âme, car tout ce qui devient consubstantiel à une substance en devient à jamais inséparable, tel le mouvement du feu qui est inséparable du feu.' *Le Dévoilement des choses cachées: Recherches de philosophie ismaélienne* [Kashf al-maḥjūb], ed. and trans. Henry Corbin (Lagrasse: Verdier, 1988), 30. Cf. *Kashf al-mahjûb: Le dévoilement des choses cachées*, ed. Henry Corbin, Bibliothèque iranienne (Tehran; Paris: Institut Franco-iranien; Maisonneuve, 1949), 2–3. Jambet, *Résurrection d'Alamût*, 149.

[77] اذ التأويل انما هو البيان ونقش الصور العقلية في قلوب المرتادين
'[L]'herméneutique du symbole [*ta'wīl*] consiste à expliciter les pures formes spirituelles et à les graver dans les cœurs des chercheurs.' *Trilogie ismaélienne: Textes edités avec traduction française et commentaire* [Kitāb al-Yanābīʿ; Risālat al-Mabdaʾ wa-l-Maʿād; Baʿzī az Taʾwīlāt-i Golshān-i Rāz], ed. and trans. Henry Corbin, Bibliothèque iranienne (Tehran; Paris: Institut franco-iranien; Adrien Maisonneuve, 1961), Kitāb al-Yanābīʿ §184; 121; 93.

[78] *Résurrection d'Alamût*, 100. Cf. the comparison between the Cross and the *Shahāda* in *Trilogie ismaélienne*, Kitāb al-Yanābīʿ §§ 143–148; 100–101; 73–75.

One way of thinking about the resurrection, or *Qiyāma*, therefore, is as a spiritual revolution; as the triumph of the spiritual under the aegis of the Imām. And this triumph inaugurates a new world – as Jambet puts it, the essence of this sort of Messianism is that it is interpretation made world:

> In that instant [of resurrection], hidden reality overturns the domination of the apparent, day and night swap powers, and an infinite joy puts an end to ancient servitude. This is what the messianism of Alamūt demands that we understand: how a certain version of the infinite can be founded on an interpretive vision of the world. All of this presupposes a doctrine of meaning whereby everything becomes the sign of a hidden reality, where signs repress and reverse their meaning, to the point where the invisible bar that separates the visible from the hidden attests to the antagonism between them. Interpretation is the passage from the hidden to the apparent. Once this traversal of the sign is allowed on the stage of the messianic event, it ushers in a practical transmutation of values and a new weighting of institutions and morals. Messianism is the becoming-world of interpretation.[79]

The Great Resurrection sets us free from literalist thinking. It marks a victory over spiritual death, compared with which victory over physical death pales into insignificance. Spiritual death is what happens when one obeys only the exoteric (*Ẓāhirī*) law, which is from this point of view motivated by fear of death and a deity who only

[79] 'Dans l'instant, la réalité cachée renverse la domination de l'apparent, le jour et la nuit échangent leur pouvoir, et une joie infinie veut mettre fin à l'antique servitude. C'est cela que le messianisme d'Alamût nous impose de comprendre: comment une certaine figuration de l'infini, de la liberté infinie, peut reposer sur une vision interprétative du monde. Nous le verrons, tout cela suppose une doctrine du sens, ou toute chose devient le signe d'une réalité occultée, où les signes refoulent et renversent ce qu'ils signifient, au point que la barre invisible qui sépare l'apparent du caché témoigne de leur antagonisme. L'interprétation est le passage du caché vers l'apparent, et cette traversée du signe, lorsqu'elle est permise sur le théâtre de l'événement messianique, invite à la transmutation pratique des valeurs et à une pesée nouvelle des institutions et des mœurs. Le messianisme est le devenir-monde de l'interprétation.' Jambet, *Résurrection d'Alamût*, 48.

knows vengeance. Once this fear disappears, liberation arrives.[80] There is a real sense in which the exoteric becomes the enemy during the resurrection – an early treatise defines the purification of the self as 'purifying oneself of the conduct of the literalists [*Ẓāhiriyyīn*].'[81] Elsewhere, the aforementioned al-Sijistānī explicitly identifies paradise, or the reward of the just, with the liberation of the esoteric from the shackles and veils of language, and its coming forth in the most beautiful form.[82] For this is the most interesting aspect of life in Alamūt. Far from being a free-for-all where people do whatever they want, far from the possibility of anomia, what happens instead is a conversion to a new discursive, political and legal order based on the manifold spiritual meanings that are revealed. Past that point, the only crime is not recognising the absolute character of that revelation, and submitting that absolute to the contingent authority of the law.[83]

These paradoxical freedoms are best represented in the current context by the Nizārīs of Alamūt: entirely faithful to God and the Imām/Resurrector, they find their freedom in the event of the Resurrection that he embodies and realizes – in short, that he *is*.[84] In Jambet's account, the key to the reformed, post-Alamūt world of the Nizārīs (and, by extension, of any revolutionary inhabiting a post-revolutionary space) is *dualitude*. In the context of the Great Resurrection of Alamūt, Jambet's exposition of *dualitude* comes through a reading of the Muslim

[80] *Résurrection d'Alamût*, 125–126.

[81] *Résurrection d'Alamût*, 105.

[82] 'Lorsque les temps seront accomplis, et que ces hautes connaissances seront fixées en leur ipséité [c'est-à-dire en leur état de connaissance pures], ayant rejeté la pesanteur des mots et du langage, elles se présenteront avec la plus belle des formes et au rang le plus sublime.'

فاذا بلغت غاياتها واستقرت في هويتها و رمت بثقلها، استقرت بأحسن هيئة و أشرف رتبة بما لا عين رأت ولا أذن سمعت ولا خطر على قلب بشر

Corbin, *Trilogie ismaélienne*, Kitāb al-Yanābīʿ §131; 88; 67.

[83] '« Il est coupable de ne pas reconnaître et accomplir l'absolu. » Il est coupable de donner une forme relative, soumise au schème général de la loi, à l'absolu et à l'impératif.' *Résurrection d'Alamût*, 105.

[84] *Résurrection d'Alamût*, 100.

confession of faith (*shahāda*), and a refutation of Corbin's reading thereof.[85] Corbin reads the statement of the *tawḥīd* – there is no God (*lā ilāha*) except for God (*illā Allāh*) – as a double negation, whereby the radical atheism of the first half of the statement is negated in turn by the second, thus resulting in a declaration of the establishment of the God revealed in Being. Jambet cautions against the Hegelian implications of this reading, however: there is no *Aufhebung* in the confession of faith, whereby the negation of a negation somehow results in a positive affirmation and institution (understood as establishment, *instauration*). Following exegeses of the confession of faith by al-Ṭūsī and al-Sijistānī, Jambet reads it as a double affirmation that concludes that there is a division internal to the One: 'L'Un n'est pas Un, l'Un est un.'[86] This does not mean that the One is composed of two realities, but rather that the One is divided, and this internal division implies that the dual is ontologically prior to the One. Or, in Lacanian terms, we might say that nothing – not even the One – is everything. Jambet finds here the saying that he claims was common among the Althusserians and Maoists of his youth: 'One divides into two.'[87] An anonymous Arabic verse cited by al-Ṭūsī as a gloss on the confession of faith – *huwa huwa wa lā huwa fa huwa huwa* [roughly, 'He is He and not He; therefore, He is He'][88] – leads Jambet to argue for the inherent alterity of the One, so that the statement might be translated as 'The Other is the Other and not the Other; therefore, the Other is the Other.'[89]

85 *Résurrection d'Alamût*, 227 n.

86 *Résurrection d'Alamût*, 227 n; *Trilogie ismaélienne*, Kitāb al-Yanābīʿ §§ 109–115, 76–80, 56–59. See also Jambet's extended commentaries in Naṣīr al-Dīn Muḥammad ibn Muḥammad al-Ṭūsī, *La Convocation d'Alamût: Somme de philosophie ismaélienne = Rawdat al-taslim : le jardin de la vraie foi*, ed. and trans. Christian Jambet (Lagrasse; Paris: Verdier & Editions UNESCO, 1996), 28–31; Naṣīr al-Dīn Muḥammad ibn Muḥammad al-Ṭūsī, *Paradise of Submission: A Medieval Treatise on Ismaili thought* [Rawḍat al-taslīm], trans. S. J. Badakhchani, Ismaili texts and translations series (London; New York: I.B. Tauris in association with Institute of Ismaili Studies, 2005), 179–184.

87 'Some comments,' 37.

88 *Paradise of Submission*, §7, 14, 18. On the *huwa lā huwa* formulation specifically, see also *Trilogie ismaélienne*, Kitāb al-Yanābīʿ §22, 34–36, 16.

89 'L'Autre est l'Autre et n'est pas l'Autre – donc l'Autre est l'Autre.' *Résurrection d'Alamût*, 226.

The most serious consequence of this division is the multiplication of the forms of liberty that populate the Nizārī world. The abolition of the law, the rebirth of the faithful, the need for new ethics – Jambet sees all of these as indicators of a 'persistent operation of *dualitude* at the heart of being.'[90] It is this *dualitude* that will form the basis of post-Alamūt ethics, at once faithful and disabused of the concept of the One. This is the ethics of pedagogy, of *ta'līm*. The *dualitude* that lies at the heart of this brave new world is that of the Imām/Resurrector himself, who embodies, in his person, the principle of divine freedom. *Qua* human embodiment of divine freedom the Resurrector is thus in a 'paradoxical' position, representing two heterogeneous freedoms that cannot be reduced to each other.[91] As the subject of the Resurrection, the Imām/Resurrector combines three roles that enable the apocalyptic event: as agent he reveals the Resurrection, as spiritual pole (*quṭb*) he focalises the community's material and spiritual attention, and as outcome he is the person that is revealed as the Resurrector, something concealed since the beginning of Creation. His divided and manifold character is then transmitted throughout the world by the faithful, who reflect the Imām/Resurrector's freedom in their own lives and behaviour, like an infinite array of mirrors reflecting his radiance.[92] This process of transmission continues long after the dissolution of Alamūt through the interiorization of the knowledge of the Imām, and through the act of spiritually identifying and acknowledging the Resurrector in the Imām of every subsequent age.[93] In a remarkable conflation of Sufi and Ismāʿīlī methods, this also grants the believer access to the originary divine unity. The believer becomes the trace of the divine imperative (*amr; kun!*) through which the universe was created, and which continues to act through his or her person. The principle that operates

90 'exercise insistant d'une dualitude au sein de l'être.' *Résurrection d'Alamût*, 225.
91 *Résurrection d'Alamût*, 295.
92 *Résurrection d'Alamût*, 295–296.
93 *Résurrection d'Alamût*, 336–337.

the community is therefore that of a profusion of reproductions of the divided One through an infinite reproduction of the face of the Imām.[94]

The ethics of reproduction and transmission continues after the fall of Alamūt, and until the final Resurrection (*Qiyāmat al-qiyāmāt*) through the imperative of teaching, *ta'līm*. Teaching maintains the structure of *dualitude* in a transhistorical perspective. The establishment of teaching as a practice central to Nizārī ethics owes a great deal to Ḥasan-i Ṣabbāḥ's reformulation of the Shīʿī doctrine of *ta'līm*.[95] Originally conceived as a quality-control mechanism for ensuring the transmission of authoritative spiritual knowledge from the Imām to the community of the faithful, the principle is further expanded by Ḥasan-i Ṣabbāḥ to accommodate the times and spaces where the Imām is not immediately accessible. Specifically, the figure of the *Ḥujja* (literally, 'proof'), whose existence proves the authority of the Imām, becomes the second pole of the structure of *dualitude* across history.[96] Furthermore, Ḥasan-i Ṣabbāḥ's insistence that the structure of knowledge requires two opposed principles that can only be recognised through each other, coupled with the dual basis for any and every pedagogical relationship (not least because of the insufficiency of individual human reason in spiritual matters), bolsters the importance of the structure that frames both the Imām and the *Ḥujja*, both the teacher and the disciple. And, since the Nizārī community operates on the principle of the reproduction of the Imām in every person in the community, the structure of *dualitude* is propagated successfully. The authority of the single Imām that was the

[94] 'Le modèle de la communauté sera donc une effusion de visages qui reproduisent, sans l'épuiser, la dualitude de l'Un paradoxal, laquelle s'est réfléchie dans la dualitude de l'imâm, figuration de la forme humaine de Dieu, et face humaine, trop humaine de l'espérance messianique.' *Résurrection d'Alamût*, 357.

[95] Daftary, *The Isma'ilis* 339–342.

[96] One major difference between Daftary's and Jambet's readings of duality is that Daftary considers the binary structures of and around knowledge 'dialectical', while Jambet's definition of *dualitude*, as we have seen, is that it is a binary structure whose members cannot be reduced to a dialectical relationship. *The Isma'ilis* 341.

mainstay of Imāmī jurisprudence is now transformed into a transhistorical network of teachers and students, each of whom reproduces the division inherent to the Imām and the One. In Imāmī jurisprudence, there was only one teacher and everyone was his student; in Nizārī jurisprudence, everyone is a teacher, and everyone is a student. This is no mere act of rebellion: this is a necessary framework for the life of the community after the fall of Alamūt.

Jambet maps the desire for and of the Imām as the desire for and of the other. He also maps the Imām/*Ḥujja* dyad onto the Lacanian opposition between the truth and knowledge: the Imām, alias the truth, emerges as the truth that appears in a brief flash during a short period of time, while the *Ḥujja* continues the work of disseminating knowledge with and within the community across time.[97] Jambet's conclusion further confirms the Lacanian and Platonic dimension of his and Ḥasan-i Ṣabbāḥ's reading of the Imām:

> In Platonic fashion, he [Ḥasan-i Ṣabbāḥ] demonstrates that the necessary condition for the coming forth of the truth, and its sustenance by a master, is that a desire in a certain subject calls for its emergence. The desire for the master is the desire of the other, so that the master does not behave like a subject supposed to know, but that he offers a discursive configuration to the alterity that constitutes the subject to whom he responds, but which alterity also constitutes the truth for which he is responsible. It is the subject's desire for the truth that prompts the appearance of the Imām and that demonstrates the necessity of the Imām's act of being.[98]

[97] *Résurrection d'Alamût*, 358–362.

[98] 'En un style platonicien il [Ḥasan-i Ṣabbāḥ] démontre que la condition pour que la vérité surgisse, et pour qu'un maître la soutienne, c'est qu'un désir en appelle l'émergence chez un certain sujet. Le désir du maître c'est le désir de l'autre, de sorte qu'à son tour le maître ne se comporte pas en sujet supposé savoir, mais qu'il offre une configuration discursive à l'altérité qui constitue le sujet auquel il répond, mais qui constitue tout aussi bien la vérité dont il répond. C'est le désir de la vérité chez le sujet qui suscite l'apparition de l'imâm et qui démontre la nécessité de son acte d'être.' *Résurrection d'Alamût*, 366.

The Lacanian vocabulary of this passage (desire of the master, desire of the other, subject-supposed-to-know) leads to a key Platonic comparison: the Imām is like Socrates (or rather, Socrates is the Imām), constantly acting as a midwife for ideas in his disciples' souls:

> Ismāʿīlism demands the simultaneous emergence of the truth and the initiatory transmission of knowledge. It thus resembles the Platonic master, who creates in the soul an autonomous and eternal source of the truth, but who also runs the constant risk of seeming to be a master who hides this truth under an imaginary absolute truth.[99]

Jambet extends this bold comparison to the *Symposium*, whereby the relationship between Imām and disciple (a category that includes the *Ḥujja*) is mapped onto the relationship between Alcibiades and Socrates. The net result is a conclusion that reaffirms those of *Apologie de Platon* and *L'Ange*: the utter impossibility of having an outlaw master, or rather, the futility of imagining that an outlaw master is the figure best suited to an infinite quest for knowledge.[100] The disillusioned tone of this ending reveals some of the reasons for Jambet's interest in the esoteric. The Nizārī community of Alamūt is, like the desert fathers and the Great Proletarian Cultural Revolution, an example of an angelic community and revolt.[101] And yet even here, the ontological forces that drive the production of political and spiritual meaning reproduce the forms of mastery that we saw elsewhere: monasticism

[99] 'L'ismaélisme veut tout à la fois l'émergence de la vérité et la transmission initiatique du savoir. Il rejoint ainsi le maître platonicien, dont le souci est d'enfanter en l'âme, pour l'éternité, une source autonome de vérité, mais qui risque sans cesse de paraître sous les traits du maître qui occulte cette vérité dans l'imaginaire d'un savoir absolu.' *Résurrection d'Alamût*, 367. On Lacan's reading of Socrates, see Juan Pablo Luchelli, 'Lacan avec Platon: le Socrate de Lacan' (Thèse de doctorat, Université Panthéon-Sorbonne - Paris I, 2015), https://tel.archives-ouvertes.fr/tel-01321044. It comes as no surprise to learn that Lacan considered Plato a Lacanian. *Séminaire XIX*, 131.

[100] *Résurrection d'Alamût*, 369.

[101] In his introduction to his translation of *Rawḍat al-taslīm*, Jambet links the angelic to the inevitable failure of the Nizārī state: 'Si mélancolie il y eut, ce fut la conséquence inéluctable d'une folie divine, de la folie de la divinisation, versant sombre du devenir angélique de l'homme.' al-Ṭūsī, *Convocation d'Alamût*, 21.

did not prevent the establishment of a universal church, nor did Mao's last revolution end in a reign of universal justice.

Far from being an antinomian free-for-all, Alamūt becomes a place where the abolition of the law requiring the five canonical prayers of Islam gives way to a world where daily life is perpetual authentic prayer, made possible by the fact that people now, in the words of ʿAṭā-Malik Juwaynī (the Sunni Persian historian of the Mongol conquests that destroyed Alamūt, and much else), 'always have God in their hearts and constantly turn the faces of their souls towards the divine presence.'[102] These faces and souls turned towards God for all eternity are, in effect, opening themselves up wholly and absolutely to the Other. Ismāʿīlī ethics, in Jambet's reading, care nothing for individuality and personal rights. What matters in this ethical framework is the *devenir soi-même de l'autre*, the becoming oneself of the other.[103] What the faces turned towards God in Juwaynī's description see (according to Jambet) is nothing other than themselves: like the story of the birds who realize that the mythical *Simurgh* is none other than themselves in ʿAṭṭār's *Conference of the Birds*, or the sunflower that turns towards the sun and then becomes the sun. If this structure of a mass of faces turned towards one entity deemed supreme sounds familiar, that's because it is: it parallels the rallies that Jambet would have attended in Tian An Men during his Maoist days, with the substitution of God – or rather His living representative;

[102] 'Il a été établi dans la loi positive que les hommes doivent adorer Dieu cinq fois par jour et être avec Lui. Cette charge était seulement apparente, mais maintenant, dans les jours de résurrection, ils doivent être toujours avec Dieu dans leur cœur et tenir les visages de leurs âmes constamment tournés en direction de la présence divine, pour une prière authentique.' Juvaynī, *Tārīkh-i Jahāngushay*, qtd. *Résurrection d'Alamût*, 102. Jambet's translation of Juvaynī's account conceals the latter's highly partisan and critical tone. Cf. ʿAlāʾ al-Dīn ʿAṭā Malik Juvaynī, *Genghis Khan: The History of the World Conqueror*, trans. John Andrew Boyle (Manchester; Paris: Manchester University Press; UNESCO Publishing, 1997), 695–696. A more balanced account may be found in the *Paradise of Submission*, though this does not contain the parts about people facing the Imām or God; just perpetual prayer. al-Ṭūsī, *Paradise of Submission*, §§ 321–322, 111.

[103] *Résurrection d'Alamût*, 206.

namely the Imām – for Mao. Nor indeed is it any accident that in other contexts Jambet speaks of Mao as a gnostic and dwells on his gnosis of history.[104] The difference, of course, is that the Resurrection of Alamūt happens without any of the death and destruction that accompanied the Cultural Revolution, or indeed of the cynical ploys by which Mao tried to regain control of the Party by setting up China's people against each other. Resurrections, like the Great Resurrection of Alamūt, make us more alive, and take our being to its most intense level.

These mechanisms by which facing the Other leads to an ontological metamorphosis of the self clearly owe a great deal to Plotinus, whose presence should be constantly presupposed in early Islamic philosophy. But this return to the One, to a Creative deity or visible representative of that deity, simultaneously returns chronology to the moment of Creation itself. Jambet speaks of 'l'être mis à l'impératif' during the resurrection – the being subject to the imperative. The imperative in question here is the imperative 'be!' (*kun!*) The Nizārī Imām, who reveals the Resurrection, is himself revealed as the embodiment of that divine imperative, understood as the capacity to create by uttering the word *kun*. By subordinating themselves to the command of the Imām, and thus placing their being under the aegis of the imperative (both physically manifest and intelligible), the Nizārīs might be called the most creative of all revolutionaries. By returning all of creation to the moment of creation, when God commanded the universe to be, the revolutionary resurrection might be read as an invitation to be fully; to be ourselves by becoming the other. And it does so. But this returned, resurrected Being also has to be read as change, both desired and unpredictable, even as it echoes the dawn of creation.

[104] *Logique des Orientaux*, 100.

The resurrection happens in the here and now, not in another world.[105] The world, however, will go on, and not everyone will participate in the resurrection. Those who do are in the world but not of it. Worse yet, the resurrection reveals the abyss between creation and the Creator: there is an important distinction to be made between witnessing the absolute and attaining the absolute.[106] The ecstasy of the resurrection is accompanied by the melancholy of unknowability: the One [God] who desires to be known, and yet remains unknown, by Creation, and those creatures who grasp this situation. Put differently, the One who transcends being descends into being through this desire to be known.[107] Ibn al-Walīd even links the name of the divinity to the overwhelming sadness and longing (*walah*) resulting from this abyss.[108] The divine imperative (*Be!*) that creates the universe also separates Creator from creation for all eternity, and not even the resurrection will bridge that gap. Jambet selects a passage from the *Four Quartets* – poems where Eliot is arguably at his most 'Jansenist'[109] – to think through the paradoxical emotions involved. *Four Quartets* is also a text where Eliot attempts to make words mean something 'beyond words, constantly pushing the limits of imagery, reference, and rhythm to the point where the spiritual dominates the empirical.'[110] If we equate the term 'spiritual' with *Bāṭin*, it would be no exaggeration to say that 'Burnt Norton' is not far from the revelations of the resurrection in Alamūt:

> Into the world of perpetual solitude,
> World not world, but that which is not world,

[105] *Résurrection d'Alamût*, 319.
[106] *Résurrection d'Alamût*, 217–218.
[107] Corbin, *Imagination créatrice*, 134–135; Jambet, *Caché*, 57–63.
[108] *Trilogie ismaélienne*, Risālat al-Mabda' wa-l-Ma'ād §7, 88, 103.
[109] Steven Ellis, *The English Eliot: Design, Language and Landscape in 'Four Quartets'* (London: Routledge, 1991), 127.
[110] A. David Moody, '*Four Quartets:* Music, Word, Meaning and Value,' in *The Cambridge Companion to T.S. Eliot*, ed. A. David Moody (Cambridge: Cambridge University Press, 1994), 147–150.

Internal darkness, deprivation
And destitution of all property,
Desiccation of the world of sense,
Evacuation of the world of fancy,
Inoperancy of the world of spirit;
[This is the one way, and the other
Is the same, not in movement
But abstention from movement; while the world moves
In appetency, on its metalled ways
Of time past and time future.][111]

Burnt Norton deliberately devalues the temporal to the 'status of the unreal.'[112] This goes hand in hand with an opposition between worlds – temporal vs divine in Eliot's case, resurrected vs unresurrected in Jambet's. In this passage, Eliot contrasts the horizontal movement of secular time and its never-ending character with the vertical movement of the messianic, stressing the mechanical character of the former with the vivid nature of the latter.[113] The temporality of *Burnt Norton* parallels that of the moment of resurrection: it is a time outside time, and a historical event outside history; part of what both Corbin

[111] *Burnt Norton*, III, 117–129, qtd. *Résurrection d'Alamût*, 220. Jambet only cites the passage up to 124: 'Inoperancy of the World of Spirit'. In the Leyris translation cited by Jambet the entire passage reads as follows:

Dans le monde de la solitude perpétuelle
Un monde, non pas un monde, mais cela même qui n'est pas monde,
Obscurité interne, privation,
Destitution de toute propriété
Dessiccation du monde du sentir
Évacuation du monde des images
Inopérance du monde de l'esprit;
[C'est là l'un des deux chemins, l'autre
Étant le même, non mouvement
Mais l'abstention de mouvement ; cependant que le monde se meut
Dans l'appétence, sur les voies métalliques
De temps passé, de temps futur.]

T. S. Eliot, *Poésie*, trans. Pierre Leyris, Éd. bilingue (Paris: Seuil, 1976), 165.

[112] Ellis, *English Eliot*, 125.

[113] Ellis, *English Eliot*, 68.

and Jambet designate as *métahistoire* or *hiérohistoire*.[114] As such its arrival can never be expected or predicted: it can only be beckoned. Even the resurrection does not satisfy the desire for this exit from history. The resurrected are therefore eternally calling out to God for the moment of revelation, the moment of union with the divine presence. Jambet communicates this eternal invitation to the divine via Blanchot.[115]

Jambet cites the long closing sentence of Blanchot's *L'Arrêt de mort*. Here the narrator addresses himself for all eternity to a thought in a moment in time, marked by both death and the impossibility of narrating that death, and says 'Come!'[116] Derrida has analysed the semantic and figurative fields associated with the word *viens*, demonstrating its numerous significations in Blanchot's idiom – approximation (understood as de-distancing), gift, death.[117] Perhaps most significantly, Derrida sees in Blanchot's *viens* an attempt at

[114] The originality of Jambet's reading is striking. John Hayward's notes to this passage in the Leyris translation of the *Four Quartets* read it as an allusion to the ghosts in the *Odyssey* 24.5–9: 'Cf. La description des spectres criards dans l'Hadès.' Eliot, *Poésie*, 224. This is perhaps an overinterpretation in the direction of the many allusions to hell that are seen in 'The Waste Land'. Even Helen Gardner's *Art of T.S. Eliot*, whom Hayward's notes recommend, does not feature such a reading: instead, she makes a case for *Burnt Norton* as a poem about grace. *The Art of T. S. Eliot* (London: Cresset Press, 1949), 163–164. Jambet's reading situates the descent quoted above as an encounter with the muteness of *this* world, not the afterlife: 'Mais la tristesse de l'être témoigne plutôt de l'inexpressivité foncière du monde, de la solitude du principe et de la rupture dont l'impératif est la cause.' *Résurrection d'Alamût*, 220.

[115] Blanchot was an early favourite of Jambet's, who describes him as 'l'auteur de mes seize ans.' Jambet, Interview.

[116] 'Moi-même, je n'ai pas été le messager malheureux d'une pensée plus forte que moi, ni son jouet, ni sa victime, car cette *pensée*, si elle m'a vaincu, n'a vaincu que par moi, et finalement elle a toujours été à ma mesure, je l'ai aimée et je n'ai aimé qu'elle, et tout ce qui est arrivé, je l'ai voulu, et n'ayant eu de regard que pour elle, où qu'elle ait été et où que j'ai pu être, dans l'absence, dans le malheur, dans la fatalité des choses mortes, dans la nécessité des choses vivantes, dans la fatigue du travail, dans ces visages nés de ma curiosité, dans mes paroles fausses, dans mes serments menteurs, dans le silence et dans la nuit, je lui ai donné toute ma force et elle m'a donné toute la sienne, de sorte que cette force trop grande, incapable d'être ruinée par rien, nous voue peut-être à un malheur sans mesure, mais, si cela est, ce malheur je le prends sur moi et je m'en réjouis sans mesure et, à elle, je dis éternellement: « Viens », et éternellement, elle est là.' Maurice Blanchot, *L'Arrêt de mort* (Paris: Gallimard, 1948), 127; Jambet, *Résurrection d'Alamût*, 222.

[117] Jacques Derrida, *Parages* (Paris: Galilée, 1986), 34, 80, 111.

writing the wholly other and going beyond being – if such a thing were possible – through language.[118] Blanchot writes elsewhere that no injunction, prayer, or expectation, can be commensurate with that called-for moment.[119] Furthermore, the plot and characters of *L'Arrêt de mort* consistently play with themes resonant with those of *La Grande Resurrection d'Alamût*: the constant presence of resurrection, its coexistence with life and death, and the space (as opposed to opposition) between living and living on.[120] The titular death sentence is also a perpetual spacing out and deferral of the simultaneity of death and resurrection. The logic of Blanchot's narrative thus prefigures that of Jambet's analysis of Alamūt.[121] If the narrator keeps inviting the moment of resurrection come (*viens*), and with it the alterity of the other world and other life, it is in part because he can do nothing else: we cannot *make* the other come, we can only let the other come, by making space for the other in our lives and souls.[122] This logic follows on from the key constraint of the resurrection; namely, the impossibility of knowing, or calculating, exactly when it will happen. The eternal 'presence' of the resurrection only occurs in response to the narrator's *viens*, or to the Alamūtī's desire for the resurrection and the Imām. At the same time, it is the resurrection, with its revelation of the identity of the Imām and the *Bāṭin* – the becoming-world of the interpretation – that makes the Alamūtīs who they are. The production and echo of the call to the other thus operates as the binary constitutive of the free, resurrected people of Alamūt.

[118] *Parages*, 34, 66, 101.

[119] '*Viens, viens, venez, vous auquel ne saurait convenir l'injonction, la prière, l'attente.*' Maurice Blanchot, *Le Pas au-delà* (Paris: Gallimard, 1973), 185. qtd. Derrida, *Parages*, 50.

[120] *Parages*, 174–199.

[121] It also prefigures the centrality of the resurrection within the circle of human temporality. See below.

[122] Jacques Derrida, *Psyché. Inventions de l'autre* (Paris: Galilée, 1998), 60; *Parages*, 209.

Making It Last: Mullā Ṣadrā

After Plato, Corbin, and the Ismāʿīlīs, one name dominates Jambet's work during the past two decades: Mullā Ṣadrā. So important is this figure that Jambet routinely compares him to Spinoza and Hegel, referring to him at one point as 'le Hegel de l'Islam'.[123] Mullā Ṣadrā marks the culmination of ontology in Islamic philosophy.[124] He expresses the purest desire of philosophy ('le plus pur désir de la philosophie').[125] His integration of the finite within the infinite makes him a privileged point of comparison with the likes of Leibniz, Schelling, and Bergson.[126] Although these names are far removed from *L'Ange*, there are strong lines of continuity joining Jambet's early and late work. Jambet considered the seventeenth-century philosopher a kindred spirit ever since the 1980s: 'Reading Mullā Ṣadrā, we find something fitting; discrete, subterranean links with us.'[127] This might at first sight seem surprising, given the apparent contrast between Jambet's interest in revolution and rebellion, and Mullā Ṣadrā's very orderly philosophical system.[128] Commenting on Mullā Sadrā's own account of receiving metaphysical secrets from God, Jambet compares him to the first rebel, Socrates, in an account that also recalls the Jambet of *L'Ange*:

[123] *Logique des Orientaux*, 312–313; Jambet, *Mort et résurrection*, 13; Jambet, Interview.

[124] Christian Jambet, *L'Acte d'être. La philosophie de la révélation chez Mollâ Sadrâ* (Paris: Fayard, 2002), 149.

[125] *Logique des Orientaux*, 314.

[126] *Se rendre immortel, suivi du Traité de la résurrection*, trans. Christian Jambet (Saint-Clément: Fata Morgana, 2000), 9.

[127] 'Lisant Mollâ Sadrâ, nous trouvons un air de convenance, des rapports discrets, souterrains, avec nous.' *Logique des Orientaux*, 26.

[128] In this Mullā Ṣadrā is not necessarily unique, but he is superlative. Jambet argues that all Islamic philosophy is necessarily a philosophy of order, founded on divine unity and marked by a taste for the organised, hierarchical coherence of all beings. *Philosophie islamique*, 244–249. With respect to Mullā Ṣadrā, this theme receives extensive treatment in *Le Gouvernement divin: Islam et conception politique du monde. Théologie de Mullā Ṣadrā* (Paris: CNRS, 2016).

> He [Mullā Ṣadrā] has understood [...] that philosophy is the true religion; the philosophy of the gnostic solely preoccupied with his soul and its destiny.
>
> This narrative, whose parallels with Socrates and the Socrates of the Muslim tradition are visible, is the account of a return to the question of the soul as the central focus of metaphysics and theology.[129]

What the one substance was to Spinoza, and what the spirit was to Hegel, perpetual intra-substantial motion (*al-ḥaraka al-jawhariyya*) is to Mullā Ṣadrā. In the Ṣadrian doctrine everything is always moving, either to or from God. The consequences of this process for ontology and eschatology are profound – so much so that Jambet published two separate translations of Mullā Ṣadrā's *Epistle on Resurrection* (*Risālat al-Ḥashr*); the first in 2000 and the second in 2017, with an additional study and translation of the themes of death and resurrection in Mullā Ṣadrā in 2008 (*Mort et resurrection en Islam*).[130] Jambet considers the *Epistle on Resurrection* to be the key to Mullā Ṣadrā's entire philosophical system. Everything, for Mullā Ṣadrā, is caught up in the movement to and from God, and therefore everything, at any given instant, is both nothing and/or God.[131]

[129] 'Il [Mullā Ṣadrā] a compris [...] que la vraie religion est la philosophie, celle du gnostique uniquement préoccupé de l'âme et de son destin.
Ce récit, dont les similitudes avec le Socrate de la tradition et avec le Socrate de la tradition musulmane sont visibles, est celui d'un retour à la question de l'âme, foyer central de la métaphysique et de la théologie.' *La Fin de toute chose. Apocalypse coranique et philosophie* [Risālat al-Ḥashr], trans. Christian Jambet (Paris: Albin Michel, 2017), 153.

[130] With characteristic humility, Jambet explains the existence of the two translations as attempts undertaken because he did not fully understand *Risālat al-Ḥashr*. The two translations are dominated by a key intellectual interlocutor: al-Suhrawardī in *Se rendre immortel* and Plotinus in *La Fin de toute chose*. That said, the two translations and commentaries are not mutually exclusive. One key question that drives Jambet's translation and analysis is the seeming absence of any reference to the return of the Mahdī in Mullā Ṣadrā's work. Given the impossibility of such an absence being deliberate in the work of the greatest Shīʿī philosopher, Jambet argues that in fact the Mahdī is the hidden (*Bāṭin*) referent behind the intellect and the intra-substantial movement – the Mahdī comes and goes incessantly, rather than being a figure who will only appear in the parousia. The seeming absences in Mullā Ṣadrā's text bear witness to an esoteric messianic omnipresence. *Se rendre immortel*, 105; *Fin*, 183–198.

[131] Jambet, Interview.

One clear consequence is a transformation of Jambet's ideas about theodicy. In the 1970s, theodicy was always an ancillary text in the service of the Master. By 2008, he concedes that there can be theodicies that serve liberation. Furthermore, such theodicies can found an ethics of perpetual revolution and resurrection. The idea of what constitutes theodicy also changes: 'Hegel would say: "History is a theodicy." Ṣadrā would say that, in sum, the intra-substantial movement of being is theodicy.'[132] In the history of Islamic philosophy, theodicy operates as a way of separating Islamic belief from the tragic, warring and divided cosmologies of Manicheanism, Marcionism and the gnostic religions.[133] This new theodicy entails a radical rethinking of palingenesis and the post-mortem fate of the soul, as well as a re-positioning of the locus of freedom, from the exterior to the interior of the self, and from unrestricted social freedom to autarchy and self-possession.[134]

The experience of internal freedom requires fidelity, in the Badiolian sense: an adherence to the reality of an event that reveals the truth about our situation.[135] Once the Great Resurrection of Alamūt takes place, we cannot live as if it had not occurred, nor can we live as if further resurrections will never occur. Ethically and ontologically, we are subject to the truths revealed during the resurrection. This is the dominant perspective in *Se rendre immortel*, where Jambet devotes an important footnote comparing Badiou and Mullā Ṣadrā:

[132] 'Hegel nous dira : « 'L'histoire est une théodicée.' » Sadrâ dira en somme que le mouvement substantiel de l'être est théodicée.' *Mort et résurrection*, 122.

[133] *Philosophie islamique*, 246–247.

[134] *Mort et résurrection*, 68.

[135] There are numerous references throughout Badiou's *œuvre* to this idea: *L'Être et l'événement*, L'Ordre philosophique (Paris: Seuil, 1988), 257–265; *L'Éthique. Essai sur la conscience du mal* (Caen: Nous, 2009), 67–86. See also Peter Hallward, *Badiou: A Subject to Truth* (Minneapolis, MN: University of Minnesota Press, 2003), 128–130.

Badiou writes, 'Let us be faithful to the event that we are.'[136] According to Mullā Ṣadrā, fidelity to the event of oneself is the insistence and perseverance in the intensification of oneself, and there would be some profit in comparing the ethics of the contemporary French philosopher and the Shīʿī ethics of the philosopher from Iran. They seem to meet at a nodal point: the primacy of the event-based decision (*décision événementielle*). They diverge insofar as Mullā Ṣadrā treats the event as the trace of the necessity of the One, an absolutely free imperative, while Badiou sees therein the irruption of the Two; he thinks the event through the category of the ultra-one. If we demonstrate, however, that the Ṣadrian One is an infinity of infinities – a paradoxical One in our terms – then one of the divergences disappears. There remains the question of the Two, which we cannot pose with respect to Mullā Ṣadrā, who does not say, 'We are nothing, let us be everything,' but rather, 'We are not yet everything, let us be everything in order to be nothing but that everything,' with the understanding that the 'everything' is absorbed in the 'nothing' (the absence of quiddity) of pure existence. The nothing of the One is the end-point of intensification.[137]

[136] 'Soyons fidèles à l'événement que nous sommes.' *L'Être et l'événement*, 261. In Badiou's text, this was a gloss on the verse 'nous ne sommes rien, soyons tout!' from Pottier's lyrics to the *Internationale*. It is therefore worthy of note that revolution is still uppermost in Jambet's mind even as he works on that most orderly of philosophers, Mullā Ṣadrā. In his review of *L'Être et l'événement* for *L'Annuaire philosophique*, Jambet also focuses on this phrase: 'Une fidélité est toujours particulière, elle n'est pas *une*, et l'on peut dire qu'elle n'est pas, puisqu'elle n'appartient pas aux multiples comptés par l'état. Elle s'organise selon des enquêtes finies qui sont des « suites d'atomes de connexion pour une fidélité ». Son mot d'ordre exprime une éthique: « Soyons fidèles à l'événement que nous sommes. » Enfin et surtout, la procédure de fidélité, dont l'enquête est l'intervention, se lie à l'événement par un processus qui méritera le nom du *sujet* (p. 264).' 'Alain Badiou, *L'Être et l'événement*,' in *Annuaire Philosophique 1987–1988* (Paris: Seuil, 1988), 175.

[137] '« Soyons fidèles à l'événement que nous sommes » écrit Badiou. Selon Mollâ Sadrâ, la fidélité à l'événement de soi est l'insistance et la persévérance de l'intensification de soi, et il y aurait quelque curieux profit à comparer l'éthique contemporaine du philosophe français et l'éthique shi'ite du philosophe iranien. Il nous semblent se rencontrer en un point nodal: le primat de la décision événementielle. Ils divergent en ce que Mollâ Sadrâ traite l'événement comme une trace de la nécessité de l'Un, impératif absolument libre, tandis que A. Badiou y déchiffre l'irruption du Deux, il pense l'événement sous la catégorie de l'ultra-un. Mais si l'on démontre que l'Un sadrien est infini d'infinis, Un paradoxal selon notre terminologie, une des divergences s'estompe. Reste la question du Deux, que l'on ne peut poser chez Mollâ Sadrâ, qui ne dirait pas « nous ne sommes rien, soyons tout », mais « nous ne sommes pas encore tout, soyons tout afin de n'être rien que ce tout. » Étant entendu que le « tout » s'absorbe dans le « rien » (l'absence de quiddité) de l'existence pure. Le rien de l'Un est le terme de l'intensification.' *Se rendre immortel*, 184 n.

This passage contains much of what Mullā Ṣadrā stands for in Jambet's later work: the persistence of questions about freedom and its forms, within an ontological framework informed by the unitary (i.e. the One God of Abraham and/or the neoplatonic One) and within which the irreducible Two, hitherto fundamental in Jambet's thought, threatens to disappear.[138] The primacy and intensity of existence are also axiomatic: for Mullā Ṣadrā, existence – or as he puts it, the act of being (*al-wujūd*) – precedes essence, and the intra-substantial movement places every being on a circular scale of intensity at any given point in time, with intensity decreasing with distance from the One.[139] The *Risālat al-Ḥashr* describes events at the point of maximum intensity, when all beings are returned to the One. Paradoxically, this point of maximum intensity corresponds to the moment where the soul, having attained perfection, is ready to leave the body and unite with the One.[140] In this version of human existence, we are at our liveliest when we die; for death marks the moment of the rebirth of the soul.[141]

For Jambet, Mullā Ṣadrā provides a good way of thinking about the relationship between freedom and intensity of being in terms that recall his reading of Foucault. Interpretation is the royal road to freedom.[142] This refers, first and foremost, to the freedom to abandon exoteric readings of law and liturgy, in favour of interpretations that push the interpreter along on the path of gnosis (*ʿirfān*). Interpretation (*taʾwīl*) is also anamnesis and anagnorisis, the soul's awakening to its immortality and the infinity of its knowledge.[143] The act of

[138] On the tension between monism and pluralism in Mullā Ṣadrā's thought, see Fazlur Rahman, *The Philosophy of Mullā Sadrā (Sadr al Dīn al-Shirāzī)* (Albany, NY: State University of New York Press, 1975), 37–44.
[139] *Se rendre immortel*, 9; Muḥammad ibn Ibrāhīm Ṣadr al-Dīn Shīrāzī, *Risālat al-Ḥashr*, ed. and trans. Muḥammad Khvājavī (Tehran: Intishārāt-i Mawlī, 1983), 118–119.
[140] *Mort et résurrection*, 29–30.
[141] *L'Acte d'être*, 254.
[142] *Se rendre immortel*, 12.
[143] *Se rendre immortel*, 13.

interpretation goes beyond the assignation of meaning; it is the very experience of the letter in the spirit of the subject, in the very locus of the revelation of the eternal truth about God.[144] Freedom is thus a process rather than a state; a process initiated by interpretation. The liberation of the soul that begins with interpretation accelerates the soul's journey towards the One, and with it the intensification of the self. Jambet situates Mullā Ṣadrā's ethics of intensity in the lineage of Plotinus, for whom the aim was the purification of the soul from the body,[145] and al-Suhrawardī, whose doctrine of mystic lights is in some senses completed by Mullā Ṣadrā.[146] It is intensification that defines the core stage of the process of freedom in this scheme: freedom is autarchy, the independence and sovereignty of the soul with respect to its physical substrate.[147] Remaining faithful to this process, with its twin engines of interpretation and intensification, defines the ethics of resurrection in this first reading by Jambet of the Treatise of Resurrection.

Towards the end of his introduction to the first translation of *Risālat al-Ḥashr*, Jambet uses a particularly resonant term; namely, the care of the self, *le souci de soi:*

> People progressively configure their act of being, deciding over the course of their lives more or less consciously, what their paradise or hell will be. The faithful, who have been initiated into the gnosis of the Imām, are alerted by esoteric and moral teaching. Only they

144 'C'est pourquoi pratiquer le *ta'wîl*, comme le fait ici Mollâ Sadrâ, ce n'est pas donner un sens caché quelconque à un discours littéral, mais éprouver la lettre en esprit, là où elle révèle à celui qui la reçoit la vérité de ce qu'il connaît, en Dieu, de toute éternité.' *Se rendre immortel*, 13.

145 Pierre Hadot, *Plotin, ou La simplicité du regard* (Paris: Plon, 1963), 23–24.

146 *Se rendre immortel*, 78–79.

147 Jambet insists on autarchy as the translation of *ghinā* ', which is accurate enough, but his arguments also relate to *autarkeia* (understood as internal freedom and self-sufficiency), along with *ataraxia* and the holistic cosmic perspective, as one of the three pillars of the ancient Greek understanding of wisdom. Cf. Jambet, *L'Acte d'être*, 286; Pierre Hadot, *Exercices spirituels et philosophie antique*, Nouvelle édition revue et augmentée ed. (Paris: Albin Michel, 2002), 309.

> can take the necessary care of the self and elevate themselves towards the paradise fashioned within by their faithfulness to the person and lessons of the Imām. Self-intensification, ethical purification, moral self-awareness and the realization of the paradisiacal body are all practices co-ordinated with the knowledge of the Imām.[148]

The care of the self constitutes the vector by which every individual creates the body of the resurrection. The practices listed in the extract above – self-intensification, ethical purification, awareness of the moral logic of one's behaviour and so on – take us away from the suddenness and intensity of the resurrection as described in Ismāʿīlī terms, and towards something steadier and more habitual. Indeed, the *habitus* determines the fate of the soul. We now have a strong link between the care of the self and freedom. The election of virtue is closely related to being faithful to the ethics of intensification and resurrection. The path to autarchy and self-sufficiency is the result of constant practice and rehearsal rather than sudden metamorphosis:

> According to Mullā Ṣadrā, repeated vicious or virtuous conduct is dependent on the intra-substantial movement of the soul. A soul used to vice translates the weakness of its act of existing; it tends towards a poverty of being, which makes it even more likely to root itself in a bad *habitus*. Damnation is itself its own cause and movement, while virtuous habits on the other hand entail a reinforcement of the soul that expressed them in the first place.

[148] 'L'homme configure progressivement son acte d'être, décidant, au long de sa vie, plus ou moins consciemment, de ce que sera son paradis ou son enfer. Le fidèle initié à la gnose de l'Imâm est alerté par l'enseignement ésotérique et moral, il peut seul prendre le souci de soi et s'élever vers le paradis que façonne en lui la fidélité à la personne et aux leçons de l'Imâm. L'intensification de soi, la purification éthique, la connaissance des motifs moraux, la réalisation du corps paradisiaque sont des pratiques qui, toutes, sont ordonnées à la connaissance de l'Imâm.' *Se rendre immortel*, 95.

> Good habits are the fruit of liberty, and enable an even more intense liberty, and a greater ease in choosing the right path.[149]

Freedom and resurrection are thus spiritual exercises, in the sense proposed by Pierre Hadot. It will be remembered that for Hadot, ancient philosophy was a spiritual exercise, a way of learning to live rather than mastering doctrine, and – following a formulation by Georges Friedmann that prefigures Jambet's title – as a way of becoming eternal through self-overcoming ('s'éterniser en se dépassant').[150] Spiritual exercises are conversions towards the One that make us more fully alive, and bring us to a condition of inner peace (*ataraxia*), freedom (*autarkeia*) and a holistic vision of the world. Together with the ethics of self-rehearsal (understood as 'self-tryout' and as the practice of virtue),[151] this perspective constitutes the culmination of Jambet's first analysis of *Risālat al-Ḥashr*, and dominates his analysis of this same text in 2017.

Spiritual exercises and their outcomes are also central to Islamic philosophy – so much so that Jambet argues that, for those who lead the philosophic life, all philosophy is resurrection.[152] Understanding and rehearsing and the resurrection are thus key to the philosopher's methodology and teleology. For Mullā Ṣadrā, the resurrection is the extra-worldly inscription of the meaning of this world: 'Sadrian eschatology is not a philosophy of history. The resurrection is not of this world, but belongs to the order of realities *interior* to the world, it gives us the *meaning* of the world, because it is both the *inverse* and

[149] 'Selon Mollâ Sadrâ, la conduite répétée dans le vice ou la vertu est dépendante du mouvement intra-substantiel de l'âme. Lorsqu'une âme s'habitue au vice, elle traduit l'affaiblissement de son acte d'exister, elle tend vers la pauvreté d'être, de sorte qu'elle est plus entraînée encore à s'enraciner en *l'habitus* mauvais. La damnation est à elle-même sa propre cause, son propre mouvement, tandis qu'inversement l'habitude vertueuse ou spirituelle entraîne un renforcement de l'âme qu'elle a, d'abord, exprimé. La bonne habitude est le fruit de la liberté, et permet une liberté plus intense encore, une plus grande aisance à choisir la voie droite.' *Se rendre immortel*, 105.

[150] Hadot, *Exercices spirituels et philosophie antique*, 21; Georges Friedmann, *La Puissance et la sagesse* (Paris: Gallimard, 1970), 359.

[151] Hadot, *Exercices spirituels et philosophie antique*, 307; Foucault, *L'Usage des plaisirs*, 15.

[152] *Philosophie islamique*, 160–162.

the *truth* of this world as it appears.'[153] It is also that which lies at the heart of meaning, at the deepest level of the *Bāṭin*. All interpretation points to the resurrection.[154] The location of the resurrection outside history means that it is less a time than a way of being, and this way of being bears a strong resemblance to those that interested Jambet at the start of his career. He argues that Mullā Ṣadrā derives resurrection from a revolution of being:

> [Resurrection] is the result of a revolution in being, a revolution of the very act of existing (*tabdīl fī-l-wujūd*) [. . .] It is a revolution in the literal sense, that changes us by changing our very substance, and returns us to our origin. It is also a moral revolution, for which Ṣadrā assigns responsibility to our actualization of our knowledge and faith, and to the assiduous practice of the pillars of the revealed religion [. . .] It is truly a *métanoïa*, a conversion that changes people (*l'homme*) at the deepest possible level. The theme of *métanoïa* inevitably recalls another; that of *reversal*.[155]

Were it not for the nominal and textual references to Mullā Ṣadrā, one might be forgiven for thinking that this passage came from the *Apologie de Platon*, where we find the same ideas and vocabulary: revolutions that operate at the deepest part of the self, conversion, and reversal. This is the conversion that must be prepared assiduously through the aforementioned spiritual exercises.

[153] 'L'eschatologie sadrienne n'est pas une philosophie de l'histoire. La résurrection n'est pas de ce monde, mais de l'ordre des réalités *intérieures* au monde, elle offre le *sens* du monde, parce qu'elle est à la fois l'*inverse* et la *vérité* de ce monde tel qu'il apparaît.' *Mort et résurrection*, 157.

[154] As in this image from Mullā Ṣadrā's *Mafātīḥ al-ghayb*: 'La résurrection est dans l'ésotérique à l'intérieur des voiles des cieux et de la terre; elle est à ces voiles ce que l'embryon est à la matrice de sa mère.' *Mort et résurrection*, 157.

[155] 'Elle [la résurrection] est le résultat d'une révolution dans l'être, d'une révolution de l'acte même d'exister (*tabdîl fî l-wujûd*) [. . .] Il s'agit d'une révolution au sens propre, qui nous change en notre substance même, et qui nous reconduit à notre origine. C'est aussi une révolution morale, dont Sadra assigne la tâche à l'actualisation de la science et de la foi et à la pratique assidue des piliers de la religion révélée. [. . .] Il s'agit bien d'une *métanoïa*, d'une conversion qui change l'homme en ce qu'il a de plus profond [. . .] Le thème de la *métanoïa* en appelle un autre invinciblement, celui du *renversement*.' *Mort et résurrection*, 161–163.

How, then, is thinking and rehearsing the resurrection a spiritual exercise? Whereas the focus in *Se rendre immortel* was on *al-ḥaraka al-jawhariyya*, here it is on another key principle of Mullā Ṣadrā's; namely the connection between the intellect and the intelligible (*ittiṣāl al-ʿāqil bi-l-maʿqūl*). This is the new path to liberation and autarchy: 'Spiritual salvation, the possession of intelligibles, is true happiness. Mullā Ṣadrā considers spiritual happiness to be the only true liberation of the human soul. Real happiness [. . .] is the presence of the Agent Intellect in the soul.'[156] Whereas Mullā Ṣadrā's reading of eschatology and resurrection is overtly literal,[157] Jambet's analysis of *Risālat al-Ḥashr* pleads for the primacy of the moral sense of resurrection, inscribing its dynamics squarely within a vocabulary drawn from Hadot. The Resurrection is now fully a spiritual exercise, and, it is desire, rather than *habitus*, that now drives the resurrection:

> All are resuscitated according to their desire [. . .] This definition of the final gathering transforms exegetically an event predicted by prophesy into a moral test equivalent to the spiritual exercises theorised and practised by ancient Stoicism [. . .] The ultimate aim of these exercises in the framework inherited from the Sufi lexicon is the extinction of the self (*fanāʾ*), which is itself merely a version of the Stoic sage's *apatheia*. According to Mullā Ṣadrā, the pious man and the sage will, after their second birth, see and become what they hope, intuit, and above all know about themselves in this world thanks to the spiritual exercise that leads the best people to *apatheia*.[158]

156 'Le salut spirituel est le bonheur véritable, la possession des intelligibles. Mullā Ṣadrā considère que le bonheur spirituel est la seule véritable libération de l'âme humaine. Le bonheur réel, non le bonheur entendu de façon imagée, est la présence réelle de l'Intellect agent dans l'âme.' Jambet, *Fin*, 21.

157 *Mort et résurrection*, 77.

158 'Chacun ressuscite selon la forme de son désir [. . .] Cette définition du rassemblement transforme, de manière exégétique, un événement prédit par la prophétie en une épreuve morale qui équivaut à l'exercice spirituel que le stoïcisme antique a théorisé et pratiqué [...] Selon nous, la finalité ultime de ces exercices dans le schème légué par le lexique du soufisme, finalité qui est l'extinction de soi (*fanā'*), n'est autre qu'un succédané de l'apathie du sage stoïcien. Selon Mullā Sadrā, dans sa vie dernière, en sa deuxième naissance, l'homme pieux et le sage verront et deviendront ce qu'ils ont pressenti et espéré ou, mieux, ce qu'ils auront su d'eux-mêmes ici-bas grâce à l'exercice spirituel conduisant les meilleurs à l'apathie.' *Fin*, 36–37.

The self-rehearsals and self-observations along the path of wisdom make life after the resurrection (though not the exact hour of the resurrection itself) comprehensible and knowable.

Jambet's equation of *fanā'* with Stoic *apatheia* also implies a failure of reason and a need for spiritual discipline as a path towards such a state of serenity, an apathy. The recourse to the vocabulary of the Sufis in both Jambet's and Mullā Ṣadrā's texts takes us to the end of reflection as a route to the resurrection. Inducing the desire that will result in a good resurrection is not a matter of logical argument: it is, rather, a question of spiritual exercise leading, ultimately, to the extinction of the self in God (*al-fanā' fī-l-tawḥīd*).[159] This is in keeping with the principle of maximum intensity of being taking place at the moment when the soul leaves its bodily enclosure and re-unites with the One. Jambet links this cultivation of desire to Massignon's reading of the being of God as desire (via al-Ḥallāj).[160] For Jambet, via Mullā Ṣadrā, the being of the soul is also desire: the desire to leave the body and emigrate far from nature. The circularity of the intra-substantial motion coupled with the image of two desires – one human, and the other divine – meeting each other defines the trajectory of the seeker's desire. The aim of the spiritual exercise is to enable the desire of the human soul to re-encounter God's desire, whence it arose.[161]

These spiritual exercises trace an arc from faith (*īmān*) to certainty (*īqān*) through the abandonment of the lower world, moral purification, and a constant interrogation on the relationship between the resurrection and human temporality.[162] This relationship is not one of futurity; it is one of simultaneity. The resurrection is to the

[159] *Fin*, 45.
[160] Jambet, *Fin*, 84. Cf. Massignon, *EM*, 1:478.
[161] With Mullā Ṣadrā we are still very much in a monadological universe where all entities reflect each other, albeit at some remove from that of Leibniz, and certainly far from Jambet's claims about the latter's relationship to *Le Maître*. See *L'Acte d'être*, 74–77, 83–86, 153–154.
[162] *Fin*, 131–133.

present as centre is to circumference: the resurrection sits at the centre of this world, not between this one and the next. There it generates the circles of meaning and temporality that define our lives.[163] Mullā Ṣadrā thus proposes an ahistoric, or rather ultra-historic, eschatology. Far from erasing the *eschaton* from our daily consciousness, this location beyond history inscribes it in every instance of our human lives. The resurrection is always with us; it is the centre around which our lives turn and the *Bātin* of everything we know and understand. The spiritual exercises of the *ʿārif* are those that keep these realities firmly in mind, framing an ethics that has much in common with Platonic models of acquiring wisdom:

> This model commands us to flee from the world, this prison of the senses, without delay, in order to escape from the detractors and their false goods. Knowing the end of everything and what the last days and return to God will entail is not just reaching the most important truth of a human life, it is also being encouraged to leave this world in order to live according to the ways of the next. To know in all certainty that this world will end is to prepare oneself to leave it, in full realization of what this spiritual *hijra* will be: passing from the apparent to the hidden meaning of the universe.[164]

Here we find the motivation for Jambet's second translation of *Risālat al-Ḥashr*: the repeated motifs of permanent revolution, permanent

[163] See Mullā Ṣadrā's commentary *ad* Q36:48 ('They [the unbelievers, the blasphemers, the *kuffār*] say: "When will this promise be fulfilled if you speak the truth?"'). The importance of the resurrection to human reality in the here and now is such that Mullā Ṣadrā defines *kufr* as ignorance of the reality of the resurrection (أي الجهل بحقيقة الساعة واليوم الآخر) in his commentary *ad* Q36:64 ('Here is the hell you were promised: today let it scorch you for what you blasphemed!').

[164] 'Ce modèle commande de s'évader sans tarder de ce monde, de la prison sensible, pour échapper aux négateurs et à leurs faux biens. Connaître la fin de toute chose, savoir ce qu'il en est de la vie dernière et du retour en Dieu, ce n'est pas seulement accéder à la vérité la plus importante pour la vie humaine, c'est aussi recevoir un vif encouragement à quitter ce bas-monde pour vivre selon la vie de l'autre monde. Savoir que ce monde finira, le savoir en toute certitude, c'est se préparer à le quitter, en sachant ce que sera cette hégire spirituelle : le passage du sens apparent de l'univers à son sens caché.' *Fin*, 161.

resurrection, constant rebellion defined as an *exitus* from the world and total devotion to the immortality of the soul. The political and metaphysical nexus with which Jambet's career began is still operative today, despite the shifts in locus from externally-oriented, social freedom to internally-focused, personal freedom. Jambet uses his vast knowledge of gnostics and esoterics – a category that includes Plato and Mao as well as Mullā Ṣadrā – to think through the implications.

The permanent memory of the resurrection is no morbid obsession, however; for the moment of resurrection is also, as we have seen, the return to the moment of creation. Jambet's preoccupation with this moment both confirms and subverts his engagement with philosophies of order.

Conclusion

The conflation of resurrection and creation brings us to a state of maximum liveliness and intensity. This maximal state entails significant ethical implications, not the least of which is the absence of antinomianism. Ethically speaking, one thing we cannot do, or rather should not do, is act as if the end had not happened; as if the resurrection – or the revolution – were mere accidents, or momentary lapses of theologico-political reason. We must be 'faithful to the event of ourselves.' In light of Jambet's reading of Alamūt and Mullā Ṣadrā, we are never more faithful to ourselves than at the moment of the resurrection.

The word 'event' is applicable not only to us, but *a fortiori* to the universe, to which it applies as the most general property.[165] Every reality, every soul, every self occurs in time. The world is not eternal. We must therefore be faithful to the event of ourselves within this created, temporal context. This fidelity necessarily implies keeping in

[165] '*L'événement* est la propriété la plus générale de l'univers.' Jambet, *L'Acte d'être*, 182.

mind, and keeping faith with, the moment of creation (*kun!*) and the moment of resurrection, the second birth of the soul which marks an exit from history. This exit must bring with it the abandonment of hidebound certainties in favour of what might be, or indeed of who we might be. We must allow the imagination to do its work, and make way for an imaginary re-institution of society. In a reading of the ethics of Naṣīr al-Dīn al-Ṭūsī, Jambet argues that the resurrectionary–revolutionary political ideal demands that social relations be re-imagined, and that the name given to these social relations at their most intense is love. This is the condition that makes possible the extra-worldly city of angels, held together by *philia* and love.[166] Being subject to the imperative implies being in love, at least a little. Love, moreover, is the name of the maximal state of being that represents the political Real: 'Ideal politics can only think the political Real by conceiving the *maximum link*. Love is the name of this link, where differences are abolished. It is not the destruction of sociability, but its maximal intensity that can and must represent the political Real.'[167]

We can no more will these change in ourselves than we can know when we will fall in love. We cannot know when the resurrection will come, we can be open to it, and know that it will happen repeatedly. The coming of the resurrection is marked by desire; the desire for the

[166] 'La communauté idéale est une communauté angélique, en ce que ses membres vivent unis comme s'ils n'étaient pas dans les corps. Les malheurs du politique viennent des points d'arrêt qu'opposent à l'unification les discordances corporelles, tandis que le bien politique se situe à cette limite ou doit se produire la résurrection spirituelle de l'homme. Les hommes sont aptes à une telle métamorphose salvifique en ce qu'ils sont capables de la *philia*. Naṣīr Ṭūsī fait de la *philia*, dont le thème rappelle irrésistiblement Aristote [Éthique à Nicomaque IX, 12, 1171b–1172a. Voir *Akhlâq* p. 321 et sq.], la possibilité de l'amour. *Philia* et amour se soutiennent et produisent l'harmonie mutuelle des sujets et la vie de citoyen.' 'Idéal du politique et politique idéale selon Naṣīr al-Dīn Ṭūsī,' in *Naṣīr al-Dīn Ṭūsī: philosophe et savant du XIIIe siècle. Actes du colloque tenu à l'Université de Téhéran, 6–9 mars 1997*, ed. Naṣr Allāh Pūrjavādī and Živa Vesel, Bibliothèque iranienne (Tehran: Institut Français de recherche en Iran; Presses Universitaires d'Iran, 2000), 51.

[167] '[L]a politique idéale ne peut penser le Réel du politique qu'en concevant le *lien maximum*. L'amour est le nom que reçoit ce lien maximum, où les différences s'abolissent. Ce n'est pas la ruine de la sociabilité, mais son intensité maximale qui peut et doit figurer le Réel du politique.' 'Idéal du politique,' 56.

other that is embodied in the figure of the Imām. Over and above the Lacanian dimension of this formulation, we would do well to remember some of Derrida's arguments about the invention of the other in order to shed light on the full richness of Jambet's articulation of this idea. Derrida's invention of the other is a process that implies finding (*invenire*), discovering, as well as designing and making the other. He extends invention to places where it would not normally be expected, such as ideas, reproduction, God and the truth.[168] Invention is the advent, the coming of the event of the truth (the coming of the truth as event). Across all the semantic variations of the term 'invention', the idea of the coming surprise remains central.[169] Invention depends on the ability to say and respond to the imperative, 'come [*viens*].'[170] We – as rebels, and as angelic revolutionaries – call out to the resurrection and the advent of the Imām. At the same time, the resurrection calls to us from its location at the centre of time and meaning. We both produce and are made by that call. The call of the resurrection (or revolution) recalls what Derrida says of the other in *Psyché*: the other calls us to come forward, but that (both the call and the coming) only happens in the plural.[171]

This is, perhaps, the key lesson of Jambet's reading of revolution: that meaningful change – change in the angelic sense, change that destroys tyranny rather than repeating or compounding it – must always come from the Other, from a place that can neither be mapped nor predicted. Despite the ordered universes that preoccupy Jambet, we can never really tell where revolutions or resurrections come from. The locus of this alterity (or rather the locus that alterity comes from) has gone by many names in history – God, the Messiah, the sovereign,

[168] *Psyché*, 14, 37, 43–44.
[169] 'Dans tous les cas et à travers tous les déplacements sémantiques du mot "invention", celle-ci reste le *venir*, l'événement d'une nouveauté qui doit surprendre'. *Psyché*, 36.
[170] *Psyché*, 53–54.
[171] 'L'autre appelle à venir, et cela n'arrive qu'à plusieurs voix.' *Psyché*, 61.

the masses, the proletariat – but we must remember its utterly heterogeneous, extra-worldly, unpredictable, incalculable, and extra-historical character. We should also never lose sight of the perpetually manifold character of resurrection. We say *the* resurrection, *the* revolution, we still use the singular to speak of freedom and sovereignty, but it would be far more accurate to speak of all these things in the plural: freedoms, revolutions, resurrections, and so on. The fact that history and messianism are orthogonal, and can only intersect at certain unpredictable times, means that the task of messianism, as Jambet puts it, is infinite. Only by making room for these others, to whom we call out and which always come in plural forms, only by being alert to the meaning hidden behind every apparition, and by re-enchanting the world by re-interpreting it, can we save our souls and be at our freest, our liveliest, and our most loving.

EPILOGUE

On Being True to Oneself: Esoteric Authenticities

Lionel Trilling starts his incisive *Sincerity and Authenticity* thus: 'Now and then, it is possible to observe the moral life in the process of revising itself.'[1] A similar description might apply to the ideas and phenomena covered in this book. Trilling builds his argument around the opposition between the 'honest soul' and the 'disintegrated consciousness', terms taken from Hegel's reading of Diderot's *Le Neveu de Rameau* in his *Phenomenology*.[2] The disintegrated – or alienated – consciousness (*der sich entfremdete Geist*) is the term applied to Rameau's immoral, but utterly brilliant, nephew; a character that Hegel uses to describe the spirit in one of its key stages of development towards omniscience. The vast modern influence of the notion of the immoral revolutionary, who engages in objectionable behaviour in the service of a good cause, need not detain us here. What matters is the rejection of that mode by Massignon, Corbin, and Jambet, all of whom knew their Hegel, and much else, and all of whom refuse the idea of a dialectical passage through dissolution – which might be read as a form of self-betrayal – in favour of moral and ontological systems that go from the good to the real: *al-Ḥaqq*.

Desire, certainty, resurrection: these are three experiences during which we are arguably as close and intimate as it is possible to be to ourselves. A more cynical reading would also claim that they are ones

1 Lionel Trilling, *Sincerity and Authenticity* (Cambridge, MA: Harvard University Press, 1972), 1.
2 Trilling, *Sincerity and Authenticity*, 33–47; Hegel, *HW*, 3:364–366.

where we are at our most deluded. The esoteric operates as a self-cure against the possibility of that delusion. The consequences of being too true to oneself can range from the ridiculous – as in Molière's M. Jourdain – to the disastrous, as in Massignon's experiences in Iraq. The esoteric functions as a safety valve that simultaneously enables such fidelity without the risk of excessive rigidity: we are certain because we are forever with our angels; we are free to abandon ourselves to the *ḥaqq* of desire because of the laws of hospitality, we can adhere to our ideals to the very end because of the reality of resurrection. The esoteric operates as a road map to our own selves; to the ideal self embodied in the notion of the *Insān Kāmil* – variously understood as a perfected physical or personal entity – to which we might be true.

If we were to ask what, or where, this self is located, we would encounter the hoary division between the map and the territory: the esoteric can lead us to selves and locations but cannot be substituted for the experience of the self. The representative space that leads us to the self, and might even contain versions thereof, is all that is communally available to us. One way of bridging the gap between idealised representation and esoteric reality is the inclusion of the universe, no matter how sprawling, in that representation. Esoteric cosmologies thus work by spelling out the implications of *hen panta*, and the all that is containable in the one. In the esoteric register, being true to oneself means being true to everything.

And so Massignon's lessons about fidelity to *al-Ḥaqq* are so many routes to the catholic, desiring self. If we recall al-Ḥallāj's poems on the primordial nature of desire and the involution of the vision of the self in the divine, we understand that saying *Anā al-Ḥaqq* not only works as an echo of the Gospel of John and justification of al-Ḥallāj as *le Christ coranique*, but also as an account of *al-Ḥaqq* as the truth of the self, and of primordial desire (*ʿishq*) as a longing to be that self. Furthermore, Massignon's doctrine of hospitality reminds us that the self to which we must be true can only come from, and be, the other, the guest that we receive in order to be ourselves. Similarly, the central place of vision in Corbin's account of the esoteric might be considered a solution to the Calvinist idea of an inscrutable God: seeing what the believer has seen, as the believer has seen it, effectively dislodges that inscrutability and makes way for a more certain idea of the divine that guides better because it can be better seen. Last, but by no means least, Jambet's work on political and spiritual revolution as a resurrection of the soul, and of the end of everything as the return of everything to its beginnings, systematises fidelity to the idea of a secular, immortal self that is always located somewhere between creation and re-creation.

What is curious about these versions of fidelity is the way in which they play with the rules-based idea of the self that dominates the Abrahamic monotheisms even as they draw on these very monotheisms for their foundation and formulation. For Massignon, the very fact that al-Ḥallāj was deemed a heretic and crucified proves that the Sufi was both faithful to *al-Ḥaqq* and that, consequently, his memory must itself be a part of that faithfulness. Corbin's vast systems linking everything from gnosticism to Sufism to Goethe and Heidegger inscribes the marks of the divine vision everywhere in our being rather than in any one location. And Jambet's avowed atheism finds its strongest expression in accounts of the belief central to the Abrahamic monotheisms; namely, that life in this world is mere preparation for the next, and that justice will be served as part of that process.

So many versions of fidelity beg the question of the knowability of the self in question. Whether or not the esoteric might be listed as yet another variation on the many fantasies of omniscience that have characterised systems of belief, ethics, metaphysics, and psychoanalysis is not the aim here. The recurrence of that fantasy in all such systems is, however. The pattern of ideas and words that hold forth the promise of fully knowing oneself – and, consequently, fully knowing everything –

that such systems share gives us a clue as to the value of the esoteric and the importance of its constant irruption into twentieth-century thought. When claims to total knowledge fail, as they must, the esoteric keeps alive the hope that the path to omniscience remains open, and that even if the destination is never reached, the ethical, intellectual, and spiritual rewards of the path are considerable.

The unbetrayed self as guest, vision, resurrection. That is the promise of the esoteric. One version of that self may be glimpsed via the account of the gnostic soul presented by Hans Jonas in *The Gnostic Religion*. The soul thrown into a dark and chaotic universe seeks authenticity.[3] Now, authenticity is a term that has exercised numerous minds in the twentieth century; some of whom, like Heidegger and Sartre, worked in the same theoretical, philosophical, and political universe as the thinkers we have encountered in this book. And yet the version of the unbetrayed, authentic self in play here is far from the version that we find in *Being and Time* or *Being and Nothingness*.[4] Once again, Trilling's analysis of authenticity might be more useful: authenticity points, he says, to 'our anxiety over the credibility of existence and of individual existences.'[5] Following Sartre, Trilling describes inauthenticity as the 'Hell of dehumanization' that comes about through our dependence on other people just to feel that we are.[6] The esoteric saves us from all of this. Postulating a self that overcomes the threat of nothingness through a continuous connection with the divine enables the credible assembly of the scattered, alienated self into something that can be called 'authentic'; a self with respect to whom imposture would be unthinkable. An idea of selfhood that depends on hospitality, or a vision, or rebirth as an utterly maximal

3 Jonas, *Gnostic Religion*, 63–64; 330.
4 Jonas's account of authenticity does, in fact, owe a great deal to Heidegger, but he takes pains to separate his account of gnostic authenticity from that found in Heidegger's work, especially *Being and Time*. *Gnostic Religion*, 334–337.
5 Trilling, *Sincerity and Authenticity*, 93.
6 Trilling, *Sincerity and Authenticity*, 102.

version of the self, incorporates alterity into itself: the divine guest, the otherworldly scene, and the immortally good self all give us permission to be fully ourselves without regard for the risks that such a way of being might carry in a hostile universe or corrupt society. Such a self would be immune to betrayal; it could never be in-credible.

What is especially striking about this version of authenticity is how out of place it seems in the contemporary political and social setting. We have grown accustomed to certain versions of authenticity reminiscent of (or derived from) Hegel's alienated consciousness, as well as recognisable forms of rebellion and revolt, to the well-rehearsed scenario of marchers and demonstrators invading the world. Far too unfamiliar are rebellions that depend on letting the world into our homes, lives, and spaces, not only as moments of solidarity and generosity, but as acts and ways of being, or ways of knowing the world that depend explicitly on such hospitalities. Even less familiar are meaningful (as opposed to merely reactionary) forms of rebellion based on being good, without the putatively necessary passage through evil as a means to an end whose justification is always in doubt. The esoteric promises progress without alienation, towards a something novel and better, and yet in its novelty strangely familiar: a place where we can be at our most angelic, our most loving, our maximal selves, and at the closest proximity to resurrection in a new, and much better, world.

Bibliography

al-Sijistānī, Abū Yaʿqūb. *Kashf al-mahjûb: Le dévoilement des choses cachées.* Bibliothèque iranienne. Edited by Henry Corbin. Tehran; Paris: Institut Franco-iranien; Maisonneuve, 1949.

al-Sijistānī, Abū Yaʿqūb. *Le Dévoilement des choses cachées: Recherches de philosophie ismaélienne.* [Kashf al-maḥjūb]. Edited and Translated by Henry Corbin. Lagrasse: Verdier, 1988.

al-Ṭūsī, Naṣīr al-Dīn Muḥammad ibn Muḥammad. *La Convocation d'Alamût: Somme de philosophie ismaélienne = Rawdat al-taslim: le jardin de la vraie foi.* Edited and Translated by Christian Jambet. Lagrasse; Paris: Verdier & Editions UNESCO, 1996.

al-Ṭūsī, Naṣīr al-Dīn Muḥammad ibn Muḥammad. *Paradise of Submission: A Medieval Treatise on Ismaili thought.* [Rawḍat al-taslīm]. Translated by S. J. Badakhchani. Ismaili texts and translations series. London; New York: I.B. Tauris in association with Institute of Ismaili Studies, 2005.

Amanat, Abbas. *Apocalyptic Islam and Iranian Shi'ism.* London: I. B. Tauris, 2009.

Attridge, Derek. *The Singularity of Literature.* London and New York: Routledge, 2004.

Attridge, Derek. *The Work of Literature.* First ed. Oxford: Oxford University Press, 2015.

Auerbach, Erich. *Scenes from the Drama of European Literature.* Translated by Ralph Manheim. Minneapolis, MN: University of Minnesota Press, 1984.

Awn, Peter J. *Satan's Tragedy and Redemption: Iblis in Sufi Psychology.* Leiden: Brill, 1983.

Badiou, Alain. *L'Être et l'événement.* L'Ordre philosophique. Paris: Seuil, 1988.

Badiou, Alain. *L'Éthique. Essai sur la conscience du mal.* Caen: Nous, 2009.

Baldick, Robert. *The Life of J.-K. Huysmans.* Sawtry: Dedalus, 2006. 1955.

Beaufret, Jean. *Introduction aux philosophies de l'existence. De Kierkegaard à Heidegger.* Paris: Denoël/Gonthier, 1971.

Benveniste, Emile. *Vocabulaire des institutions indo-européennes.* Paris: Minuit, 1969.

Birnbaum, Jean. *Les Maoccidents: un néoconservatisme à la française.* Paris: Stock, 2009.

Blanchot, Maurice. *L'Arrêt de mort.* Paris: Gallimard, 1948.

Blanchot, Maurice. *Le Pas au-delà.* Paris: Gallimard, 1973.

Bloom, Harold. *Omens of Millennium: The Gnosis of Angels, Dreams, and Resurrection.* New York: Riverhead, 1997.

Borch-Jacobsen, Mikkel. *Lacan: le maître absolu.* Paris: Flammarion, 1990.

Bounoure, Gabriel. 'Louis Massignon, itinéraire et courbe de vie.' In *Louis Massignon*, edited by Jean-François Six. Cahiers de l'Herne, 45–54. Paris: L'Herne, 1970.

Bourg, Julian. *From Revolution to Ethics: May 1968 and Contemporary French Thought.* Montréal, Québec: McGill-Queen's University Press, 2007.

Bourg, Julian. 'Principally Contradiction: The Flourishing of French Maoism.' In *Mao's Little Red Book: A Global History*, edited by Alexander C. Cook, 225–244. Cambridge: Cambridge University Press, 2014.

Bourseiller, Christophe. *Les Maoïstes. La Folle histoire des gardes rouges français.* Points. Paris: Seuil, 2008. 1996.

Bulliet, Richard W. *The Case for Islamo-Christian Civilization.* New York: Columbia University Press, 2004.

Camilleri, Sylvain, and Daniel Proulx. 'Martin Heidegger et Henry Corbin ; lettres et documents (1930–1941).' *Bulletin heideggérien* 4 (2014): 4–63. http://www.amiscorbin.com/wp-content/plugins/pdf-viewer-for-wordpress/web/viewer.php?file=http://www.amiscorbin.com/wp-content/uploads/2012/06/Camilleri-Proulx-Corbin-Heidegger-Lettres_et_documents.pdf.

Cavagnis, Julien. 'Corbin, Hadot, Foucault. Mise en dialogue de *Qu'est-ce que la philosophie islamique?* de Christian Jambet.' *Cahiers Philosophiques*, no. 1 (2012): 111–125. https://www.cairn.info/load_pdf.php?ID_ARTICLE=CAPH_128_0111.

Certeau, Michel de. *La Prise de parole et autres écrits politiques.* Edited by Luce Giard. Points essais. Paris: Seuil, 1994.

Chakravorti Spivak, Gayatri, and Michael Ryan. 'Anarchism Revisited: A New Philosophy.' *Diacritics* 8, no. 2 (1978): 66–79.

Cheetham, Tom. *Green Man, Earth Angel: The Prophetic Tradition and the Battle for the Soul of the World.* Albany, NY: State University of New York Press, 2005.

Cheetham, Tom. *The World Turned Inside Out: Henry Corbin and Islamic mysticism.* Woodstock, CT: Spring Journal Books, 2003.

Chittick, William C. *The Sufi Path of Knowledge: Ibn Al-Arabi's Metaphysics of Imagination.* Albany, NY: State University of New York Press, 1989.

Claudel, Paul, and Louis Massignon. *Correspondance 1908–1953: braises ardentes, semences de feu.* Les Cahiers de la *NRF*. Nouvelle édition renouvelée et augmentée. Edited by Dominique Millet-Gérard. Paris: Gallimard, 2012.

Copenhaver, Brian. 'Hermes Trismegistus, Proclus, and the Question of a Philosophy of Magic in the Renaissance.' In *Hermeticism and the Renaissance: Intellectual History and the Occult in Early Modern Europe*, edited by Ingrid Merkel and Allen G. Debus. Folger Institute Symposia, 79–110. Washington, DC; London: Folger Shakespeare Library; Associated University Presses, 1988.

Corbin, Henry. *Alone with the Alone: Creative Imagination in the Sūfism of Ibn 'Arabi.* New ed. Princeton, NJ: Princeton University Press, 1998.

Corbin, Henry. *Avicenne et le récit visionnaire.* Lagrasse: Verdier, 1999. 1952–1954.

Corbin, Henry. 'Conférence temporaire: « Recherches sur l'herméneutique luthérienne ».' *Annuaire de l'École Pratique des Hautes Études, Section des Sciences Religieuses 1939–1940* (1939): 99–102. http://www.persee.fr/web/revues/home/prescript/article/ephe_0000-0002_1938_num_52_48_17452.

Corbin, Henry. 'De Heidegger à Sohravardî: Entretien avec Philippe Némo.' In *Henry Corbin*, edited by Christian Jambet. Cahiers de l'Herne, 23–37. Paris: L'Herne, 1981.

Corbin, Henry. *En Islam iranien. Aspects spirituels et philosophiques.* 4 vols. Paris: Gallimard, 1991. 1971.

Corbin, Henry. *Face de Dieu, face de l'homme: Herméneutique et soufisme.* Paris: Entrelacs, 2008.

Corbin, Henry. *L'Imagination créatrice dans le soufisme d'Ibn ʾArabî.* Paris: Entrelacs, 2006. 1958.

Corbin, Henry. *L'Homme & son ange: initiation et chevalerie spirituelle.* Paris: Fayard, 2016. 1983.

Corbin, Henry. 'Post-Scriptum à un entretien philosophique.' In *Henry Corbin*, edited by Christian Jambet. Cahiers de l'Herne, 38–56. Paris: L'Herne, 1981.

Corbin, Henry. 'Pour l'anthropologie philosophique: un traité persan inédit de Suhrawardî d'Alep.' *Recherches philosophiques* 2 (1933): 371–423.

Corbin, Henry. 'Qu'est-ce que la métaphysique?'. Translation. *Bifur* 8 (June 1931): 5–27.

Corbin, Henry. 'Regards vers l'Orient.' *La Tribune indochinoise* (Paris), 15/8 1927, 4–5.

Corbin, Henry. 'Théologie au bord du lac.' In *Henry Corbin*, edited by Christian Jambet. Cahiers de l'Herne, 62–63. Paris: L'Herne, 1981.

Corbin, Henry. *Trilogie ismaélienne: Textes edités avec traduction française et commentaire.* [Kitāb al-Yanābīʿ; Risālat al-Mabdaʾ wa-l-Maʿād; Baʾzī az Taʾwīlāt-i Golshān-i Rāz]. Edited and Translated by Henry Corbin, Bibliothèque iranienne. Tehran; Paris: Institut franco-iranien; Adrien Maisonneuve, 1961.

Daftary, Farhad. *The Isma'ilis: Their History and Doctrines.* Second ed. Cambridge: Cambridge University Press, 2007. 1990.

Deleuze, Gilles. *Le Pli: Leibniz et le baroque.* Paris: Minuit, 1988.

Derrida, Jacques. 'Hostipitality.' In *Acts of Religion*, edited by Gil Anidjar, 358–420. New York and London: Routledge, 2002.

Derrida, Jacques. *Parages.* Paris: Galilée, 1986.

Derrida, Jacques. *Psyché. Inventions de l'autre.* Paris: Galilée, 1998.

Derrida, Jacques, and Anne Dufourmantelle. *De l'hospitalité.* Paris: Calmann-Lévy, 1997.

Destremeau, Christian, and Jean Moncelon. *Louis Massignon.* Tempus. Paris: Perrin, 2011. 1994.

Dodds, E. R. 'The Parmenides of Plato and the Origin of the Neoplatonic "One".' *The Classical Quarterly* 22, no. 3/4 (1928): 129–142.

Ehrmantraut, Michael. *Heidegger's Philosophic Pedagogy.* London; New York: Continuum, 2010.

Eliot, T. S. *Collected poems, 1909–1962.* London: Faber, 1974.

Eliot, T. S. *Poésie.* Translated by Pierre Leyris. Éd. bilingue. Paris: Seuil, 1976.

Ellis, Steven. *The English Eliot: Design, Language and Landscape in 'Four Quartets'.* London: Routledge, 1991.

Ferrari, G. R. F. *City and Soul in Plato's Republic.* Chicago: University of Chicago Press, 2005.

Foucault, Michel. *Dits et écrits: 1954–1988.* Edited by Daniel Defert and François Ewald. 4 vols. Paris: Gallimard, 1994.

Foucault, Michel. *L'Usage des plaisirs. Histoire de la sexualité.* Paris: Gallimard, 1984.

Foucault, Michel. *Le Souci de soi.* Histoire de la sexualité. Paris: Gallimard, 1984.

Friedmann, Georges. *La Puissance et la sagesse.* Paris: Gallimard, 1970.

Gardner, Helen. *The Art of T. S. Eliot.* London: Cresset Press, 1949.

Gibson, Andrew. *Intermittency: The Concept of Historical Reason in Recent French Philosophy.* Edinburgh: Edinburgh University Press, 2012.

Goémé, Christine, and Judith d' Astier. *Michel Foucault, l'art de penser.* Paris: Institut National de l'Audiovisuel (INA), 1991. Sound Recording.

Goethe, Johann Wolfgang von. *Sämtliche Werke nach Epochen seines Schaffens, Münchner Ausgabe.* Edited by Herbert Georg Göpfert, Norbert Miller, Gerhard Sauder and Karl Richter. Munich: Hanser, 1985.

Griffiths, Richard. *The Reactionary Revolution: The Catholic Revival in French Literature, 1870–1914.* London: Constable, 1966.

Gude, Mary Louise. 'J.K. Huysmans, Louis Massignon, and The Language Of Mysticism.' *Religion & Literature.* 30, no. 2 (1998): 81–96.

Gude, Mary Louise. *Louis Massignon: The Crucible of Compassion.* Notre Dame, IN: University of Notre Dame Press, 1996.

Gugelot, Frédéric. *La Conversion des intellectuels au catholicisme en France, 1885–1935.* Paris: CNRS, 2010. 1998.

Gutas, Dimitri. 'Forward to the Past.' Review of Christian Jambet: *Qu'est-ce que la philosophie islamique? Philosophy East and West* 64, no. 4 (2014): 1042–1047. https://doi.org/10.1353/pew.2014.0068.

Guyon, Bernard. 'Jalons pour une étude du style de Louis Massignon.' In *Louis Massignon*, edited by Jean-François Six. Cahiers de l'Herne, 106–114. Paris: L'Herne, 1970.

Hadot, Pierre. *Exercices spirituels et philosophie antique.* Nouvelle édition revue et augmentée. Paris: Albin Michel, 2002. 1981.

Hadot, Pierre. *Plotin, ou La simplicité du regard.* Paris: Plon, 1963.

Hallward, Peter. *Badiou: A Subject to Truth.* Minneapolis, MN: University of Minnesota Press, 2003.

Hallward, Peter. *Out of this World: Deleuze and the Philosophy of Creation.* London; New York: Verso, 2006.

Hegel, Georg Wilhelm Friedrich. *Werke.* Edited by Eva Moldenhauer, Karl Markus Michel and Helmut Reinicke. 20 vols. Frankfurt am Main: Suhrkamp, 1986.

Heidegger, Martin. *Basic Writings: From Being and Time (1927) to The Task of Thinking (1964).* Edited and Translated by David Farrell Krell. Second ed. San Francisco, CA: HarperSanFrancisco, 1993.

Heidegger, Martin. *Being and Time.* Translated by Joan Stambaugh. SUNY Series in Contemporary Continental Philosophy. Revised ed. Albany, NY: SUNY Press, 2010.

Heidegger, Martin. *Gesamtausgabe: I Abteilung: Veröffentlichte Schriften, 1910–1976.* Frankfurt am Main: Klostermann, 1975.

Heidegger, Martin. *Pathmarks.* Edited and Translated by William McNeill. Cambridge; New York: Cambridge University Press, 1998.

Heidegger, Martin. *Qu'est-ce que la métaphysique?: Suivi d'extraits sur l'Être et le temps et d'une conférence sur Hölderlin.* Edited and Translated by Henry Corbin. Paris: Gallimard, 1938.

Hemming, Laurence Paul. *Heidegger's Atheism: The Refusal of a Theological Voice.* Notre Dame, IN: University of Notre Dame Press, 2002.

Huntington, Samuel P. *The Clash of Civilizations and the Remaking of World Order.* London: Touchstone, 1998.

Jambet, Christian. 'Alain Badiou: *L'Être et l'événement*.' In *Annuaire Philosophique 1987–1988*, 141–183. Paris: Seuil, 1988.

Jambet, Christian. *Apologie de Platon: Essais de métaphysique.* Paris: Grasset, 1976.

Jambet, Christian. 'Constitution du sujet et pratique spirituelle. Remarques sur *l'Histoire de la sexualité*.' In *Michel Foucault philosophe. Rencontre internationale, Paris 9,10,11 janvier 1988*, edited by Association pour le Centre Michel Foucault. Des Travaux, 271–287. Paris: Seuil, 1989.

Jambet, Christian. *Henry Corbin et Louis Massignon.* Paris: www.amiscorbin.com, 2011.

Jambet, Christian. 'Idéal du politique et politique idéale selon Naṣīr al-Dīn Ṭūsī.' In *Naṣīr al-Dīn Ṭūsī: philosophe et savant du XIIIe siècle. Actes du colloque tenu à l'Université de Téhéran, 6–9 mars 1997*, edited by Naṣr Allāh Pūrjavādī and Živa Vesel. Bibliothèque iranienne, 31–57. Tehran: Institut Français de recherche en Iran; Presses Universitaires d'Iran, 2000.

Jambet, Christian. 'Interview with Christian Jambet.' By Ziad Elmarsafy. 10 July 2018.

Jambet, Christian. *L'Acte d'être. La philosophie de la révélation chez Mollâ Sadrâ.* Paris: Fayard, 2002.

Jambet, Christian. *La Fin de toute chose. Apocalypse coranique et philosophie.* [Risālat al-Ḥashr]. Translated by Christian Jambet. Paris: Albin Michel, 2017.

Jambet, Christian. *La Grande Résurrection d'Alamût. Les formes de la liberté dans le shi'isme ismaélien.* Lagrasse: Verdier, 1990.

Jambet, Christian. *La Logique des Orientaux. Henry Corbin et la science des formes.* Paris: Seuil, 1983.

Jambet, Christian. *Le Caché et l'Apparent.* Mythes et religions. Paris: L'Herne, 2003.

Jambet, Christian. *Le Gouvernement divin: Islam et conception politique du monde. Théologie de Mullā Ṣadrā.* Paris: CNRS, 2016.

Jambet, Christian. *Mort et résurrection en islam. L'Au-delà selon Mullâ Sadrâ.* Paris: Albin Michel, 2008.

Jambet, Christian. 'Philosophie angélique.' In *Henry Corbin*, edited by Christian Jambet. Cahiers de l'Herne, 97–106. Paris: L'Herne, 1981.

Jambet, Christian. *Qu'est-ce que la philosophie islamique?* Folio Essais. Paris: Gallimard, 2011.

Jambet, Christian. 'Repères biographiques.' In *Henry Corbin*, edited by Christian Jambet. Cahiers de l'Herne, 15–20. Paris: L'Herne, 1981.

Jambet, Christian. 'Retour sur l'insurrection iranienne.' In *Michel Foucault*, edited by Philippe Artières, Jean-François Bert, Frédéric Gros and Judith Revel. Cahiers de l'Herne, 372–376. Paris: L'Herne, 2011.

Jambet, Christian. *Se rendre immortel, suivi du Traité de la résurrection.* Translated by Christian Jambet. Saint-Clément: Fata Morgana, 2000.

Jambet, Christian. 'Some Comments on the Question of the One.' *Angelaki* 8, no. 2 (2003): 33–41. https://doi.org/10.1080/0969725032000162558.

Jambet, Christian, and Guy Lardreau. *L'Ange. Pour une cynégétique du semblant.* Paris: Grasset, 1976.

Jambet, Christian, and Guy Lardreau. *Le Monde. Réponse à la question, Qu'est-ce que les droits de l'homme?* Paris: Grasset, 1978.

Janicaud, Dominique. *Heidegger en France.* 2 vols. Paris: Albin Michel, 2001.

Jonas, Hans. *The Gnostic Religion: The Message of the Alien God and the Beginnings of Christianity.* Second, enlarged ed. Boston, MA: Beacon Press, 1963.

Juvaynī, ʿAlāʾ al-Dīn ʿAṭā Malik. *Genghis Khan: The History of the World Conqueror.* Translated by John Andrew Boyle. Manchester; Paris: Manchester University Press; UNESCO Publishing, 1997. 1958.

Kleinberg, Ethan. *Generation Existential: Heidegger's Philosophy in France, 1927–1961.* Ithaca, NY and London: Cornell University Press, 2005.

Koyré, Alexandre. *Mystiques, spirituels, alchimistes du XVIe siècle allemand.* Collection Idées. Paris: Gallimard, 1971.

Lacan, Jacques. *Autres écrits.* Paris: Seuil, 2001.

Lacan, Jacques. *Écrits.* Paris: Seuil, 1966.

Lacan, Jacques. *Le Séminaire de Jacques Lacan. Livre VII. L'Éthique de la psychanalyse.* Paris: Seuil, 1986.

Lacan, Jacques. *Le Séminaire de Jacques Lacan. Livre XIX, . . . ou pire.* Paris: Seuil, 2011.

Lacan, Jacques. *Le Séminaire de Jacques Lacan. Livre XVIII. D'un discours qui ne serait pas du semblant.* Paris: Seuil, 2008.

Lacan, Jacques. *Le Séminaire de Jacques Lacan. Livre XX. Encore.* Points. Paris: Seuil, 1999. 1975.

Lacan, Jacques. *Le Triomphe de la religion.* Paris: Seuil, 2005.

Lacan, Jacques. *The Triumph of Religion: Preceded by Discourse to Catholics.* Translated by Bruce Fink. Cambridge: Polity, 2013.

Laude, Patrick. *Pathways to an Inner Islam: Massignon, Corbin, Guénon and Schuon.* Albany, NY: State University of New York Press, 2010.

Laurens, Henry. *La Question de Palestine. Tome premier: 1799–1922, l'invention de la Terre sainte.* Paris: Fayard, 1999.

Le Châtelier, Alfred. 'États-Unis d'Orient.' *Revue du Monde Musulman* 36 (1918–1919): 10–14.

Leibniz, Gottfried Wilhelm. *Discours de métaphysique suivi de Monadologie et autres textes.* Edited by Michel Fichant. Folio Essais. Paris: Gallimard, 2004.

Lévi-Strauss, Claude. *Les Structures élémentaires de la parenté.* Second ed. Berlin: Mouton de Gruyter, 2002. 1968.

Lévi-Strauss, Claude. *Œuvres.* Edited by Vincent Debaene. Bibliothèque de la Pléiade. Paris: Gallimard, 2008.

'Note sur l'ouvrage de Tom Cheetham, The World Turned Inside Out: Henry Corbin and Islamic Mysticism.' www.amiscorbin.com, 2005, http://www.amiscorbin.com/note-sur-l-ouvrage-de-tom-cheetham-the-world-turned-inside-out-henry-corbin-and-islamic-mysticism/ (accessed 8 August 2015).

Luchelli, Juan Pablo. 'Lacan avec Platon: le Socrate de Lacan.' Thèse de doctorat, Université Panthéon-Sorbonne – Paris I, 2015. https://tel.archives-ouvertes.fr/tel-01321044.

Luther, Martin. *Lectures on Romans.* Edited and Translated by Wilhelm Pauck Louisville, KY: Westminster John Knox Press, 2006. 1961.

MacFarquhar, Roderick, and Michael Schoenhals. *Mao's Last Revolution.* Cambridge, MA; London: Harvard University Press, 2008. 2006.

Mason, Herbert. *Al-Hallaj.* New York and Abingdon: Routledge, 1995.

Mason, Herbert. 'Louis Massignon, Catholicism, and Islam: A Memoir Reflection.' *Spiritus: A Journal of Christian Spirituality* 8, no. 2 (2008): 202–206. https://doi.org/https://doi.org/10.1353/scs.0.0021.

Mason, Herbert. *Memoir of a Friend: Louis Massignon.* Notre Dame, IN: University of Notre Dame Press, 1988.

Massignon, Louis. 'Documents sur la situation sociale dans l'Inde.' *Revue du monde musulman* 44–45 (1921): 53–204.

Massignon, Louis. *Écrits mémorables.* Edited by Christian Jambet. 2 vols. Paris: R. Laffont, 2009.

Massignon, Louis. *Essai sur les origines du lexique technique de la mystique musulmane.* Paris: Cerf, 1999. 1968.

Massignon, Louis. *Essay on the Origins of the Technical Language of Islamic Mysticism.* Translated by Benjamin Clark. Notre Dame, IN: University of Notre Dame Press, 1997.

Massignon, Louis. 'In Memoriam Sir Mark Sykes: Remarks on the Present Disruption of British Policy in the Near East.' *Revue du Monde Musulman* 37 (1918–1919): 15–22.

Massignon, Louis. *La Passion de Husayn Ibn Mansûr Hallâj: martyr mystique de l'Islam, exécuté à Bagdad le 26 mars 922: étude d'histoire religieuse.* 4 vols. Paris: Gallimard, 1990. 1975.

Massignon, Louis. 'Le Problème des réfugiés et son incidence sur le Proche-Orient.' *Politique étrangère* 14, no. 3 (1949): 219–232. https://www.persee.fr/doc/polit_0032-342x_1949_num_14_3_2806.

Massignon, Louis. *Les Trois prières d'Abraham.* Paris: Cerf, 1997.

Massignon, Louis. *Opera minora.* Edited by Youakim Moubarac. 3 vols. Beirut: Dar Al-Maaref, 1963.

Massignon, Louis. *Parole donnée.* Paris: Union Générale d'Editions, 1970.

Massignon, Louis. *The Passion of al-Hallāj: Mystic and Martyr of Islam.* Translated by Herbert Mason. Bollingen Series. 4 vols. Princeton, NJ: Princeton University Press, 1982.

Massignon, Louis. *Testimonies and Reflections: Selected Essays of Louis Massignon.* Edited and Translated by Herbert Mason. Notre Dame, IN: University of Notre Dame Press, 1989.

Massignon, Louis, and Mary Kahil. *L'Hospitalité sacrée.* Paris: Nouvelle Cité, 1987.

Mao Zedong. 'Sixteen Points on Cultural Revolution.' *Peking Review*, 12 August 1966. https://www.marxists.org/subject/china/peking-review/1966/PR1966-33g.htm.

Meesemaecker, Laure. *L'Autre visage de Louis Massignon.* Versailles: Via Romana, 2011.

Meisner, Maurice J. *Mao Zedong: A Political and Intellectual Portrait.* Cambridge: Polity, 2007.

Miller, Mitchell H. *Plato's Parmenides: The Conversion of the Soul.* Princeton Legacy Library. Princeton, NJ: Princeton University Press, 2017. 1986.

Millet-Gérard, Dominique. 'Massignon et Huysmans: « silhouette d'or sur fond noir ».' *Bulletin de l'Association des Amis de Louis Massignon*, no. 20 (2007): 6–33.

Moody, A. David. '*Four Quartets:* Music, Word, Meaning and Value.' In *The Cambridge Companion to T.S. Eliot*, edited by A. David Moody, 142–157. Cambridge: Cambridge University Press, 1994.

Paugam, Jacques. *Génération perdue: ceux qui avaient vingt ans en 1968? ceux qui avaient vingt ans à la fin de la guerre d'Algérie? ou ni les uns ni les autres?* Paris: R. Laffont, 1977.

Pavel, Thomas. *La Pensée du roman.* Paris: Gallimard, 2003.

Rahman, Fazlur. *The Philosophy of Mullā Sadrā (Sadr al Dīn al-Shirāzī).* Albany, NY: State University of New York Press, 1975.

Reinhardt, Hartmut. 'Geheime Wege der Aufklärung. Goethe, die Illuminatenorden, und das Epos-Fragment ›Die Geheimnisse‹.' In *Die Weimarer Klassik und ihre Geheimbünde*, edited by Walter Müller-Seidel and Wolfgang Riedel, 145–176. Würzburg: Königshausen & Neumann, 2002.

Renan, Ernest. *Averroès et l'Averroïsme. Essai historique.* Paris: Calmann-Lévy, 1869. 1852.

Ridgeon, Lloyd V. J. *Morals and Mysticism in Persian Sufism: A History of Sufi-futuwwat in Iran.* London: Routledge, 2010.

Rocalve, Pierre. *Louis Massignon et l'islam. Place et rôle de l'islam et de l'islamologie dans la vie et l'œuvre de Louis Massignon.* Damascus: Presses de l'Institut français du Proche-Orient (IFPO), 1993. http://books.openedition.org/ifpo/4660.

Ruspoli, Stéphane. *Le Message de Hallâj l'expatrié. Recueil du 'Dîwân', 'Hymnes et prières', 'Sentences prophétiques et philosophiques'.* Paris: Cerf, 2005.

Ryffel, Heinrich. *ΜΕΤΑΒΟΛΗ ΠΟΛΙΤΕΙΟΝ: Der Wandel der Staatsverfassungen.* Reprint ed. New York, Arno Press, 1973.1949.

Ṣadr al-Dīn Shīrāzī, Muḥammad ibn Ibrāhīm. *Risālat al-Ḥashr.* Edited and Translated by Muḥammad Khvājavī. Tehran: Intishārāt-i Mawlī, 1983.

Said, Edward W. *The World, the Text and the Critic.* Cambridge, MA: Harvard University Press, 1983.

Sedgwick, Mark J. *Western Sufism: From the Abbasids to the New Age.* New York: Oxford University Press, 2017.

Seng, Helmut. *Un livre sacré de l'Antiquité tardive: les Oracles Chaldaïques.* Turnhout: Brepols, 2016.

Six, Jean-François. 'Louis Massignon Prophète du dialogue entre Orient-Occident.' In *Louis Massignon*, edited by Jean-François Six. Cahiers de l'Herne, 259–273. Paris: L'Herne, 1970.

Smith, Anthony Paul. 'NATURE DESERVES TO BE SIDE BY SIDE WITH THE ANGELS: nature and messianism by way of non-islam.' *Angelaki* 19, no. 1 (2014): 151–169. https://doi.org/10.1080/0969725X.2014.920640.

Smith, Anthony Paul. 'The Speculative Angel.' In *Speculative Medievalisms: Discography*, edited by The Petropunk Collective, 45–64. Brooklyn, NY: Punctum Books, 2013.

Soster, Maria. 'Henry Corbin pendant les années trente.' Première journée Henry Corbin, EPHE, Paris, 17 December 2005. www.amiscorbin.com.

Starr, Peter. *Logics of Failed Revolt: French Theory after May '68*. Stanford, CA: Stanford University Press, 1995.

Suhrawardī, Yaḥyā ibn Ḥabash Shihāb al-Dīn al-. *L'Archange empourpré. Quinze traités et récits mystiques traduits du persan et de l'arabe*. Edited and Translated by Henry Corbin. Paris: Fayard, 1976.

Suhrawardī, Yaḥyā ibn Ḥabash Shihāb al-Dīn al-. *Œuvres philosophiques et mystiques II. 1. Le Livre de la théosophie orientale 2. Le Symbole de foi des philosophes 3. Le Récit de l'exil occidental*. Bibliothèque iranienne. Nouvelle série. Second ed. Edited by Henry Corbin. Tehran; Paris: Académie Impériale Iranienne de Philosophie; A. Maisonneuve, 1977.

Thomas, William Isaac. *Primitive Behavior: An Introduction to the Social Sciences*. New York: McGraw-Hill, 1937.

Trilling, Lionel. *Sincerity and Authenticity*. Cambridge, MA: Harvard University Press, 1972.

Trouillard, Jean. *L'Un et l'âme selon Proclos*. Paris: Les Belles Lettres, 1972.

van Lit, Lambertus Willem Cornelis. *The World of Image in Islamic Philosophy: Ibn Sīnā, Suhrawardī, Shahrazūrī, and Beyond*. Edinburgh: Edinburgh University Press, 2017.

Walbridge, John. *The Leaven of the Ancients: Suhrawardī and the Heritage of the Greeks*. Albany, NY: State University of New York Press, 1999.

Walbridge, John. *The Wisdom of the Mystic East: Suhrawardī and Platonic Orientalism*. Albany, NY: State University of New York Press, 2001.

Wetsel, David. *L'Écriture et le reste: The Pensées of Pascal in the Exegetical Tradition of Port-Royal*. Columbus, OH: Ohio State University Press, 1981.

Index

www.ingramcontent.com/pod-product-compliance
Lightning Source LLC
Chambersburg PA
CBHW070640300426
44111CB00013B/2190
9781350200180